THE BEST OF CZECH COOKING

EXPANDED EDITION

THE BEST OF CZECH COOKING

EXPANDED EDITION

Peter Trnka

HIPPOCRENE BOOKS, INC.
New York

Paperback Edition, 2009.

For information, address:
HIPPOCRENE BOOKS, INC.
171 Madison Ave.
New York, NY 10016
www.hippocrenebooks.com

Library of Congress Cataloging-in-Publication Data

Trnka, Peter.
The best of Czech cooking / Peter Trnka.--Expanded ed.
p. cm. -- (Hippocrene international cookbook series)
Includes index.
ISBN-13: 978-0-7818-0805-7 (hb) / ISBN-10: 0-7818-0805-7 (hb)
ISBN-13: 978-0-7818-1210-8 (pb) / ISBN-10: 0-7818-1210-0 (pb)
1. Cookery, Czech. I. Series.

TX723.5.C9 T76 2001
641.59437--dc21

2001024925

Acknowledgments

This book is dedicated to two women: to my mother, Nina, who fed me well but not so well as to take away my own desire to play in the kitchen and who taught me most of what I know about Czech food; and to Alexandra, my daughter, who shows signs of loving food as much as I do. And thanks to all the friends whom I have had the pleasure to cook for during the past few years.

Table of Contents

Preface to the Expanded Edition

The new edition of *The Best of Czech Cooking* is revised and expanded. The major additions are three new chapters: "Pork," "Mushrooms," and "Beers, Wines, and Spirits." The revisions are corrections to English and Czech spelling and minor alterations to ingredients and quantities in a few recipes. The book contains several new game recipes, due both to the increasing popularity of wild food and my own greater exposure to such food (without becoming a hunter) while living in Newfoundland. The profusion of affordable hare (*zajic*), elk or moose, caribou or reindeer (*dančy*), and game birds such as grouse greatly extends the variety of meats available to the adventurous chef. A note of caution is due, however, since game may be tough and dry if it is old or cooked inappropriately. I provide recipes that minimize the hazard of such unfortunate results. The other new additions are in the realm of sweets, where I have tried to remedy the injustice of the first edition's relatively small set of offerings.

Each of the new chapters is here for a different reason. It was not until a few months after the first edition was published that it was brought to my attention that *vepřo-knedlo-zelo*—the classical Czech dish of roast pork, cabbage, and dumplings—was not in the book. I surveyed the volume in haste only to find that there were basically no pork recipes at all. I found the missing chapter, "Pork," on my computer but I had neglected to finish it or send it to my publisher. I then contemplated a whole new book to make up for my mistake, provisionally entitled "The Forgotten Pig," but the opportunity of this second edition allows me another remedy. The new chapter on pork constitutes a major addition to the recipes for Czech main dishes.

The new chapter on mushrooms addresses a new obsession of mine, due in part, again, to the natural food resources of Newfoundland and, in part, to memories of walks as a child with my mother, gathering mushrooms in the woods of southern England. My obsession with forms of edible fungi is quite a typical Czech preoccupation and reflects the profusion and variety of mushrooms in a broad range of Czech dishes. Some of these recipes are to be found in the first edition, but I have added new ones here, using a wider variety of both fresh and dried wild mushrooms. The new chapter also addresses the promises and problems of hunting for fungus and some techniques for preparing and drying mushrooms.

The third new chapter, on drinks, concerns the aperitifs that precede meals, the beers and wines that accompany them, and the digestives that follow. The emphasis in this chapter is on the truly world historical moment among Czech beverages, namely, Czech Pilsner Urquell beer. If you do not know to what I refer and I have whetted your appetite, go directly to the final chapter.

A note about the title. My original plan for the book was to call it *New Czech Cooking* though this did not go over well with my publishers, who opted for a more traditional name. Given the rapid, haphazard, and tourist-oriented changes to what is now served as Czech food in the Republic, especially in Prague, I am quite satisfied with *The Best of Czech Cooking.*

Finally, a historical correction and a few additions to my "Acknowledgements." First, my daughter Alexandra, now five, has moved beyond "signs of loving food" to a deep and broad appreciation of all types of food and a skill in cooking things herself. I would also like to thank my father, Jiři Trnka, especially for his discussion of beers, wines, and spirits, and for the chess games that usually follow our suppers. Finally, I would like to thank all those writers on food, that I read when I was young. I first learned about this practical art by reading and it was as much the literacy of good food writers that maintained my interest in cooking as it was the food itself. Among those to whom I owe a debt is Dione Lucas, whose *French Cooking* I devoured from front to back when I was eleven or twelve, and whose recipes I still rely upon.

Peter Trnka
St. John's, Newfoundland
June 2001

INTRODUCTION

Many of the recipes collected in this book are, first and foremost, stories. Some are stories of how my mother taught herself how to cook Czech food once most of our family had left Prague, and others recount my own experiments in the kitchen which started when I was eight or nine years old and continue on today. There are stories about particular ingredients and cooking techniques, textures and colors, reductions and combinations, and about a long process of the education of taste. Many of these dishes also have social stories: of how certain foods are talked about and distinguished, of what happened at various dinner parties where such and such was served, of many memories of friends sharing in the ritual of dinner. For those who believe that cooking is an art, it is ephemeral at times, the product of long labor often disappearing quickly, but so grows the love of food, the care of its selection, preparation, and shared consumption. I hope that this book may, thus, be read in at least two ways. First, as a helpful resource for how to make a wide range of delicious and healthy Czech dishes. And, second, as an assembly of anecdotes about and suggestions for how to eat well.

The recipes in this book vary from the very simple to the quite complicated and time-consuming. They should thus appeal to the cook who is in a rush and also to one who, at least on occasion, has some time to spend on what they consider to be a skilled craft. The recipes are designed so that a relative newcomer to the kitchen should have little trouble creating a tasty meal but there are also remarks here and there for how a more ambitious cook might adjust or modify basic approaches.

Czech cooking is distinguished by some unique characteristics, primary among those being the large savory dumplings that are cut into slices like loaves of bread, but it also resembles other European cuisines, especially those of Russian, Polish, Hungarian, and German heritage. I have chosen dishes that exemplify the central Czech traditions but I have also modified some preparations. The extensive use of butter, lard, and cream is prohibitive to some and in many cases unnecessary for a rich and memorable meal, so I often cut down on quantity or suggest alternative forms of achieving similar results. I emphasize the many uses of different types of vegetables where some might be content to focus on meat, though there is no escaping the Czech inclination to make meat the centerpiece of one's meal. When it comes to meat, I use less fatty forms and suggest cooking finer cuts for shorter periods than some Czechs might prefer.

For someone new to Czech cooking, there will be a few surprises and novelties with regard to ingredients and modes of preparation, but none of these are too complicated or strange. The most important rule in cooking is to begin with quality, fresh ingredients and here Czechs are no exception. Learning how to use the right amount of salt, relying on freshly cracked pepper instead of a tasteless powder, choosing bread that has flavor, and knowing when to spice things up and when to leave things alone are simple principles that any cook needs to know. Some Czech peculiarities may need a little more explaining, though.

To begin with, many Czech dishes are simply made, with very few herbs or spices, except perhaps for some fresh parsley or caraway seeds here or there. This is not to say that few herbs or spices are known in Czech cooking but that their place is well-defined. Fresh herbs, such as parsley, dill, and chives, are used on many things, and paprika, caraway seeds, marjoram, bay, nutmeg, and thyme are also common. Other, less likely spices, such as ginger, cloves, and allspice are also used, and not only in baking but in piquant sauces for meat and fowl.

All herbs and spices, when dried, have a limited shelf-life. If you've had something sitting around for more than a year it is most likely useless and you should get rid of it. Some spices, such as pepper and nutmeg, clearly benefit from being ground or grated just before using. Since paprika is a key ingredient, take some time finding a good-quality one (some are completely bland and tasteless and add nothing but color to a dish). The same applies for prepared mustard: avoid the pure vinegar taste that generic American mustards tend to have and go for a stronger flavor. I recommend a good Dijon, though this may be too sharp for some palates.

As in many other cuisines, onions play a foundational role for many Czech foods, but the use of garlic is not as universal and usually it appears only in small quantities. You may want to adjust the amount of garlic suggested depending on your taste: many of the recipes would take more garlic in stride and would also not suffer if it were omitted. To fry onions and garlic, as well as vegetables and meat, Czechs use either vegetable oil, butter, or lard. Of these three fats, lard is preferred and often takes the form of drippings that are saved from frying bacon or other meats. If you like to use drippings this way, simply collect them in a jar that you keep in the fridge. Otherwise, store-bought lard is fine, though you can readily substitute vegetable oil for it or butter if you so choose.

Some butter or lard melted in a frying pan and then sprinkled with flour makes the typical thickening for Czech soups, stews, and sauces. This version of French roux is easy to make and has the benefit that the longer you fry the flour the darker hue it will add to your dish. If you wish to avoid the addition of fat when thickening something, simply mix together flour, water, and some of the hot cooking liquid, and add this to the sauce or soup.

On the liquid side of things, knowing how to make a good meat or fish broth will serve you well when it comes to preparing a soup, stew, or sauce. I include a couple of simple recipes for broth which do not discriminate excessively regarding the kinds of meats or fishes to be used. As long as you simmer a meat broth slowly and flavor it well just about any collection of meats and bones, with some exceptions, does well. If you do not have any homemade broth, using cubes is fine, as is plain water.

Czechs also use wine and beer to flavor food, though perhaps not as extensively as the French or Italians. Czech beer is very good, either of the pilsner or the dark variety, so using it instead of what I find to be blander American sorts is a good idea. Czech wine can also be quite nice but is sometimes hard to get and no great injustice will be done if you use something else. Cheaper wines are usually a good idea for cooking, though avoid cooking wine, which is excessively salty, and in dishes with a large quantity of wine choose a fairly tasty one as the flavor will pervade the dish.

The most familiar combination of vegetables in Czech cuisine consists of carrots, parsnips, and celeriac. This trio is common in soups and stews and is often also the foundation of a marinade or sauce. Celeriac or celery root is the least well-known of these vegetables but also perhaps the finest. It is more readily available in supermarkets and grocers now than a few years ago, though some still shy away from its dirty appearance. Celeriac is usually sold encrusted with earth and cleaning it may appear tricky but isn't: simply slice off a thin layer of the skin and then wash it well. The other commonly used vegetables are all familiar—potatoes, spinach, leeks, zucchini, cauliflower, beans—except, perhaps, for kohlrabi, a small to medium-size green bulb that tastes a little like young turnip.

When it comes to mushrooms things are more complicated. The ubiquitous white mushroom is excellent in many contexts but Czechs pride themselves on their use of wild mushrooms. More varieties of domestic and wild mushrooms are available now, both fresh and dried, and if unschooled in mushroom picking it is best to seek them out this way. Good, fresh portobello or porcini/*Boletus* mushrooms will do very well in just about any of the dishes calling for mushrooms. If you cannot find fresh wild mushrooms, use the dried ones for perhaps less spectacular but intensively flavorful effects. To use dried mushrooms, simply soak them in some warm water for about fifteen minutes and then clean off any dirt they may have clinging to them. The soaking water should not be thrown out but strain it and add to any soup or sauce.

The Czech use of meats and fishes poses one or two problems for other markets. In general there are many similarities between Czech favorites and things available elsewhere, but there are a few exceptions. First, the range of delicatessen meats that are available in the Czech Republic is enormous and many of these meats are used not only as appetizers or sandwich fillings but as the basis for certain dishes. Unless you live in a larger city with an Eastern European deli, you will have to simplify to some extent given what is available to you. Second, game is eaten quite extensively, and while some types of meat, such as rabbit or venison, are easy to find just about anywhere, wild boar and hare are not. Third, Czechs use almost all of the animal in cooking and so organ meats are more common than in many other cuisines. I will not press fried brains or poached tongue upon any reluctant guest, but for the curious such dishes hold great promise since organ meats, well-made, can be sublime.

Fourth, and finally, when it comes to fish Czechs are largely limited by their land-locked borders to freshwater fish and, of these, carp is the undoubted favorite. Carp are available in many fish markets but they often tend to be larger than the three- to four-pound optimal size. Large carp may have too pronounced a flavor and should be avoided. Other freshwater fish may easily substitute: bass and pickerel will do fine, as will, surprisingly, catfish or mackerel. Trout and salmon are also used a fair amount. The most important thing about fish is that it is fresh and that you do not overcook it. Most of the fish recipes in this book are quite simple and can easily use other kinds of fish than the ones specified. Salmon may be the only exception here since its color and flavor are quite unique. Czechs use parts of the fish that may be looked down upon elsewhere, especially the eggs or roe and the head. Fishheads are brilliant in soup. They also make for a splendid spectacle when kept on a whole fish and roasted.

A typical Czech meal often starts with a soup, though a simple hot or cold appetizer may be served prior to this. A lovely way to introduce a dinner is to serve a few thin slices of a smoked or spiced meat with a tasty bread. This principle is complicated somewhat to make *chlebíčky* or canapés, slices of good bread decorated with salami, ham, smoked trout, cheese, pickles, eggs, and so on. Eggs are used not only to decorate canapés but are also scrambled or made into omelettes, combined with vegetables or meats (especially calf's brain), or hold together pancakes or fritters. Many of the hot appetizers included here will make for a fine light lunch, especially the favorite potato pancakes or *bramboráky*.

Czech soups are usually quite hearty, often more like stews, especially those based on meat. Of these the most well known are *guláš* (goulash) or meat-soups flavored with paprika and a variety of vegetables, commonly potatoes, carrots, parsnips, cabbage, and/or sauerkraut. Tripe soup is probably one of the most distinctive of the Czech meat soups and when made well, cooked slowly until the tripe is incredibly tender, it is a real treat.

There are also all kinds of vegetable soups and while these are ordinarily made with a meat broth, using water instead makes them into excellent vegetarian meals. Vegetable soups may feature one main ingredient, such as cauliflower, cabbage, potatoes, or beets, or they may combine various types; they may be thickened with flour fried in butter or a mixture of cream and egg; and, finally, they are often served with croutons made from cubes of fine bread fried in butter or lard.

Croutons are essential for one of the signature dishes of Czech cuisine, the carp soup that begins the traditional Christmas Eve supper. One or two heads of the fish are ideal for this soup, but any combination of fish fillets will do. For the Christmas supper, the heads are used for soup and then the fillets are breaded and fried and served with a fancy potato salad. Last of all comes a Christmas cake called *vánočka* that is served in slices with butter and honey.

While potatoes certainly dominate a corner of the Czech salad repertoire, many other vegetables are served singly or in combination either before or with a main meal. Pickled beets or coleslawed cabbage are common, as is a sweetish cucumber salad. Salads are also made of all types of fresh or smoked meats and fish and such heartier dishes can easily be turned into complete lunches. Leftover roasts of beef or chicken are ideal for this purpose.

As for main dishes, fish are usually prepared quite simply, fried in a little butter, coated in flour or egg or a more complicated batter. Fish are also roasted, poached, or cooked "*na modro*" (blue) by using plenty of vinegar. All types of poultry apart from chicken can be found quite readily. Roasted duck or goose, served with dumplings and cabbage, is a typical dish, as are various stews featuring wild mushrooms or sauerkraut. Ducks and geese are also served with sweet or fruity accompaniments but this is certainly not invariably true.

What one can be quite sure of, however, is that beef and veal form the center of the Czech culinary heritage. Pork and, to a lesser extent, lamb have their place, but beef rules. From the simplest beef steak, fried in butter, adorned with nothing more than some pepper and parsley, to stuffed beef birds or braised sweetbreads, there is almost an endless array of fine dishes. *Svíčková* is the classic example. For this dish, beef tenderloin is marinated for a day in plenty of vinegar, herbs, spices, and root vegetables. The meat is then roasted and its marinade puréed and thickened with cream. Slices of the tenderloin are served with dumplings and plenty of rich sauce.

Savory, large bread or potato dumplings are served with many kinds of dishes and are more popular than the very popular potato. Czech dumplings may take some time to learn to make properly. The first trick is to get the right type of flour. A too fine flour is of no use. I find that a combination of regular white flour and semolina works well. Working the dough for dumplings takes a bit of muscle but requires no special skill, unlike the slicing of them. Czech dumplings are the size of small loaves of bread and so are served in slices about ¼ inch thick. To slice them right you shouldn't use a knife. A knife will compress the dumpling, whereas a piece of thread wrapped around the loaf and then brought together will yield a fluffier result.

Small dumplings of all sorts—flour, semolina, liver, spinach—are used widely in soups. Dumplings similar to Polish perogi or Italian ravioli are stuffed with seasoned ground meat or farmer cheese and served with lemon and melted butter. Czechs also make fruit dumplings for dessert, or, like in my family, as a meal in themselves. These small, fist-size dumplings are filled with plums, apricots, or strawberries and served with sugar, melted butter, and farmer cheese.

Fruit plays a major role in many Czech desserts. Thin fruit cakes, where the batter is studded with halved plums or cherries, strudels, pancakes, doughnuts, and fritters abound. Fruit preserves are also widely used, especially the dark, rich plum jam favored in many eastern European countries. Desserts are also often filled with a sweetened farmer cheese or a poppy seed mixture. Of the many cakes that are made, I include a few of the most common: *bábovka* (the Czech version of coffeecake) and *vánočka* (the Christmas cake). I also include a chestnut cake to show the frequent combination of flour and nuts in cake batter.

The selection of recipes in this book in no way forms an exhaustive or even near exhaustive account of the great variety of dishes that make up Czech cooking but represents an attempt to capture the best of parts of that tradition. I hope this book will be of use in your own experiments in the kitchen as well as in the stories about our lives that so often revolve around food.

1

Appetizers

Czech meals often begin with soup but something simple may come before: a little smoked meat, for example, with some pickles or capers and sliced, sweet onion. The simplicity of appetizers reflects, in part, the variety of prepared delicatessen foods available. All kinds of roasted and smoked meats, pork and beef, lean and fatty, mild or spiced, line the counters of a good delicatessen. Head cheese and smoked tongue are a couple of my favorites.

This simple presentation of meat takes on a more sophisticated life in the form of decorated canapés or *chlebíčky*. The combinations of meat, cheeses, eggs, pickles, and herbs are literally endless. Making these canapés involves a sense of color and design: you have to make sure that everything fits in a small space and that the ingredients project a vivid image.

It is crucial to use high quality ingredients for dishes such as these. Choose a nice, fresh bread with some texture and flavor. Find a good delicatessen. Use freshly grated pepper for seasoning. Serve with a glass of good wine or beer. And, not least, have a jar of mustard that will enhance the food you are serving. I find Dijon mustard does well, though many Czechs prefer a milder blend.

If you want to stay away from meat there are many hot vegetable dishes that make good appetizers. Whether stuffing or frying, make sure your greens are fresh and that you do not cook them too long.

Eggs are also popular and can be combined with meats or vegetables to create impressive appetizers or light meals. Get beyond the modern prejudice that holds that eggs should be served only for breakfast. Eggs are lovely scrambled, omeletted, or baked. And the same applies to them as to vegetables: do not overcook them. The difference between eggs scrambled with wild mushrooms made well and made badly is infinite.

Remember, scramble eggs on a fairly high heat in a good quantity of butter, stirring frequently. All it takes is a minute or two.

If not featured as the main ingredient, eggs play a part in many dishes, such as the various vegetable pancakes and fritters at the end of this chapter. As elsewhere, greens such as spinach and kale play a big role here. Used more and more these days, greens are tasty, colorful, and adapt to all kinds of uses. They also take rich ingredients like sour cream very well.

Ham Canapés
(Obložené Chlebíčky)

Thinly sliced French baguette, rye bread, or pumpernickel, spread with butter, mustard, or mayonnaise, and decorated with a choice of meat, cheese, eggs, pickles, and parsley makes for a favorite starter to meals. Really no rules apply apart from good taste and a sense of color. You may move away from the meat theme altogether and use a good spreadable cheese or a creamy potato salad. Make two or three kinds, arrange them on a fancy platter, and you have a very pretty and substantial beginning to your dinner. The following are a few examples of what can be done.

1 French baguette
3 tablespoons butter
3 tablespoons good quality mustard, mild to medium hot
½ pound good quality ham (Prague or Black Forest), sliced
2 hard-boiled eggs, sliced
2 pickles, sliced thinly lengthwise
several sprigs fresh parsley
salt and freshly ground pepper

Slice the baguette thinly along a shallow diagonal. Butter each piece and then spread on some mustard. Lay on a slice of ham. Place a slice of egg on top and a strip of pickle on its side, then tuck a sprig of fresh parsley somewhere convenient. Season with salt and pepper.

SERVES 4 TO 6.

Salami Canapés

Find a good quality Czech- or Polish-type salami with a little spice but not too hot. A Swiss cheese complements the salami well and its holes add to the decorative factor, but choose whatever mild cheese you like best. All kinds of meat may be used on bread in this way, be they specially smoked delicatessen meats or leftover roasts. Smoked tongue is especially nice.

8 slices rye bread, in quarters sliced thin
3 tablespoons butter
3 tablespoons good mustard
⅓ pound good salami, mild to medium hot
¼ pound Swiss cheese
thin slices sweet onion
2 pickles, sliced thinly lengthwise
sprigs of fresh parsley
salt and freshly ground black pepper

Spread the rye bread pieces with butter and then mustard. Place a slice of salami on each and cover with a piece of cheese. Add a few rings of onion, lay on a pickle slice, and a sprig of parsley, and lightly sprinkle with salt and pepper.

SERVES 4 TO 6.

Farmer Cheese Canapés

Find a tasty farmer cheese, ricotta, or even cream cheese to use for these canapés. If the cheese has a lot of liquid, hang it in a sieve for 30 minutes to get rid of the excess. If you like a little more spice in your food, combine the paprika with a pinch of cayenne pepper. Or mix a little horseradish or a crushed garlic clove into the cheese.

1 French baguette
3 tablespoons butter
1 cup farmer cheese, drained
½ cucumber, peeled and seeded
1½ tablespoons chopped fresh dill
1 teaspoon paprika
salt and freshly ground black pepper

Slice the French bread thinly across a shallow diagonal and butter each piece. Spread the bread with a coat of cheese. Lay on a couple of thin slices of cucumber. Sprinkle with dill, paprika, salt, and pepper.

SERVES 4 TO 6.

Smoked Trout Canapés

Smoked trout and salmon, though very different, are both nice as appetizers. You can try this with anchovies or herring as well, or, indeed, with any cured or smoked fish that is to your liking. Using chives instead of parsley varies the flavor a little.

1 French baguette
3 tablespoons butter
2 hard-boiled eggs, sliced
¼ pound smoked trout
salt and freshly ground black pepper
2 tablespoons chopped chives
1 lemon, cut into wedges

Slice the French bread thinly across a shallow diagonal. Butter the bread and then place an egg slice and a piece of trout on each portion. Sprinkle with salt, pepper, and chopped chives. Serve with lemon wedges.

SERVES 4 TO 6.

Stuffed Eggs

Stuffing eggs is as simple an enterprise as decorating bread. As long as you pay attention to what ingredients go together and what looks nice, the outcome will be a success. What follows is a basic recipe flavored with some sweet onion and fresh dill. Add some crushed anchovies or red pepper and capers for a more complex flavor. Caviar, or some other kind of roe, sprinkled on top of the eggs, is also very good.

6 hard-boiled eggs
3 tablespoons mayonnaise
1 tablespoon minced sweet onion
1 tablespoon chopped fresh dill
salt and freshly ground black pepper
1 teaspoon paprika
several sprigs fresh dill

Carefully slice the hard-boiled eggs in half lengthwise. Remove the yolks and place in a small bowl. Mash the yolks lightly with a fork. Mix in the mayonnaise until well incorporated. Mix in the sweet onion, chopped dill, and salt and pepper to taste.

Using a teaspoon, fill the egg whites with the stuffing. Sprinkle on paprika and decorate with a sprig of dill.

SERVES 6.

Mushrooms Stuffed with Spinach

Czechs, like most people, stuff just about anything that has a cavity, including tomatoes, peppers, cucumbers, onions, celeriac, and mushrooms. The spinach and mushroom coupling is excellent. Choose large white champignon mushrooms if this is all that is available, but otherwise opt for portobellos or porcinis.

- 12 large mushrooms
- 1 pound fresh spinach
- 2 strips bacon, diced
- 1 small onion, finely chopped
- ½ teaspoon marjoram
- 2 egg yolks
- bread crumbs (optional)
- salt and freshly ground black pepper
- ½ cup grated Gruyère cheese

Wipe the mushrooms clean and cut off the end of the stalk if it contains dirt. Pull the stalks apart from the caps and chop the stalks finely.

Clean the spinach and blanch it in boiling salt water for 2 minutes. Remove, squeeze dry, and chop. Preheat the broiler.

Fry the bacon in a pan until well done but not crisp. Add the onion and fry until almost golden, stirring occasionally. Add the chopped mushroom stalks and fry for a few more minutes. Take the pot off the stove. Mix in the spinach and marjoram. Mix in the egg yolks. Add some bread crumbs if the mixture needs thickening. Season with salt and pepper. Fill the mushrooms with the stuffing, cover with grated cheese, and broil 10 minutes, or until the cheese is bubbly and golden.

SERVES 4 TO 6.

Stuffed Green Peppers

Double the quantities in this recipe for a fine main course. If substituting large tomatoes for the peppers, reduce the baking time a little. The following uses meat in the filling, but you may try chopped mushrooms instead.

4 tablespoons (½ stick) butter or vegetable oil
2 medium onions, chopped
1 clove garlic, crushed
½ pound ground pork
4 tablespoons chopped fresh parsley
2 teaspoons marjoram
1 cup cooked rice
salt and freshly ground black pepper
4 large green peppers
1 can (28 ounces) crushed tomatoes
1 cup sour cream

To make the filling, melt 2 tablespoons of the butter in a frying pan and fry half the chopped onion and all of the garlic on medium-low heat until almost golden. Raise the heat and add the ground pork. Cook for 5 or 6 minutes until the meat is well browned, stirring occasionally. Mix in 2 tablespoons of parsley, 1 teaspoon marjoram, the rice, and salt and pepper to taste. Remove from heat.

Slice off the bottoms of the peppers and reserve. Pare the insides of the peppers and wash them and their bottoms. Fill the peppers with the stuffing and close them by replacing the bottoms.

To make the sauce, fry the remaining onion in the remaining 2 tablespoons butter until almost golden. Add the remaining 2 tablespoons parsley and 1 teaspoon marjoram, and salt and pepper to taste. Add the crushed tomatoes, bring slowly to a boil, and simmer, uncovered, for 30 minutes.

Preheat the oven to 350°F.

Place the peppers in a baking dish, cover them with the tomato sauce, and bake for 30 minutes. Serve with sour cream on top.

SERVES 4.

Kale Rolls

Kale, like other greens, is coming back into style and here it is used instead of the common cabbage. Nutritious, versatile, tasty, and cheap, greens may be simply braised on their own, added to soups or stews, or stuffed as below. If you want to keep the dish meat free, substitute a combination of mushrooms and carrots for the ground beef or pork.

1 large head kale
4 tablespoons (½ stick) butter or vegetable oil
1 medium onion, chopped
1 clove garlic, crushed
¼ pound mushrooms, sliced
½ pound ground beef or pork
1 cup cooked rice
salt and freshly ground black pepper
1 teaspoon marjoram
½ teaspoon grated nutmeg
1 egg (optional)
1 cup beef broth or water
1 cup sour cream

Cut off the harder stems of the kale leaves and chop these up for later use in the stuffing. Take the whole leaves and blanch them very quickly in boiling, salted water for 15 to 30 seconds. Remove and let dry.

For the filling, melt 2 tablespoons of butter or oil in a frying pan on medium-low heat. Add the onion and the garlic and fry until almost golden, stirring occasionally. Add the mushrooms and fry for a couple of minutes. Add the ground beef and brown for 5 minutes. Add the chopped kale stems and cook a few minutes longer. Add the cooked rice. Season with salt, pepper, marjoram, and nutmeg. Remove from heat. If the filling is loose, bind it by mixing in a whole egg.

Preheat oven to 375°F.

Spread out one of the kale leaves, put 2 or 3 tablespoons of filling in the center, and roll it up. Repeat until all the leaves are filled. Put the kale rolls in an ovenproof dish, pour on the broth, and dot the rolls with the remaining 2 tablespoons butter or oil. Bake for 30 minutes. Serve with sour cream.

SERVES 4 TO 6.

Ham Baked in Pastry

A large, thick slice of ham serves as a nice appetizer when covered with cheese and phyllo pastry, especially when you can pick up this delicate, rich pastry ready-made at the grocery store.

1 package (1 pound) phyllo pastry
¾ cup grated Gouda or Gruyère cheese
1 thick slice ham
1 egg
pickles

Preheat the oven to 375°F.

Roll the phyllo pastry out fairly thin, fold it over, and roll it out again. Sprinkle on half the cheese, place the ham slice on top, and cover with the rest of the cheese. Fold the phyllo pastry over the filling and make it into a nice, tightly closed package. Beat the egg and brush it on the pastry. Bake the pastry in a buttered dish until golden, about 30 minutes. Serve with pickles.

SERVES 4.

Ham Baked with Celeriac

The simple combination of ham and celery root covered with sliced tomatoes and cheese makes a splendid, casserole-type starter. This is a wonderful way to use leftovers from a baked ham.

- ½ pound thick-sliced, good quality ham
- ½ small celeriac
- 2 tablespoons butter or lard
- 1 small leek
- 1 large potato, boiled, peeled, and sliced
- 1 teaspoon marjoram
- salt and freshly grated black pepper
- 2 ripe tomatoes, sliced
- ½ cup grated Gruyère cheese

Slice the ham into thin strips about 1½ inches long. Clean the celeriac well, then cut into strips the same size as the ham. Blanch the celeriac strips in salted, boiling water for about 10 minutes or until tender. Remove the celeriac and drip dry.

Preheat the oven to 400°F.

Melt the butter or lard in a frying pan on medium-low heat. Slice the leek into fine circles and fry, stirring occasionally, for 2 minutes. Add the ham and celeriac and fry for a few minutes longer. Add the sliced potato. Season with marjoram, and salt and pepper to taste.

Place the mixture in an ovenproof dish. Cover with sliced tomatoes. Finally, cover with the grated cheese. Bake for 15 minutes. The cheese should be bubbling and golden brown when done.

SERVES 4.

Poached Carp

One small carp, weighing 2 to 3 pounds, will feed 4 people as an appetizer. If carp is not available or is not to your liking, you may also use fillets of pickerel, bass, trout, or mackerel. Fish fillets may also be fried in butter or baked in a hot oven with some wine and lemon juice. Do not overcook the fish: 10 minutes per inch of thickness is a good gauge.

- 4 small carp fillets
- salt and freshly ground black pepper
- 1 tablespoon caraway seeds, crushed
- 2 tablespoons butter
- 1 small onion, thinly sliced
- ½ teaspoon cayenne pepper
- ½ cup dry white wine
- juice of ½ lemon
- 2 tablespoons chopped fresh parsley
- 1 lemon, quartered

Season the fillets with salt, pepper, and the crushed caraway seeds.

Heat the butter in a frying pan over low heat. Fry the fillets very gently for no more than 2 minutes per side. Add the sliced onion and sprinkle on the cayenne pepper. Add the wine and lemon juice, and bring to a low boil. Season with salt and pepper. Poach, covered, for 5 minutes.

Remove the fillets from their liquid. Reduce the liquid on a high heat, whisking in a little more butter. Pour the sauce on the fillets, sprinkle them with parsley, and serve with lemon quarters and white bread.

SERVES 4.

Caviar Lívanečky

A delicate savory pastry is baked in butter and then topped with caviar and sour cream: rich, decadent, and impressive. If you can afford real, expensive caviar, go for it. Otherwise, any type of roe will do fine. Bliny are made by frying such pastries in butter.

- ½ ounce (1 packet) dry yeast
- ½ cup milk or light cream
- 1 cup smooth flour
- 2 eggs
- 4 tablespoons (½ stick) butter, melted
- 1 cup sour cream
- 2 to 3 ounces caviar or roe
- 1 lemon, cut into wedges

Put the yeast in a cup with 1 tablespoon warm milk and 1 tablespoon flour. Cover with a damp cloth and leave in a warm place to ferment for 30 minutes.

Warm the remaining milk in a small pot, but do not boil it. Take it off the heat, let cool for a few seconds, and break in the eggs, one at a time. Mix well. Add the yeast mixture and stir well. Add the milk mixture to the remaining flour and make a ball of dough. Leave for 1 hour, covered, in a warm place, to rise.

Preheat the oven to 400°F.

Roll the dough out quite thin and cut out diamonds about 2 inches long. Brush these with melted butter and bake for 20 minutes. Put on serving plates. On each livánec, add a dollop of sour cream and some caviar. Serve with lemon wedges on the side.

SERVES 4 TO 6.

Asparagus Baked with Eggs

Eggs used to be much more common than they are these days, both as appetizers and main dishes. Yet they may be prepared in so many ways and are cheap and tasty. Scramble them simply or with the addition of fancier ingredients. Or add one more degree of complexity and unify the scramble into an omelette and wrap it around something good. Eggs are also very nice baked. If you have them, individual ramekins or custard dishes make this dish more than pretty.

1 pound asparagus
1 cup milk
4 tablespoons (½ stick) butter
4 tablespoons flour
salt and freshly ground black pepper
½ teaspoon grated nutmeg
8 large eggs
½ cup grated Gruyère cheese
2 tablespoons chopped fresh parsley

Break off the tough ends of the asparagus and discard them. Wash the asparagus and steam in salted water for 4 to 5 minutes, or until almost tender. Remove the asparagus from the liquid.

Make a béchamel sauce as follows: Warm the milk in a small pot on medium heat. Melt the butter in a frying pan on medium heat, add the flour and fry for a couple of minutes, stirring well. Mix in the warm milk, stirring constantly, and bring slowly to a boil. Cook another couple of minutes to achieve a fairly thick sauce. Remove from the heat and season with salt, pepper, and nutmeg.

Preheat the oven to 350°F degrees.

If you have ramekins, great, but if you don't, use one large oven dish and make one big version of what follows. Butter each ramekin. Place 3 or 4 stalks of asparagus in each dish. Break 2 eggs on top of the asparagus. Cover with some of the béchamel sauce. Sprinkle on grated cheese. Place the ramekins in a large pan of water and bake until the eggs are set but the yolks are still soft, 15 to 20 minutes. Sprinkle with parsley and serve.

SERVES 4.

Eggs Baked with Chicken Livers

A rich dish that transforms some ordinary ingredients into a sophisticated appetizer. In this recipe, as in many others, I choose to use Gruyère cheese for cooking since it melts well and has a distinct but not strong flavor.

½ cup peas, fresh or frozen
2 tablespoons butter
1 small onion, finely chopped
1 clove garlic, crushed
⅓ pound chicken livers, chopped
3 tablespoons chopped fresh parsley
salt and freshly ground black pepper
8 large eggs
½ cup grated Gruyère cheese

Preheat oven to 375°F.

Cook the peas in boiling water until almost tender. Drain.

Melt the butter in a frying pan on medium-low heat. Fry the onion and garlic until almost golden. Add the chopped livers and cook for 5 minutes. Mix in the peas and 2 tablespoons of the parsley. Season with salt and pepper.

Butter 4 ramekin or custard dishes. Fill each with some of the liver mixture and make two small wells. Crack 2 eggs into each well. Sprinkle on the grated cheese.

Bake until the eggs are set but not hard, about 15 minutes. Serve sprinkled with the remaining 1 tablespoon of parsley.

SERVES 4.

Scrambled Eggs with Calf's Brains

Obviously not a dish for the squeamish, but if you like calf's brains this will appeal to you. The consistency of soft scrambled eggs is very close to that of brains: when combined, the two taste like a cloud.

- juice of 1 lemon
- ½ pound calf's brains, cleaned
- 2 tablespoons butter
- 6 large eggs
- salt and freshly ground black pepper
- cream (optional)
- 2 tablespoons finely chopped fresh parsley or chives

Bring a pot of salted water to a boil. Add the lemon juice. Add the brains and poach until tender, about 30 minutes. Remove, drip dry, and keep warm in the oven.

Melt the butter on medium heat in a large frying pan. Break the eggs into a bowl and whisk very well. Add salt and pepper. Scramble the eggs quickly in the frying pan, making sure they do not dry out (a little cream may be added when they are done).

Slice the calf's brains fairly thin. Place on serving plates, cover with the scrambled eggs, and sprinkle on salt, pepper, and parsley or chives.

SERVES 4.

Cauliflower Scrambled with Eggs

From real brains we go to a dish that uses eggs and cauliflower to imitate them, sort of. The texture is wonderful and if you like this enough, you may soon move on to the real thing. Other vegetables may be substituted for the cauliflower, such as spinach or kale, and mixing in some grated cheese is also nice.

- ½ small cauliflower
- 8 large eggs
- 2 tablespoons butter
- 4 scallions, sliced
- 1 teaspoon caraway seeds, crushed
- 1 tablespoon chopped fresh chives

Cook the cauliflower in salted boiling water until tender, about 20 minutes. Drain and chop roughly.

Beat the eggs well in a bowl.

Melt the butter in a frying pan on low-medium heat. Fry the scallions for 2 minutes. Mix in the chopped cauliflower and the crushed caraway seeds.

Raise the heat a little under the frying pan. Add the eggs and, stirring well, fry them until just done, which should take 2 or 3 minutes at most. Serve sprinkled with chives.

SERVES 4.

Scrambled Eggs with Mushrooms

If pressed, you may use ordinary white champignon mushrooms for this dish, but the eggs go best with a wilder taste like that of porcinis or portobellos. As in other recipes, the eggs are good here for presenting the essence of one other ingredient. When well made, the eggs are creamy and light: again, beware of overcooking them.

½ pound fresh porcini or portobello mushrooms, chopped
12 large eggs
2 tablespoons butter
2 tablespoons chopped fresh parsley

Wipe the mushrooms clean and cut off the end of the stems if there is dirt attached. Slice them fairly thick, about ¼ inch.

Beat the eggs well in a bowl.

Melt the butter on fairly high heat in a frying pan. Throw in the mushrooms and brown them quickly. Lower the heat a little under the frying pan and add the eggs. Stirring well, cook the eggs quickly and remove from heat. Serve sprinkled with parsley.

SERVES 4 TO 6.

Spinach Omelette

Just one example of how lovely an omelette may be as an appetizer or main dish, again featuring greens. If available, try substituting red Swiss chard for the spinach for an interesting color contrast.

1 pound fresh spinach
4 tablespoons (½ stick) butter
1 small onion, chopped
½ teaspoon grated nutmeg
salt and freshly ground black pepper
5 large eggs
½ cup grated Gruyère cheese

Clean the spinach and blanch in salted boiling water for 2 minutes. Remove and squeeze dry.

Melt 2 tablespoons butter in a frying pan on low-medium heat. Fry the onion until almost golden. Remove and mix with the spinach. Season with nutmeg, salt, and pepper.

Beat the eggs in a small bowl.

Melt the remaining 2 tablespoons butter on medium heat in the frying pan. When quite hot, pour in the eggs and stir them around with a fork, as they cook for the first minute or two. Lower the heat and let the eggs almost set, stirring the surface of the omelette with your fork. Place the spinach on half the omelette. Cover with the grated Gruyère. Fold the omelette over with a spatula and cook for a couple more minutes, until the cheese has melted.

SERVES 2.

Fried Cauliflower

This dish may be served with a cheese sauce: make a béchamel sauce (as in the recipe for Asparagus Baked with Eggs, see page 27) and add some grated cheese when done. I like cauliflower made this way simply with lemon juice and mayonnaise.

1 small cauliflower
3 eggs
salt and freshly ground black pepper
¼ cup milk
¾ cup flour
4 tablespoons (½ stick) butter
1 lemon, cut into wedges
mayonnaise

Wash the cauliflower and let dry. Break the vegetable apart into florets. Blanch in boiling salted water for 5 minutes.

Break the eggs into a bowl, season with salt and pepper, and mix in the milk. Add the flour and mix into a medium-thick batter.

Melt the butter on medium-low heat in a large frying pan. Dip the florets in batter, coating them well, and then place in the frying pan. Fry on all sides until golden brown, about 10 minutes altogether. Serve with wedges of lemon and big dollops of mayonnaise.

SERVES 4 TO 6.

Potato Pancakes
(Bramboráky)

Readily available in the smallest of kitchens or roadside stands, potato pancakes are staples of Czech cooking. Crisp and tender, they are rich enough to serve as is, with a sprinkle of parsley, or with a little sour cream.

- 6 large potatoes
- 1 teaspoon salt
- 2 cloves garlic, crushed
- 1 teaspoon marjoram
- 2 eggs
- ¼ cup flour
- 4 tablespoons (½ stick) butter

Peel the potatoes and grate them roughly, either by hand or in a food processor. Squeeze out the excess liquid that the potatoes release. Add salt, crushed garlic, marjoram, eggs, and the flour. Mix well.

Melt some butter in a frying pan on medium heat. Add large dollops of potato mixture and flatten them out to make pancakes. Fry until golden, 3 to 4 minutes, then flip and repeat. Keep frying the pancakes in batches, keeping the finished ones warm in the oven, until all are done.

SERVES 4 TO 6.

Spinach Pancakes

Like other recipes for greens, substitute whatever is available for what may be specified in a recipe. Mustard greens, Swiss chard, or kale will do just as well as spinach.

- 1 pound fresh spinach, cleaned
- 4 tablespoons (½ stick) butter
- 2 eggs, separated
- 1 teaspoon salt
- ⅓ cup flour
- freshly ground black pepper
- ½ teaspoon grated nutmeg
- 1 cup sour cream

Preheat the oven to 375°F.

Blanch the spinach in salted boiling water for 2 minutes. Remove and squeeze dry. Chop roughly.

Cream together the butter, egg yolks, and salt in a bowl. Mix in the spinach. Then add the flour. Beat the egg whites until stiff, then add to the mixture and combine well. Season with pepper and nutmeg.

Butter a flat baking pan. Mold large pancakes from the spinach mixture, place on the baking pan, and bake for about 20 minutes. Serve with sour cream.

SERVES 4 TO 6.

Vegetable Fritters

A more complicated version of the pancake idea, using yeast-risen dough and a mixture of vegetables: choose whatever is fresh. A mixture of ground beef, or pork fried with onions, may be substituted for the vegetable filling.

1 cup mixed chopped vegetables, e.g. carrots, peas, celeriac, etc.
¼ ounce (1 packet) dry yeast
¼ cup milk
¾ cup flour
1 egg
salt
¼ pound mushrooms, sliced
4 tablespoons (½ stick) butter or oil, divided
1 small onion, thinly sliced
2 tablespoons chopped fresh parsley plus additional sprigs for garnish
freshly ground black pepper
1 cup sour cream

Blanch the vegetables in salted boiling water for 5 minutes. Drain and reserve.

To make the dough, first mix the yeast with a little warmed milk and a little flour. Cover with a warm, damp cloth and put in a warm place. Let rise for 5 to 10 minutes.

Mix the remainder of the flour with the egg, the remaining milk, and the risen yeast mixture. Add a little salt. Cover and let rise in a warm place for 30 minutes.

Fry the mushrooms in 1 tablespoon butter until golden brown, then set aside.

To make the fritters, flatten out oval-shaped portions of dough, the size of a small pancake, on a floured board. Place a scoop of the blanched vegetables on the dough. Add some sliced onion, mushrooms, and parsley. Season with salt and pepper. Close the fritters and seal them by pinching the dough. Make all the fritters this way.

Fry the fritters on medium heat in the remaining butter until golden on both sides, about 10 minutes. Serve sprinkled with parsley and a dollop of sour cream.

SERVES 4 TO 6.

2

Soups

Served either as a first course or as meals in themselves, soups form a major part of Czech cuisine. Soups are an economical way to feed a number of family members or guests, especially when one wants a small portion of meat to go a long way. The richness of a soup used to be judged in part by measuring the "eyes" that formed on the surface: the more droplets of fat floating on the top of the soup, the greater the generosity of the host. Traditionally, most meat and vegetable soups begin with a broth made from meat and bones, usually beef, but often a mixture of different kinds. The Czech obsession with meat need not be followed to take advantage of the variety of soups found in the cuisine, however. Many vegetable soups are very good made with water instead of meat broth. The fish soups also may be made with water as their base, though a good fish stock enhances them.

I begin with a basic recipe for beef broth which may be modified depending on the types of meat one has at home. A broth made primarily with red meat, beef or a combination of beef, pork, and lamb, will be darker than one using all or mostly chicken. If you have them, duck bones are wonderful in a meat stock. I follow with a number of meat soups, most starting from the basic broth and adding fresh beef or pork or smoked meat or sausage, as well as a selection of vegetables.

Czechs use a familiar combination of root vegetables in many soups: carrots, parsnips, celery root or celeriac, and potatoes. You should be able to find celery root without too much difficulty. Do not be put off by the fact that it seems to be the only vegetable sold with dirt still sticking to it. When you get it home, simply cut off the thin outside layer of the root with its dirt and you will be left with a white globe which, when diced and added to soups, is quite lovely. Parsnips and celery root are often used together but you may also substitute one for the other depending on what is available.

Fish soups are made very differently from meat soups. While a good meat broth requires a few hours of slow simmering to achieve its full flavor, a fish stock may be finished in half an hour. This is because fish lets off its taste very quickly and there is no need for prolonged cooking to break down its flesh. Czechs use mostly freshwater fish in cooking, and carp is a big favorite. If carp is available, use it, making sure you buy the smaller, two- to three-pound versions. Large carp may taste muddy, but this warning does not apply to the small fish, if fresh. Carp are unjustly maligned. Their flavor is rich and the meat has a dense texture. If carp are not to be found, I often use a combination of other fishes, such as pickerel, catfish, perch, and mackerel. In most of the recipes below, you may substitute almost any kind of firm-textured fish for those listed and the result will be a tasty soup.

Perhaps the greatest variety of cooking methods and flavors may be found in vegetable soups: chunky soups and puréed soups, clear ones and creamy ones, those that bring out the essence of one vegetable and those combining many, and so on. Vegetable soups usually take less time to cook than meat soups, especially if you do not overcook the vegetables. Like meat and fish soups, they are often served sprinkled with chopped fresh parsley and fried croutons. They may also be fortified with leftover crepes, thinly sliced, or some type of dumpling or noodle. Indeed, there is such a vast array of dumplings used in Czech soups that they could easily fill a chapter of their own. I describe some basic types at the end of the chapter and the enterprising cook may easily modify these once the basic techniques are understood.

Finally, a word on thickenings. Once a soup is almost finished, you may want to thicken the broth a little. There are numerous ways of going about this. If you are using potatoes or rice or dumplings in the recipe, these additions will tend to thicken the soup on their own. Otherwise, a typical method is to add a little cream into which you have whisked an egg yolk. This is done at the last minute: you don't want to cook the egg, just heat the mixture through with the rest of the soup. Even easier perhaps, and less fattening, is to mix some flour or cornstarch with some water in a small cup, then add some of the hot liquid from the soup, then mix into the soup and boil for a couple of minutes. Adding hot liquid to the thickener before it is incorporated into the soup avoids lumps; if using cornstarch you may skip this step as cornstarch never lumps.

Yet another thickening procedure, and probably the most popular one, is to use a roux. A roux is usually made at the beginning of a soup but may also be added a few minutes before serving. To make a roux, in its most basic form, melt 4 tablespoons (½ stick) butter, add an equal portion of flour and cook for a few minutes, and then add a cup of the stock or liquid you are using, mixing well, and cook another couple of minutes. Thickening soup with a small portion of flour in this way avoids any lumps and adds flavor. Cook the flour briefly for a light color, longer for a darker hue: when making the roux, you will see the flour gradually browning the longer you keep it on the heat. Practice will tell you how long is enough for the hue required. Czechs often use lard or meat drippings, especially bacon, instead of butter: if this is to your liking, begin storing drippings in a small jar in your fridge.

Beef Broth

Beef broth is the basis for many Czech soups, though water may be substituted if desired. I prefer to use beef shank over cubed stewing beef: shank is tastier, cheaper, and comes with the bone and marrow so beneficial to stock. You need not stick strictly to beef. Any leftover meat or bone is acceptable, though too much lamb or chicken will change the flavor of the broth. Replace all the beef with chicken to make a light chicken broth. Beef or chicken broth may be turned into a simple soup with, for example, the addition of some carrots, parsnips, celery root, and onion, thickened either with a little roux or egg yolk mixed with cream. Broth may also be served poured on toast spread with a little crushed garlic, or with noodles or dumplings.

2 pounds stewing beef and bones
8 cups cold salted water
2 bay leaves
8 to 10 whole black peppercorns
1 medium parsnip, chopped
1 large carrot, chopped
½ small celeriac, chopped
1 large onion, halved

Put the meat and bones in a large pot and cover with water. Cover the pot and slowly bring to a boil. Add all the other ingredients and cook for 2 to 3 hours, skimming off any scum that forms on the surface or any excess grease. Strain the liquid from the meat and vegetables. (Instead of skimming grease from the broth as it cooks, you may refrigerate the broth when it is done, and once set, simply scoop the fat off the surface.)

MAKES 6 CUPS OF BROTH.

Beef Goulash Soup

Goulash soups are common to Czech, Slovak, Polish, and, of course, Hungarian cuisine. They may be served at the start of a meal but large portions are satisfying all on their own. Paprika is a central ingredient in goulash and other Czech soups. Try to get a good quality paprika. Paprika does come in different degrees of hotness, though all are relatively mild.

- 2 strips bacon, diced
- 1 medium onion, finely chopped
- 1 pound stewing beef, cubed
- ½ small celeriac, diced
- 2 medium carrots, diced
- 1 medium parsnip, diced
- 1 tablespoons paprika
- 2 tablespoons tomato paste
- 8 cups water or broth
- 4 medium potatoes, cubed
- salt and freshly ground black pepper
- 1 teaspoon celery seed, crushed
- 1 teaspoon caraway seed, crushed
- 2 cloves garlic, crushed
- 2 tablespoons flour

Fry the bacon in a large pot until well done, but not crisp. Add the onion and fry slowly until almost golden, stirring occasionally. Add the cubed beef and fry until browned. Add the celeriac, carrots, parsnip, paprika, and tomato paste, and fry for several more minutes.

Add the water or broth (the pot should be about ⅔ full). Bring slowly to a boil, reduce the heat, and simmer, partially covered, for about 2 hours or until the meat is tender. Add the potatoes, salt and pepper to taste, celery seeds, caraway seeds, and garlic. Simmer for another 30 minutes or so, until the potatoes are done. If the soup needs thickening, mix the flour with some water in a small cup, add some of the hot liquid from the soup, then incorporate the thickener back into the soup, mixing well and letting boil for a couple of minutes.

SERVES 4.

Pork Goulash Soup

This is a lighter version of goulash, with fewer vegetables and featuring pork instead of beef. Once you have the general idea, you can combine both meats in the same soup if you wish and choose the vegetables you prefer.

1 large onion, finely chopped
4 tablespoons (½ stick) butter
1 pound pork, cubed
6 cups beef or chicken broth
salt and freshly ground black pepper
2 tablespoons flour
2 medium carrots, diced
4 medium potatoes, diced
1 tablespoon paprika
2 cloves garlic, crushed
1 teaspoon caraway seeds, crushed
1 teaspoon marjoram

Fry the onion in 2 tablespoons of butter in a large pan on low heat until almost golden. Raise the heat to medium, add the pork and fry until browned, stirring occasionally. Pour on the broth and bring to a slow boil. Add salt and pepper to taste. Reduce heat to low and simmer, uncovered, for about 1 hour or until the meat is tender.

Spoon away the grease from the surface of the soup.

In a frying pan, melt the remaining 2 tablespoons butter on medium heat, then add the flour and fry it for 2 to 3 minutes, stirring often. Add some warm broth to the roux, mixing well; bring to a boil, then stir this mixture into the soup.

Add the carrots, potatoes, paprika, garlic, caraway seeds, and marjoram to the soup. Cook about 30 minutes until the vegetables are done.

SERVES 4.

Beef Soup with Sour Cream

This is a very simple beef soup distinguished by the combination of a flavorful broth with the sourness of the cream and vinegar that are added toward the end of its cooking. Use pumpernickel, rye, or good quality white bread to make the croutons.

1 pound stewing beef
1 tablespoon vegetable oil
6 cups cold water or broth
salt and freshly ground black pepper
1 medium onion, skinned and left whole
1 teaspoon marjoram
2 bay leaves
3 tablespoons butter
2 tablespoons flour
½ cup sour cream
2 to 4 tablespoons white wine vinegar
3 slices black or rye bread

Put the piece or pieces of stewing beef as they are into a large pot, pour on the vegetable oil, and cover with water or broth. Add salt, a good deal of pepper, the whole onion, marjoram, and the bay leaves. Bring slowly to a boil, reduce heat, and simmer, uncovered, until the meat is tender, about 2 hours.

Remove the meat and onion from the broth, discard the onion and cut the meat into fine pieces.

Melt 2 tablespoons of the butter in a frying pan and add the flour: fry gently to make a roux. Add some of the warm broth, mixing well, and bring to a boil slowly; cook for a couple of minutes, then stir into the soup and cook for 20 minutes. Return the meat to the soup and cook for a few more minutes.

Take the soup off the heat. Stir in the sour cream and vinegar to taste. Serve with croutons made from frying cubed bread in the remaining butter.

SERVES 4 TO 6.

Tripe Soup
(Drštková Polévka)

This is a classic Czech soup in which the tripe should be extremely tender and the broth creamy and rich. Many people are afraid of innards, but they can be the most tasty and tender servings when cooked well. If you buy the tripe precooked (which is normal these days) then it does not need pre-boiling to tenderize it.

- 1 pound tripe
- 1 large onion, finely chopped
- 3 tablespoons butter or lard
- 2 tablespoons flour
- ½ small celeriac, diced
- 2 medium carrots, diced
- 1 medium parsnip, diced
- 1 tablespoon paprika
- salt and freshly ground black pepper
- 2 cloves garlic, crushed
- 4 tablespoons chopped fresh parsley
- 1 teaspoon marjoram

If the tripe is not precooked, wash it well, rub it with salt, and wash again. Cook the tripe in boiling water for 30 minutes. Discard the cooking liquid. Fill a pot with 8 cups fresh salted water. Bring to a boil, add the precooked trip, reduce heat, and simmer for 2 to 3 hours or tender. Remove the tripe, reserve the broth, and chop fine.

In a large pot, fry the onion in the butter or lard. Add the flour and fry on medium heat for a couple of minutes. Add ½ cup of the reserved broth from the soup, mixing well. Bring to boil slowly. Add the rest of the broth, stirring constantly. Add the chopped tripe, celeriac, carrots, parsnip, paprika, salt, pepper, garlic, 2 tablespoons of the parsley, and the marjoram. Simmer, partially covered, until vegetables and tripe are tender. Serve sprinkled with the remaining 2 tablespoons of parsley.

SERVES 6.

Red Soup

If you have a few different types of meat left over from other dishes, this soup will suit you well. Combining beef, pork, and lamb with tomatoes and paprika gives this soup a rich red-brown color.

1 medium onion, finely chopped
3 tablespoons butter or lard
1 pound beef, pork, and lamb, cubed
2 tablespoons flour
1 tablespoon paprika
4 skinned tomatoes, chopped
2 medium potatoes, diced
salt and freshly ground black pepper
2 tablespoons chopped fresh parsley

In a large pot, fry the onion in the butter or lard on low heat until almost golden, stirring occasionally. Raise the heat to medium, add the meat and brown it all over. Add the flour and paprika, and fry for a couple of minutes. Add 6 cups water, bring slowly to a boil, reduce heat, and simmer, partially covered, until almost tender.

Add the tomatoes and potatoes, and salt and pepper to taste. Cook until tender, about 20 minutes. Sprinkle with parsley before serving.

SERVES 4 TO 6.

Smoked Meat Soup

Sauerkraut and kale are both good complements to the smoked taste of this soup. Use whichever is available, opting for the first if you desire a more sour taste and kale for a bright green color.

- ½ pound smoked pork hock
- 1 pound sauerkraut or kale, chopped
- 2 medium potatoes, diced
- 2 tablespoons butter or lard
- 1 medium onion, finely chopped
- 4 tablespoons flour
- 1 tablespoon paprika
- 1 teaspoon marjoram
- 2 tablespoons chopped fresh parsley

Put the smoked meat in a large pot and add 6 cups water. Bring slowly to a boil, reduce heat, and simmer, uncovered, until tender, about 2 hours. Remove the meat and chop into cubes, then return it to the broth. Add the chopped sauerkraut or kale and the potatoes. Bring the soup back to a boil and simmer for 15 minutes.

Make a roux: melt the butter or lard on low heat, add the onions and fry until almost golden, then add flour, paprika, and marjoram, and fry for 2 or 3 more minutes, stirring occasionally. Add ½ cup of the hot broth, mixing well, and bring to a boil while stirring. Cook the roux for a couple of minutes and then stir into the soup. (The soup may also be thickened with a mixture of milk or cream and an egg yolk instead of the roux—add this once you have taken the soup off the heat). Sprinkle with chopped parsley before serving.

Serves 4 to 6.

Chicken and Vegetable Soup

Cooking a whole chicken to make broth yields a full-flavored soup. If serving as a main course, include all the chicken in the soup; otherwise you may reserve some of this very tender meat for sandwiches or other dishes. This soup may be thickened with roux or flour and water, but it is also fine as it is.

- 1 small whole chicken
- salt and freshly ground black pepper
- 1 onion, finely chopped
- 2 tablespoons butter or lard
- 2 medium carrots, diced
- ½ small celeriac, diced
- ¼ cauliflower, in florets
- 1 cup peas, fresh or frozen
- ¼ cup long-grain white rice
- 2 tablespoons chopped fresh parsley

Remove most of the skin from the chicken and discard. Put the whole chicken in a large pot and cover with 6 cups water, add salt and pepper to taste. Bring slowly to a boil, reduce heat, and simmer, partially covered, for 1 hour.

Remove the chicken from the broth and strip off its meat. Return the bones to the broth and cook for another hour or so. Cut the meat into thick strips and reserve.

Discard the bones from the broth once the broth is finished cooking. Skim any excess fat from the broth. Keep warm.

Fry the onion in butter or lard on low heat in a frying pan until almost golden. Add the carrots and celeriac and fry for a few minutes, stirring occasionally. Transfer all the contents of the frying pan into the broth. Add the cauliflower florets and peas and bring slowly to a boil. Reduce the heat and leave to simmer, uncovered, for 10 minutes.

Add rice, chicken meat, and additional salt and pepper to taste. Cook another 20 minutes. Serve sprinkled with parsley.

SERVES 6.

Oxtail Soup

Oxtail makes for one of the finest of broths, though one needs to adopt a strategy to deal with its fat. Making the stock a day in advance if you have the time allows you to chill it and then scoop off all the grease in one go. This is recommended. The degreased broth is extremely rich and tasty and goes well with a little sherry or port, or both, though these may be omitted.

1½ pounds oxtail
2 bay leaves
1 teaspoon marjoram
8 black peppercorns
salt
1 onion, diced
4 tablespoons (½ stick) butter
2 medium parsnips, diced
3 medium carrots, diced
½ cup peas, fresh or frozen
½ cup port (optional)
2 tablespoons flour

Slice the oxtail into several sections and place in a large pot. Add the bay leaves, marjoram, peppercorns, and salt to taste. Cover with 8 cups water, slowly bring to a boil, reduce heat and simmer, partially covered, for 2 hours or until tender. Since oxtail contains much fat, you may either spoon this off during the cooking or make the broth a day in advance, refrigerate, and then scoop off the fat once it sets.

In a large frying pan, fry the onion in 2 tablespoons of butter on medium-low heat until almost golden. Add the parsnips, carrots, and peas, and cook for a couple of minutes, stirring occasionally. Add the vegetables to the broth and cook for another 15 minutes.

Remove the oxtail sections from the soup, strip off the meat and return it to the soup. Cook for 5 minutes. Add port if desired.

To thicken the soup, make a roux by melting the remaining 2 tablespoons butter in a frying pan over medium heat, mixing in the flour and frying for a couple of minutes; add some of the soup liquid, cook for another minute, then stir into the soup. Heat through and serve.

SERVES 6.

Rabbit Soup

Rabbit is a mild tasting meat that needs strong flavors to complement it. Using leeks and wine accomplishes this. For those who are squeamish, avoid the head of the rabbit, though it does benefit the taste of the broth greatly.

½ rabbit, in one piece
1 medium carrot, peeled, whole
½ small celeriac, peeled
2 small leeks, washed
salt and freshly ground black pepper
2 strips bacon, finely sliced
1 small onion, finely chopped
2 tablespoons flour
1 cup dry red wine
2 tablespoons chopped fresh parsley
3 slices black or rye bread, cubed
1 tablespoons butter

Put the rabbit in 6 cups cold, salted water and bring to a boil slowly. Reduce the heat and simmer, partially covered, for 1 hour. Add the carrot, celeriac, leeks, and salt and pepper to taste. Cook until tender, about 20 minutes. Remove the rabbit and take the meat off the bones. Strain the broth and reserve the vegetables. Chop the rabbit meat and dice the vegetables.

Fry the sliced bacon, reduce the heat, add the onion and fry until almost golden. Add the flour and fry for 2 minutes, stirring occasionally. Add the bacon and onion to the broth. Add the wine, rabbit chunks, and chopped vegetables. Cook for a few minutes to heat through. Serve with parsley and croutons made from cubed dark bread fried in the butter.

SERVES 4.

Sauerkraut and Sausage Soup
(Zelňačka)

This soup is also good made with cabbage instead of sauerkraut. Use a curly green or savoy cabbage if possible and cook a little longer than the sauerkraut.

- ¼ ounce dried mushrooms, preferably porcini
- ¼ pound barley
- 6 cups water or broth
- 2 bay leaves
- 1 teaspoon caraway seeds, crushed
- ½ pound sauerkraut
- 2 strips bacon, finely sliced
- 1 small onion, finely chopped
- 2 tablespoons flour
- 1 tablespoon paprika
- ¼ pound smoked sausage, sliced
- salt and freshly ground black pepper

Soak the mushrooms and barley in warm water for 30 minutes. Drain off the water. Put the mushrooms and barley in a large pot and cover with the water or broth. Add the bay leaves and caraway. Bring slowly to a boil, reduce the heat, and simmer, uncovered, until the barley is tender, about 45 minutes. Add the sauerkraut and simmer for another 30 minutes.

Fry the bacon until well done but not crisp. Add the onion, reduce heat, and fry until almost golden. Add the flour and paprika and fry for a couple of minutes, stirring occasionally. Add ½ cup of broth from the soup, mix well, and cook for a couple of minutes. Stir the thickener into the soup.

Add the sliced sausage and salt and pepper to the soup. When the soup is heated through, serve.

SERVES 4 TO 6.

Czech Borscht

This soup combines a large amount of beets with a fair quantity of meat for a thicker soup than borscht lovers may be used to. For this recipe the vegetables need to be julienned instead of diced: slice them lengthwise into thin strips about 1½ inches long.

½ pound stewing beef
¼ pound smoked meat
6 cups broth or water
8 to 10 black peppercorns
2 bay leaves
salt
1 tablespoon tomato paste
2 strips bacon, diced fine
1 medium onion, chopped
½ small celeriac, julienned
2 medium carrots, julienned
1 medium parsnip, julienned
½ pound fresh beets, julienned
2 tablespoons lemon juice
½ cup sour cream

Place the beef and the smoked meat in a large pot and cover with broth or water. Add the whole peppercorns, bay leaves, some salt to taste, and the tomato paste. Bring to a boil slowly, reduce heat, cover, and simmer until the meat is tender, about 1½ hours. Remove the meat and cut it into small cubes; return to the broth.

Fry the bacon on medium heat in a large frying pan until well done but not crisp. Add the onion and fry until almost golden. Add the celeriac, carrots, and parsnip, and fry for 2 minutes. Put all of this into the broth and bring to a low boil. Add the beets and lemon juice. Simmer, partially covered, until the vegetables are tender, about 20 minutes. Serve with sour cream on top.

SERVES 6.

Fish Broth

Unlike meat stock, a broth made from fish takes very little time to prepare. There is no need to let the meat give off its essence over a prolonged period since the fish quickly flavors the liquid and longer cooking does not improve it. It is best to use fish heads, but an equal quantity of fillets or steaks substitutes well. Use a variety of whatever fresh fish are available, such as perch, carp, cod, haddock, catfish, or snapper; frozen fillets are alright as well. This bouillon may be served as is, poured on toasted garlic bread, supplemented with dumplings, or used as a base for more complex fish soups.

2 tablespoons butter
2 large onions, finely chopped
2 cloves garlic, finely chopped
½ small celeriac, diced
2 medium parsnips, diced
1 medium carrot, diced
2 pounds assorted fish, heads included
1 cup peas, fresh or frozen
3 bay leaves
salt
10 white peppercorns
1 teaspoon saffron
1 teaspoon savory
1 teaspoon fennel seeds, crushed

Melt the butter in a large pot on medium-low heat. Add the onions and garlic and fry until almost golden, stirring occasionally. Add the celeriac, parsnips, and carrots, and fry for 2 minutes. Then add the fish and the peas. Let all of this cook for a few minutes and let off its juice. Add 6 cups water, bay leaves, salt, white peppercorns, saffron, savory, and fennel seeds. Bring slowly to boil, reduce heat, and simmer for 30 minutes, covered. Strain.

SERVES 4 TO 6.

Russian Fish Soup

Use a variety of fish for this soup if you can, such as catfish, snapper, haddock, and hake. Skate is an excellent soup fish, dissolving into thin strands when cooked until tender.

- 2 small leeks, finely chopped
- 5 tablespoons butter
- 1 medium onion, finely chopped
- 1 clove garlic, crushed
- ½ celeriac, diced
- 4 tablespoons chopped fresh parsley
- 6 cups water or fish broth
- 8 to 10 whole black peppercorns
- 1½ pounds assorted fish
- salt and freshly ground black pepper
- 4 skinned tomatoes, chopped
- 2 bay leaves
- 1 teaspoon celery seeds, crushed
- 1 teaspoon fennel seeds, crushed
- 2 tablespoons flour
- 3 slices dark bread, cubed

Clean the leeks well, trim off the green parts, and chop finely.

Melt 2 tablespoons of butter on low-medium heat in a large pot. Add the onion and garlic and fry until almost golden, stirring occasionally. Add the leeks to pan and fry for a few more minutes. Add the celeriac and cook for a couple of minutes. Add 2 tablespoons of the parsley and cook for 1 or 2 minutes. Add the water or fish broth and peppercorns.

Clean, debone, and cube the fish; if using skate, keep wings whole and when cooked, scrape the meat off the bone. Add the fish to the soup. Add salt and pepper to taste. Slowly bring to a boil, reduce heat, and simmer, partially covered, for 15 minutes.

Add the chopped tomatoes, bay leaves, crushed celery and fennel seeds. Simmer another 15 minutes.

To thicken the soup, melt 2 tablespoons of butter in a frying pan on medium heat, then stir in the flour and cook for 2 minutes. Pour on some of the hot broth, cook for another minute and then stir into the soup. Let the soup cook on a low boil for another minute or so, then add the remaining 2 tablespoons parsley. Serve with croutons made from cubes of bread fried in the remaining 1 tablespoon butter.

SERVES 4 TO 6.

Slovakian Fish Soup

This is a simple soup that gets a unique texture from grated potatoes. Use a variety of fish: perch, cod, or catfish will do.

1½ pounds assorted fish
2 strips bacon, diced
1 tablespoon paprika
6 cups water or fish broth
salt and freshly ground black pepper
1 teaspoon marjoram
4 medium potatoes, grated
2 skinned tomatoes, chopped
3 slices dark bread, cubed
1 tablespoon butter

Debone, skin, and cube the fish.

Fry the bacon in a large pot until well done but not crisp. Add the fish and fry for a couple of minutes until lightly colored. Add paprika, mixing well, and cover with water or broth. Bring slowly to a boil, reduce heat and simmer, partially covered. Add salt, pepper, marjoram, and the grated potatoes. Cook for 10 minutes.

Add the chopped tomatoes and cook another 10 minutes. Serve with croutons made from cubed dark bread fried in the butter, or dumplings (see page 78).

Serves 4 to 6.

Carp Soup

This soup forms the first course of a traditional Czech Christmas supper. The heads from the carp are used for the broth, the meat being reserved for the breaded fillets served as the main dish with potato salad. If fresh carp is available, choose fairly small fish, between 2 to 3 pounds, as the larger fish may be muddy in taste. Two heads make a good soup, so if you are buying only one carp, supplement the broth with fillets of carp or a similar fish. Often carp are sold live to ensure freshness and also to give you a chance to keep the fish in clean water for several hours or a couple of days. If carp is not available, use a combination of catfish, pickerel, and mackerel, which are pretty close in taste to carp.

2 fish heads, plus skin, bones, and liver, and/or fillets
salt
8 to 10 whole black peppercorns
½ teaspoon ground allspice
½ teaspoon grated nutmeg
2 bay leaves
1 teaspoon celery seeds, crushed
5 tablespoons butter
1 medium onion, chopped
1 parsnip, diced
½ celeriac, diced
2 tablespoons flour
3 slices dark bread, cubed
2 tablespoons chopped fresh parsley

If using whole fish, cut off their heads, skin them, and remove their innards, taking care not to break the spleen, which has an unpleasant taste and must be discarded. Cut the fillets from the fish, and reserve for later use. Clean the carp heads and innards. Then put heads, innards, skin, and bones in a large pot. If using fillets, cut these into large pieces and place in a large pot. Cover with 6 cups water.

Add salt and whole peppercorns, allspice, nutmeg, bay leaves, and celery seeds. Slowly bring to a boil, reduce heat, and simmer, partially covered, for 45 minutes.

Once the fish is cooked, remove it from the soup, and discard skin and bones if used. Strain the liquid through a sieve and reserve. Reserve the meat from the fish, innards if used, and the cheeks and tongue from the head—chop all of this.

Melt 2 tablespoons of the butter in the large pot and fry the onion on medium-low heat until almost golden. Add the parsnips and celeriac. Cook for a couple of minutes. Add the broth and bring slowly to a boil. Simmer for about 15 minutes or until the vegetables are almost done. Add the chopped fish and innards (if using). Simmer for 5 minutes.

To thicken the soup, make a roux by melting 2 tablespoons of butter in a frying pan over medium heat and then stirring in the flour. Cook, stirring occasionally, for 2 minutes, then add ½ cup of the hot liquid from the soup. Cook for a minute, then stir into the soup. Simmer for 5 minutes. Serve with croutons made from cubed bread fried in the remaining 1 tablespoon butter. Sprinkle with fresh parsley.

SERVES 6.

Vegetable Soup

Just about any vegetable that you can think of can go into a soup like this—cutting down on the variety below will do no harm. This soup is finished off with some grated cheese. Make sure to choose one that melts well, such as Gruyère.

- 3 strips bacon, diced (optional) or 2 tablespoons butter
- 1 medium onion, finely chopped
- 2 medium potatoes, cubed
- 3 medium carrots, diced
- 1 medium parsnip, diced
- ½ small celeriac, diced
- ¼ cauliflower, in florets
- 2 medium kohlrabi, diced
- 2 small leeks, finely chopped
- ½ cup peas, fresh or frozen
- 8 cups water or broth
- salt and freshly ground black pepper
- 2 tablespoons chopped fresh parsley
- ½ cup grated cheese, such as Parmesan or Gruyère

If using bacon, fry until well done but not crisp in a large pot; otherwise, melt butter in the pot. Reduce heat and add the onion: fry, stirring occasionally, until almost golden. Add potatoes, carrots, parsnip, celeriac, cauliflower, kohlrabi, leeks, peas (if using frozen peas, leave these aside and add to the soup 5 minutes before serving) and cook for a few minutes. Cover with water or broth, and slowly bring to a boil. Reduce heat, add salt and pepper to taste, and simmer, partially covered, until tender, about 20 minutes. Add parsley and grated cheese before serving.

SERVES 6.

Garden Soup

Another mixed vegetable soup, though finished here with cream and egg yolk to make a richer meal. Substitute vegetables available to you for those listed here, bearing in mind the essentials.

- 2 tablespoons butter or lard
- 1 medium onion, chopped
- 1 small curly, savoy cabbage, shredded
- 2 medium carrots, diced
- 2 parsnips or ½ a small celeriac, diced
- 2 stalks celery, finely diced
- 1 small cauliflower, chopped in florets
- salt
- 8 to 10 whole black peppercorns
- 8 cups water or broth
- ½ cup peas, fresh or frozen
- 2 cloves garlic, chopped
- 1 egg yolk
- ⅔ cup cream
- 2 tablespoons chopped fresh parsley

In a large pot, melt the butter or lard on medium-low heat, add the chopped onion and fry until almost golden, stirring occasionally. Add cabbage, carrots, parsnips or celeriac, celery, and cauliflower. Add salt and peppercorns. Add water or broth.

Slowly bring to a boil. Reduce heat and simmer, partially covered, for 20 minutes.

Add the peas and garlic, and simmer another 10 minutes. Take the soup off the heat. Whisk the egg yolk into the cream and then whisk this mixture into the soup. Return the soup to the heat and heat through while stirring but do not boil. Serve with chopped parsley.

SERVES 6.

Spinach Soup

Spinach makes for a brightly colored and softly textured soup. Add some cream once the cooking is complete for a little more richness, or some potatoes for a more substantial meal. This soup may also be served puréed, or with chopped, hard-boiled eggs.

1 medium onion, finely chopped
2 tablespoons butter or lard
2 tablespoons flour
6 cups water or broth
1 pound fresh spinach, cleaned and chopped
2 tablespoons lemon juice
salt and freshly ground black pepper

Fry the onion in butter or lard on medium-low heat in a large pot until almost golden. Add the flour and cook, stirring occasionally, for 2 minutes. Add the water or broth, mixing well. Slowly bring to a boil and reduce the heat. Add the spinach and lemon juice. Season with salt and pepper to taste. Simmer until done, about 15 minutes.

SERVES 4 TO 6.

Celeriac Soup

A very simple, puréed vegetable soup to which a little cream may be added just before serving once the soup has been taken off the heat. A similar treatment of carrots, turnips, or potatoes would also work well.

1 large celeriac
4 tablespoons (½ stick) butter
2 tablespoons chopped fresh parsley
salt and freshly ground black pepper
2 tablespoons flour
6 cups beef broth or water
½ cup heavy cream

Pare and clean the celeriac and chop it roughly. Blanch the celeriac for 5 minutes in boiling water, then transfer to a bowl of cold water; when cool, remove and let dry.

Fry the celeriac in a frying pan in 2 tablespoons of the butter for 2 to 3 minutes. Add the parsley. Season with salt and pepper to taste. Cover the pan and let cook on low heat until soft, about 10 minutes, stirring occasionally. Purée the celeriac in a food processor or pass through a sieve.

To make the roux, melt the remaining 2 tablespoons of butter in a large pot over medium heat. Add the flour, mix well, and cook for a few minutes until light golden brown in color. Add the broth or water to the roux, mixing well. Bring the liquid slowly to a boil, then reduce heat and simmer. Add the puréed celeriac to the broth, mixing well. Simmer for 5 minutes.

Before serving, stir the cream into the soup.

SERVES 4 TO 6.

Cauliflower Soup

Cauliflower does well in soup. What may be an awkward vegetable to use with main courses turns creamy and flavorful when puréed. As with many Czech dishes, the herbs and spices are minimal. This recipe features nutmeg, but try it also with a tablespoon of crushed caraway seeds instead. The version below is completely puréed, but you may also want to reserve some of the cauliflower florets and cook them in the purée for a slightly chunkier soup.

- 1 medium cauliflower, in florets
- 6 cups water or broth
- 1 cup peas, fresh or frozen
- 2 tablespoons butter or lard
- 2 tablespoons flour
- ⅔ cup heavy cream
- ½ teaspoon grated nutmeg
- ½ cup grated cheese, such as Gruyère
- 2 tablespoons chopped fresh parsley

Place the cauliflower in salted water or broth and bring slowly to a boil. Reduce heat and simmer, partially covered, for 10 minutes. Add peas and cook until done, about 10 minutes (less if frozen). Let cool a little, then purée in a food processor or pass through sieve.

Make a roux by melting the butter or lard on medium-low heat and frying the flour in it for a couple of minutes until slightly browned; add some broth and cook a little, then add to the soup. Simmer for a couple of minutes. Add the cream, nutmeg, cheese, and parsley. Mix well and serve.

SERVES 6.

Leek Soup

Leeks need to be washed well since they often hide dirt deep between their layers. A good method is to leave them to soak in plenty of water. Once washed, cut off all the green part at the top of the leek, reserving only the whites for use. This soup uses a different method for thickening than most of the others: the addition of oats toward the end of cooking. For a heartier soup, add 3 or 4 potatoes.

1 pound small leeks, cleaned well and sliced fine, whites only
3 tablespoons butter or lard
6 cups water or chicken broth
2 tablespoons oats (quick cooking or regular)
salt and freshly ground black pepper
1 teaspoon marjoram
½ cup heavy cream

Fry the leeks in butter or lard on medium-low heat in a large pot until wilted, stirring occasionally. Cover with broth or water and slowly bring to a boil, reduce heat, and simmer, partially covered, until done, about 30 minutes. Add the oats, salt, pepper, and marjoram. Cook until done, about 5 minutes. Stir in the cream and heat through.

SERVES 4 TO 6.

Asparagus Soup

Many people believe thin asparagus stalks are better than thick ones, but the opposite is the case: thicker stalks mean juicier and more tender meat. This soup is delicate, rich, and smooth.

- ½ pound asparagus, sliced fine
- 6 cups cold, salted water or broth
- 2 small leeks, cleaned and sliced fine, whites only
- 2 tablespoons chopped fresh parsley
- 1 cup long-grain white rice
- ½ teaspoon grated nutmeg
- salt and freshly ground black pepper
- ½ cup heavy cream
- 1 egg yolk

Put the sliced asparagus in water or broth. Add the sliced leeks and parsley and bring to a slow boil. Reduce the heat and simmer, uncovered, for 30 minutes. Add the rice and cook for another 20 minutes. Add nutmeg, salt, and pepper. Remove from heat. Mix the cream with the egg yolk and then stir into the soup, then serve.

SERVES 4 TO 6.

Mushroom Soup

Ordinary white champignon mushrooms serve well for this soup, but try this recipe with a mixture of white and portobello mushrooms, or some dried porcini mushrooms (soak these in warm water and clean them—the soaking water may be sieved and added to the broth).

- 1 pound mushrooms, finely sliced
- 3 tablespoons butter or lard
- 1 medium onion, finely chopped
- 3 tablespoons flour
- ½ small celeriac, diced fine
- 6 cups chicken broth or water
- ½ teaspoon caraway seeds
- ⅔ cup heavy cream
- 1 egg yolk
- salt and freshly ground black pepper
- 2 tablespoons chopped fresh parsley

In a large pot, fry the sliced mushrooms on high heat in 2 tablespoons of the butter or lard until golden brown. As soon as they start to let off their own juice, remove them from the pan.

Reduce the heat to medium, add the remaining 1 tablespoon butter, then add the chopped onion. Fry the onion until almost golden, stirring occasionally. Sprinkle on the flour and cook for 2 minutes. Add the celeriac and cook for 3 to 4 minutes. Pour on the broth or water, mixing well. Add the fried mushrooms and caraway seeds. Slowly bring to a boil, then reduce the heat. Simmer, partially covered, until done, about 30 minutes.

Remove the pot from the heat. Mix the cream with the egg yolk and whisk into the soup. Add salt and pepper to taste. Serve sprinkled with parsley.

Serves 4 to 6.

Tomato Soup

A homemade tomato soup made with fresh, ripe tomatoes is hard to beat. It is a distinguished dish served purely as it is. It may also be supplemented with some rice or, my favorite when I was a child, a whole egg per person cooked soft in the soup.

- 2 pounds fresh tomatoes
- 8 cups water or chicken broth
- 2 bay leaves
- salt and freshly ground black pepper
- 1 teaspoon white wine vinegar
- 1 teaspoon sugar
- 1 tablespoon butter
- ¼ cup cooked rice (optional)
- 1 egg per person (optional)
- 2 tablespoons chopped fresh parsley

Peel the tomatoes: this can be done most easily by dropping the tomatoes into boiling water, leaving them to blanch for about 30 seconds, and then peeling them with a sharp knife. The blanching process separates the skin of the tomato from the meat and makes peeling easier and less wasteful. Chop the peeled tomatoes.

Place the tomatoes in a large pot and add water or broth and the bay leaves. Slowly bring to a boil and then reduce heat. Simmer, partially covered, for 30 minutes.

Add salt, pepper, vinegar, and sugar. Purée the soup in a food processor or pass through a sieve. Reheat and add butter; cooked rice may also be included if desired, or a few whole eggs. If using eggs, one raw egg per person may be broken into the soup just before serving, and cooked gently for a couple of minutes for a fine effect. Serve sprinkled with parsley.

SERVES 6.

Green Soup with Potatoes

A very quick and simple soup that you can make with cabbage, as below, or any other kind of green, such as kale, Swiss chard, or mustard greens.

- ½ green cabbage, preferably curly or savoy, shredded
- 4 tablespoons (½ stick) butter or lard
- 1 tablespoon caraway seeds, crushed
- salt and freshly ground black pepper
- 2 medium potatoes
- 8 cups meat broth or water
- 3 slices dark bread, cubed

Finely shred the cabbage.

Melt 3 tablespoons of the butter or lard on medium-low heat in a large pot. Add the cabbage and fry for a few minutes, stirring well, until wilted.

Add the caraway seeds, and salt and pepper to taste. Add the potatoes and the broth. Bring slowly to a boil then reduce the heat. Simmer, partially covered, until done, about 30 minutes.

Serve with croutons made from cubed dark bread fried in the remaining 1 tablespoon butter.

Serves 6.

Cabbage Soup

A slightly more complicated version of the Czech favorite, using some meat (omit this if you want) and flavored with fresh dill.

- ⅓ pound smoked ham hock
- 8 cups water or broth
- ½ head green cabbage, preferably savoy, finely shredded
- 8 to 10 whole black peppercorns
- ¼ teaspoon ground allspice
- 2 bay leaves
- 2 medium potatoes, diced
- 2 tablespoons butter or lard
- 2 medium onions, finely chopped
- 2 tablespoons flour
- ½ cup sour cream
- 2 tablespoons chopped fresh dill
- salt and freshly ground black pepper

Put the smoked meat in a large pot and cover with water or broth. Bring to boil slowly, reduce heat, cover and simmer for 1 hour. Remove the meat and cut into small ½-inch cubes. Reserve the liquid.

Place the cabbage in the broth and add water to cover if needed. Add the whole peppercorns, allspice, and bay leaves. Add the diced potatoes. Bring back to a boil and keep on a simmer, partially covered.

Melt the butter or lard in a frying pan on medium heat. Add the onions and fry until almost golden, stirring occasionally. Add the flour and cook for a few more minutes, stirring occasionally. Add a little broth to the flour and onion mixture, bring to a boil and cook for a couple of minutes. Add to the soup and mix well. Add the cubed meat. Cook until the potatoes and cabbage are done, about 15 minutes.

Stir the sour cream into the soup. Mix in the chopped dill and salt and pepper to taste.

SERVES 6.

Potato Soup

(Bramborová Polévka)

Potatoes are often cooked with caraway seeds, as they are here. The addition of bacon and dried mushrooms gives a smoky taste to the soup. You may want to add a roux, though the potatoes and other vegetables should make for a thick soup on their own. For a simpler potato experience, omit the meat and mushrooms and cut down on the other vegetables.

- ¼ ounce dried mushrooms, preferably porcini
- 2 strips bacon, finely diced
- 2 medium onions, finely chopped
- 2 cloves garlic, crushed
- ½ medium celeriac, diced
- 2 medium carrots, diced
- 1 medium parsnip, diced
- 8 cups meat broth or water
- 6 medium potatoes, cubed
- 1 teaspoon caraway seeds, crushed
- 1 teaspoon marjoram
- salt and freshly ground black pepper

Soak the dried mushrooms in a little water for 15 minutes. Drain, clean the stems, and chop fine.

Fry the bacon in a large pot on medium heat until well done but not crisp. Reduce the heat and add the onions and garlic. Fry, stirring occasionally, until almost golden. Add the celeriac, carrots, and parsnip and fry for a few minutes. Cover with broth or water, bring slowly to a boil, reduce heat and keep on a simmer. Add the mushrooms, potatoes, caraway seeds, marjoram, and salt and pepper to taste. Simmer, uncovered, for about 20 minutes until done.

Serves 6.

Pea Soup

Pea soup is most appropriate for the cold winter months. The ham complements the peas extremely well, but vegetarians may omit it.

- 2 tablespoons butter or lard
- 1 medium onion, chopped fine
- ½ pound dried peas
- ¼ pound smoked ham hock
- 6 cups broth or water
- 1 teaspoon marjoram
- salt and freshly ground black pepper

Melt the butter or lard in a large pot on medium heat. Add the onion and fry, stirring occasionally, until almost golden.

Add the peas and the ham to the pot. Cover with broth or water, and bring to a boil. Reduce heat, and simmer, covered, for 1½ hours until done. Skim the fat off the surface as it forms.

Add the marjoram, salt and pepper to taste. Remove the ham, dice the meat, and reserve. If the peas have not completely dissolved, take the soup off the heat and either manually mash the peas into a rough consistency or pass half through a food processor. Return the meat to the soup and heat through.

SERVES 6.

Bean Soup

This soup may be made using other types of legumes, such as dried peas or lentils. If you forget to soak the beans overnight, precook them for about 1 hour and discard the cooking liquid.

2 cups white navy beans
8 cups water or meat broth
1 medium onion, finely chopped
3 cloves garlic, minced
3 tablespoons butter
2 medium parsnips, diced
2 medium carrots, diced
salt and freshly ground black pepper
2 tablespoons caraway seeds, crushed
⅔ cup heavy cream
4 slices dark bread, cubed
2 tablespoons chopped fresh parsley

Soak the beans overnight in a large quantity of water. Drain them the next day.

Place the beans in a large pot and cover them with water or broth. Bring to a boil and then reduce the heat. Partially cover and simmer for about 1½ hours or tender. Mash them roughly by hand or pass half the soup through a food processor.

Fry the onion and garlic in 2 tablespoons butter in a frying pan on low-medium heat until almost golden. Add the parsnips and carrots and fry for a few minutes, stirring occasionally. Add the vegetables to the soup and simmer for another 20 minutes Add salt and pepper to taste. Add the crushed caraway seeds.

Blend the heavy cream into ½ cup of the hot soup. Take the soup off the heat and mix in the cream. Serve with croutons made with cubed bread fried in remaining 1 tablespoon butter and parsley.

Serves 6.

Bean Soup with Dumplings

A thick, rich soup with plenty of vegetables, beans, and dumplings. Use good quality frankfurters if you are going to use sausage, though they may easily be left out for a good vegetarian meal.

- 2 cups white beans such as kidney or navy
- 8 cups salted water or broth
- 2 bay leaves
- 2 strips bacon, finely diced
- 1 small onion, finely chopped
- ½ small celeriac, diced
- 2 medium carrots, diced
- 1 medium parsnip, diced
- 2 tablespoons butter
- 2 tablespoons flour
- 2 tablespoons paprika
- 1 teaspoon marjoram
- ¼ pound sausage, sliced (optional)
- salt and freshly ground black pepper

FOR THE DUMPLINGS:

- ¼ cup milk
- 2 tablespoons butter
- 2 tablespoons coarse flour
- 1 egg
- 2 tablespoons chopped fresh parsley
- bread crumbs

Soak the beans in plenty of water the night before. Drain them the next day, discarding the water.

Place the beans in a large pot. Cover with salted water or broth. Add the bay leaves. Bring slowly to a boil and then reduce the heat. Simmer, partially covered, for 1 hour or until the beans are almost tender.

Fry the diced bacon in a large frying pan on medium heat until well done but not crisp. Reduce the heat and add the onion. Fry the onion until almost golden, stirring occasionally. Add the celeriac, carrots, parsnip, and the butter, and fry, stirring occasionally, for 5 minutes. Add flour and cook for a couple of minutes. Add paprika, marjoram, and sausage, if using. Cook for a few minutes, then add all this to the beans. Season with salt and freshly ground black pepper. Simmer, partially covered, for 10 minutes.

To make the dumplings, you first need to make a béchamel sauce. Put the milk and ¼ cup water to warm in a small pot. Meanwhile, melt the butter on medium heat, add the flour and cook for a few minutes, stirring well. Take the pan off the heat and mix in the milk and water; return the pan to the heat and cook a few minutes until thickened. Add the egg and parsley and as much of the bread crumbs as needed for a semithick paste, and mix well. Season with salt and freshly ground black pepper. Take spoonfuls and drop into the soup. Cook for a few minutes until done.

SERVES 6.

Barley Soup

A lovely soup for the winter and whenever you need comfort. I hated barley when I was young but a buttery treatment of the pearls transforms something potentially bland into a delectable treat.

- 2 cups barley
- 8 cups meat broth or water
- 3 tablespoons butter
- 1 medium onion, finely chopped
- 2 medium carrots, diced
- ½ small celeriac, finely diced
- 2 medium potatoes, cubed
- salt and freshly ground black pepper
- 1 teaspoon marjoram
- 1 tablespoon chopped fresh parsley

Wash the barley, place in a large pot and cover with the broth or water. Bring slowly to a boil, reduce heat, and simmer, covered, until the barley is tender, about 1 hour.

Melt the butter in a large frying pan on medium heat. Add the chopped onion and fry until almost golden, stirring occasionally. Add the carrots, celeriac, and potatoes, and fry for a few minutes until they are slightly turning color and glistening. Add the vegetables to the soup. Add salt, pepper, marjoram, and the chopped parsley. Simmer for 10 minutes.

SERVES 6.

Garlic Soup

This is a very simple but flavorful soup with a subtle taste of garlic. Use good quality dark bread, either a dark rye or pumpernickel.

- 6 cloves garlic
- 1 tablespoon salt
- 8 cups water or broth
- 1 teaspoon caraway seeds, crushed
- 2 medium potatoes, diced
- 1 teaspoon marjoram
- 3 tablespoons butter or lard
- ½ teaspoon powdered ginger
- 1 teaspoon fresh black pepper
- 4 slices dark rye bread
- 2 tablespoons chopped fresh parsley

Mash the garlic with the salt: do this either with a mortar and pestle, or use a garlic press to crush the garlic and then mix in the salt.

Place the garlic and salt in a large pot and add the water or broth. Slowly bring the water to a boil, reduce heat and keep on a simmer. Add the crushed caraway seeds, potatoes, marjoram, 2 tablespoons butter or lard, and the ginger. Simmer, uncovered, until the potatoes are tender, about 15 minutes. Add freshly ground black pepper and some more salt if needed.

Fry the slices of bread in remaining 1 tablespoon butter until golden brown. Place a slice of bread in each soup bowl and ladle the garlic soup over it. Sprinkle on parsley.

SERVES 4.

Bread Soup

Perhaps an odd idea for a soup, but the actual product is much better than it sounds. Certainly a recipe that makes almost nothing go a long way.

1 medium loaf hard bread, dark rye or pumpernickel
8 cups water or broth
1 teaspoon crushed caraway seeds
salt and freshly ground black pepper
¼ cup heavy cream
1 tablespoon butter
2 egg yolks
2 tablespoons chopped fresh parsley

Cube the bread and place it in a large pot. Add the broth or water, caraway seeds, and salt and pepper to taste. Bring slowly to a boil and then reduce the heat. Simmer, uncovered, for approximately 15 minutes but not so long as to allow the bread to dissolve completely.

Purée the soup in a food processor or pass through a strainer. Mix the cream with the butter and egg yolks and whisk into the soup to thicken it and add richness. Heat through but do not boil. Add additional salt to taste and sprinkle with parsley.

SERVES 4 TO 6.

Beer Soup
(Pivní Polévka)

Another soup with bread, this time fortified by some beer. Choose a good, strong flavored beer to use with a tasty broth.

½ loaf dark bread
1 bottle (12 ounces) good beer, such as Czech Pilsen
6 cups beef broth
1 tablespoon caraway seeds, crushed
salt
2 eggs
1 egg yolk
½ cup heavy cream

Cut the bread into small cubes and place into a bowl. Cover bread with beer and soak for a few minutes.

Bring the broth to a boil in a large pot. Add the beer and bread mixture. Cook for just a few minutes. Let cool for several minutes, then process in food processor or mash through a sieve.

Put the puréed soup back on the stove and bring to a slow boil. Add the caraway seeds, salt, whole eggs and the yolk. Take off the heat and mix in the cream.

SERVES 4 TO 6.

Strawberry Soup

Cold fruit soups served in the height of summer heat are popular throughout Europe. Raspberries and blackberries work well, as do cherries.

1 pound fresh strawberries, cleaned and hulled
2 tablespoons confectioners' sugar
1 cup plain yogurt, preferably Balkan
½ cup heavy cream
mint sprigs for garnish

Slice the strawberries, place in a bowl, and sprinkle on the confectioners' sugar. Leave to sit for about 2 hours in a cool place.

Remove ½ cup of the sliced strawberries and reserve. Mix the yogurt and cream into the bowl of strawberries. Either purée in a food processor or pass through a sieve. Serve with the reserved strawberry slices and a sprig of mint.

SERVES 4.

Noodles

Czechs use many last minute additions to soups. If you have leftover crepes, slice these thinly into julienne strips. Leftover egg or pasta noodles are also good. Or make fresh noodles.

½ cup flour
1 egg

Put the flour on a board and make a well in the center. Put the egg and 1 tablespoon water into the well. Slowly mix the flour into the egg. Leave for 30 minutes. Roll out the dough. Cut it into strips, then stack these and cut them into fine ribbons. Shake out the noodles and leave to dry for a few minutes. Cook in broth or water.

Serves 4 to 6.

Semolina Dumplings

All kinds of flour dumplings are made for use in soups. They differ in the type of flour used and the other ingredients called upon. The following recipe features semolina as a rough-grained basis for the dumpling, but substitute any sort of flour that you have for a similar result.

½ cup semolina
1 egg
3 tablespoons milk or water
a little salt

Mix together all the ingredients and leave to stand a few minutes. Cook spoonfuls in broth for 10 minutes. Parsley may also be added to the mixture.

SERVES 4 TO 6.

Liver Dumplings

All types of meat and vegetable bases may be used for dumplings. I give you two examples—the much favored liver dumpling and a spinach dumpling.

- 2 tablespoons butter
- 1 whole egg
- ¼ pound liver, crushed
- 1 teaspoon marjoram
- 1 clove garlic, crushed
- salt and freshly ground black pepper
- 1 cup bread crumbs

Mash the butter with the egg. Add the crushed liver, marjoram, garlic, and salt and pepper. Slowly mix in as much of the bread crumbs as needed to form a thick paste. Mix well. Put spoonfuls in soup or broth, cook for 10 minutes.

SERVES 4 TO 6.

Spinach Dumplings

Other greens may be substituted for the spinach or one may go to a completely different vegetable altogether. Try broccoli or tomato.

¼ pound fresh spinach
1 strip bacon, finely diced
salt
2 eggs, separated
freshly ground black pepper
1 cup bread crumbs

Clean the spinach well. Bring a pot of salted water to a boil, add the spinach, and cook until tender, about 10 minutes. Drain the spinach, squeeze out all the excess liquid, and chop.

Fry the bacon on medium heat until well done but not crisp, then drain and cool. Add salt and the egg yolks to the bacon and mix together well. Add the cooked spinach and pepper.

Whip the egg whites until stiff, then fold them into the spinach mixture. Slowly add bread crumbs as needed to make a thick paste. Make dumplings from the mixture with a tablespoon and add to soup 5 minutes before serving.

SERVES 4 TO 6.

3

SALADS

The strong tendency among Czechs to enhance a dish with meat does not stop when it comes to salads. A typical salad, served before the main course, may consist of several different types of roasted and smoked meats, bound with mayonnaise, yogurt, or sour cream, incorporating vegetables only as an afterthought: a pickled cucumber diced fine, a few wedges of tomato, or the laying of a few lettuce leaves under the meat. While not fitting the traditional concept of a green salad, such a prepared cold meat salad is reminiscent of the chicken or "chef's salad" popular in American cuisine or Vietnamese beef salads. Depending on the quality of meats and dressings used, Czech salads may range from a simple and hearty mayonnaise mixture to a fragrant and light, almost Oriental, treatment of meat. Czechs also use fish in salad, either fresh or smoked, combined with greens or root vegetables. I include a couple of these salads, again featuring the Czech favorite, carp, though trout or pickerel, for example, may be substituted.

Despite the Czech preoccupation with meat, there are many fine vegetable salads as part of the repertoire, featured in versions of common green salads, more unique bean and root vegetable salads, and in pickles. Here one may find many new ideas for serving greens: a light and slightly sweet cucumber salad, pickled blood red beets, pickled cabbage, parboiled celeriac with apples, and many more.

A note may be useful regarding the most uncomplicated of these recipes, the ordinary green salad. Many people, still, may find salads rather dull, especially salads that leave out all the good stuff and give you only the filler: lettuce. I used to hate lettuce, too, but it has slowly come to be one of my favorite greens. The trick in appreciating it, as with all simple and unadorned ingredients, is to choose the right one and treat it with respect. A few guidelines may be useful. First, if using one or a combination of lettuces, choose fresh plants with crisp leaves. No matter how good the lettuce looks, the selection process is, in part, a throw of the dice: some lettuces are rich in taste, while others are bitter or bland. Having chosen a lettuce, don't spoil the salad when it comes to cleaning your prize. Make sure that you get rid of all the dirt on the leaves, especially at their base. A bite of grit is hard to surpass in terms of indigestibility. Once washed, make sure you dry the lettuce well: a wet leaf dilutes taste and makes the salad lifeless. Either dry the leaves with paper towels, effective though labor intensive and wasteful, or pick up, for a few dollars, a plastic salad spinner.

Once the lettuce is chosen, washed, dried, and torn, it may be combined with a few or many other vegetable ingredients, but what is most important is the dressing. A full vinaigrette is used in the first recipe below, combining oil, red wine vinegar, lemon juice, and mustard. It is essential to use good quality oil and vinegar since this is where most of the taste for the salad derives. The mustard and lemon juice add complexity to the acidic element of the dressing, though they may be omitted if more vinegar is added. A little garlic serves the sauce well. It may be included, crushed, in the vinaigrette itself or rubbed into the salad bowl prior to filling.

Simple Green Salad

Choose a fine, fresh, and tasty lettuce to serve as the main ingredient here, a crisp romaine or tender Boston leaf, and avoid the tasteless and dull iceberg. A variety of lettuce types are now available in most ordinary supermarkets and some even sell a mix of greens prepared for salad making. To complicate the recipe below, use a combination of greens, adding radicchio for color, or chicory for bite, for example. Slices of endive also make a good addition without straying from the green theme. What you add to the lettuce is up to you and what is listed below is one suggestion among many. Try substituting cucumber for the radish, or parsley for the chives, and so on. For this salad I use a basic vinaigrette which, to succeed, requires good ingredients. Choose a quality oil, such as extra-virgin olive for a rich taste or sunflower for simplicity. Complement the oil with a fine red wine vinegar and a tasty mustard, such as Dijon.

1 medium head romaine lettuce
1 clove garlic
6 radishes
½ small sweet onion
1 small bunch chives
4 tablespoons olive oil
1 tablespoon red wine vinegar
1 tablespoon lemon juice
1 teaspoon mustard
¼ teaspoon salt
freshly ground black pepper

Wash the lettuce leaves well, then pat or spin dry. Rub the garlic into the salad bowl and then discard it. Tear the lettuce approximately into 2-inch squares to fill the bowl. Finely slice the radishes, onion, and chives and add to the lettuce.

Make the dressing by pouring the oil into a small bowl, whisking in the vinegar and lemon juice, and then the mustard. Make sure the mixture is well incorporated. Season with salt and pepper. Pour the dressing onto the salad just before serving and toss well.

SERVES 4.

Mixed Green Salad

Building from the base of greens in a simple salad, this recipe adds cucumber, tomatoes, and carrots. You may mix and match here as you please given what looks good at the market. A little thinly sliced fennel is nice, or some cut asparagus, and so on. Instead of a vinaigrette, the following salad uses a creamy dressing, though either type does well. Adding a fresh herb, such as parsley or dill, is nice.

1 small head romaine lettuce
½ English cucumber
2 ripe tomatoes
1 small carrot
½ small sweet onion
½ cup plain yogurt
2 tablespoons sour cream
4 tablespoons white wine vinegar
white wine (optional)
1 tablespoon chopped fresh parsley
salt and freshly ground black pepper

Wash the lettuce well and then pat or spin dry. Tear into medium-size pieces into a salad bowl. Peel the cucumber and slice it into thin rounds. Cut each tomato into 8 pieces. Peel and grate the carrot. Slice the onion into fine strips. Add all the vegetables to the lettuce.

To make the dressing, mix together the yogurt and sour cream, then whisk in the vinegar. If it is too thick, thin it with a little water or white wine. Add the parsley and salt and pepper to taste. Dress the salad just before serving.

SERVES 4.

Cucumber Salad

This is a light, slightly sweet salad that's especially good during the summer as an accompaniment to a roast or barbecued meat. For a creamier version, substitute sour cream for the oil.

1 large English cucumber
salt
½ cup white wine vinegar
¼ cup cold water
1 teaspoon sugar
2 tablespoons vegetable oil
1 clove garlic, crushed
¼ teaspoon paprika
freshly ground black pepper

Peel the cucumber and slice into very thin rounds. Put it into a deep plate or small salad bowl, sprinkle with some salt and let sit for 15 minutes. Add the vinegar, water, sugar, oil, garlic, paprika, and some pepper.

SERVES 4.

Mixed Vegetable Salad

What could almost be a Mediterranean-style salad takes its Czech signature from the inclusion of kohlrabi, a delicate tasting green bulb that may be eaten raw or cooked. If kohlrabi is not available, use cucumber instead.

2 green peppers
2 red peppers
4 tomatoes
2 medium kohlrabi
2 medium carrots
2 tablespoons chopped fresh parsley
1 clove garlic, crushed
4 tablespoons vegetable or olive oil
2 tablespoons lemon juice
salt and freshly ground black pepper

Cut the peppers into quarters, core and wash them, then slice them into thin strips. Cut each tomato into 8 pieces. Peel the kohlrabi, cut into quarters, then slice into thin strips. Place all the vegetables into a salad bowl. Peel the carrots and grate them into the bowl. Add the parsley and crushed garlic. Mix together the oil and lemon juice, season with salt and pepper, and dress the salad a few minutes before serving.

SERVES 4.

Mixed Salad with Radishes

A variant of the previous recipe, skipping the kohlrabi and using radishes, cucumber, and endive instead. An ideal salad for a hot day—fresh, crisp, and with a little bite.

10 radishes
4 tomatoes
1 small head endive
½ English cucumber
1 green pepper
1 red pepper
½ small sweet onion
1 clove garlic
2 tablespoons chopped fresh parsley
4 tablespoons olive oil
1 tablespoon red wine vinegar
1 tablespoon lemon juice
salt and freshly ground black pepper

Clean the radishes well, chop off their tops and bottoms, and slice thinly. Cut each tomato into 8 pieces. Wash the endive well and tear each leaf into 2 or 3 pieces. Peel the cucumber and slice thinly. Core the peppers, cut into quarters, and slice thinly. Finely slice the onion. Put all the vegetables into a salad bowl that you have rubbed with the garlic. Sprinkle on the chopped parsley.

Make the vinaigrette by whisking together the oil, vinegar, and lemon juice with salt and freshly ground black pepper. Dress the salad a few minutes before serving and toss well.

SERVES 4.

Celeriac Salad

Celeriac is a delicate ingredient that, either raw or cooked, stands on its own in a light dressing. I cook the root in the version below and sweeten the salad with a little grated apple. The easiest way to clean the root is to slice off thinly the dirt-encrusted outside layer and then wash under running water.

1 small celeriac
1 bay leaf
½ teaspoon allspice
salt and freshly ground black pepper
½ cup white wine vinegar
1 medium apple
¼ cup sour cream
1 tablespoon mustard

Peel and wash the celeriac, then cut it into fine strips. Bring a pot of water to boil, with the bay leaf, allspice, and salt and pepper. Add the julienned celeriac and boil lightly until tender, about 10 minutes. Drain the celeriac, place in a small salad bowl or deep plate, pour on the vinegar, and let cool.

Peel the apple and then grate it onto the cooled celeriac. Add the sour cream, mustard, and additional salt and pepper to taste. Mix well.

SERVES 4.

Green Bean Salad

A bean salad may be very simple: some yellow or green beans, boiled until almost tender, and dressed with oil and lemon juice. The version below is a bit more complicated, including other vegetables and some spice from a hot pepper, such as a banana pepper or jalapeño.

½ pound green beans
½ English cucumber
2 medium tomatoes
1 hot green pepper
½ small sweet onion
1 clove garlic
2 tablespoons chopped fresh parsley
4 tablespoons vegetable or olive oil
2 tablespoons white wine vinegar
1 tablespoon lemon juice
salt and freshly ground black pepper

Parboil the beans in boiling, salted water for 5 minutes or until just tender, drain and let cool. Slice the beans into a small salad bowl or deep plate. Peel the cucumber and slice it thinly. Cut each tomato into 8 pieces. Pare the hot pepper and slice into thin rounds. Slice the onion very fine and crush the garlic into it. Mix all the vegetables with the beans, add the parsley, oil, vinegar, lemon juice, and salt and pepper to taste. Mix well.

SERVES 4.

Coleslaw

Cabbage may be used raw or cooked in salad. Here the former is combined with some sweet apple for a crisp and tart dish. While white or green cabbage is usually chosen for this dish, red cabbage serves well too.

- ½ head green cabbage
- 1 small sweet onion
- 2 medium carrots
- 1 small apple
- ½ cup sour cream
- ¼ cup white wine vinegar
- pinch of sugar
- salt and freshly ground black pepper

Remove the outer leaves and the core from the cabbage, then shred very fine into a salad bowl. Grate the onion, peeled carrots, and apple onto the cabbage. Mix well. Add the sour cream, vinegar, sugar, and salt and pepper to taste. Mix thoroughly and chill before serving.

SERVES 6.

Cauliflower Salad

Another simple, single vegetable salad that may be dressed with mayonnaise or, as below, in a vinaigrette. You may serve this salad on its own, before the main meal, or as an accompaniment to meat or fish.

1 small cauliflower
½ small sweet onion
2 tablespoons chopped fresh dill
4 tablespoons olive oil
1 tablespoon white wine vinegar
1 tablespoon lemon juice
salt and freshly ground black pepper

Break the cauliflower into florets, discarding the hard core and green outer leaves. Bring a large pot of salted water to a boil, add the cauliflower and cook until just tender, about 10 minutes. Remove the florets, drain, and let cool.

Finely chop the onion. Place the cauliflower in a small salad bowl or deep plate, add the onion and chopped dill.

Make a vinaigrette by whisking the oil with the vinegar, lemon juice, and salt and pepper until well combined. Pour the dressing onto the cauliflower and toss well. Marinate in a refrigerator or cool place for about an hour before serving.

SERVES 4.

White Bean Salad

This salad of dried beans and vegetables makes a nice starter but may also be served with a simple roast. For a lighter version, make a vinaigrette instead of the mayonnaise dressing.

1 cup dried white beans
½ teaspoon baking soda (optional)
salt
1 bay leaf
2 medium potatoes
½ small celeriac, cleaned
2 medium kohlrabi
½ sweet onion
½ cup frozen peas
2 medium carrots
1 dill pickle
½ cup mayonnaise
1 tablespoon mustard
2 tablespoons sour cream
3 tablespoons white wine vinegar
juice of 1 lemon
2 tablespoons chopped fresh dill
salt and freshly grated black pepper

The day before you wish to serve the salad, soak the beans in a good quantity of water with baking soda, if you have it.

The next day, drain the beans, place them in a pot, and cover with water. Add some salt and a bay leaf. Bring to a boil and let simmer, covered, until tender, about 1½ hours. Drain the beans and let cool.

Boil the potatoes in their skins until just tender. Do the same with the celeriac and kohlrabi. Peel the potatoes and kohlrabi and dice. Dice the celeriac. Add the vegetables to the beans. Finely chop the onion and add it to the salad. Parboil the peas in boiling water for 2 minutes, drain, cool, and add to the salad. Peel the carrots and grate them into the mixture. Finely chop the pickle and mix well into the salad.

Add the mayonnaise, mustard, sour cream, vinegar, lemon juice, dill, and salt and pepper to taste. Mix well. Add more mayonnaise if the salad is a little dry. Chill in the refrigerator for at least 1 hour.

SERVES 4.

Beet Salad

More a pickle than a salad, this recipe may be used equally well for other vegetables, such as cauliflower, celeriac, cucumber, or green beans.

1 pound beets
1 cup white wine vinegar
2 tablespoons sugar
1 tablespoon fennel seed, crushed
1 teaspoon salt

Boil the beets whole in a good quantity of salted water until just tender, about 45 minutes. Take the pot off the heat and let the beets cool in their liquid. Remove the beets from their liquid.

Take about a cup of the liquid in which the beets have cooked and place it in a small pot. Add the vinegar, sugar, fennel seed, and salt. Bring to a boil and cook 5 minutes.

Peel the beets and then slice them, neither too fine nor too thick. Place in a large jar, then pour on the vinegar mixture to cover them. Cover the jar with wax paper and a rubberband and marinate in the refrigerator.

SERVES 6.

Pure Potato Salad

Czechs have dozens of different recipes for making salads with potatoes. I start with an eminently simple suggestion of potatoes and sweet onions in a light vinaigrette. You may make this salad more complex by adding some green beans or a finely sliced red pepper.

8 medium-size new potatoes
1 clove garlic
1 small sweet onion
2 tablespoons chopped fresh parsley
6 tablespoons olive oil
2 tablespoons red wine vinegar
2 tablespoons lemon juice
salt and freshly ground black pepper

Boil the potatoes, whole and in their skins, with some salt until just tender and let cool slightly. If using new potatoes with a thin, clean casing, you may not need to peel them; older potatoes should always be peeled.

Slice the potatoes into fairly thick pieces and place in a salad bowl which has been rubbed with the garlic. Slice the onion very thinly and add to the potatoes. Sprinkle on the parsley. Pour on the oil, then the vinegar and lemon juice, and season with salt and freshly ground black pepper. Mix well and refrigerate for at least 30 minutes before serving.

SERVES 6.

Christmas Potato Salad

From potatoes pure and simple we go to the other end of the spectrum for a salad that combines potatoes with various other vegetables, pickles, eggs, apples, and so on, and is then decorated with still additional ingredients. This salad is traditionally served on Christmas Eve with fried carp and makes for a truly impressive and tasty meal. Make lots so you have leftovers for the days afterwards. The version below is meatless, though a little ham or smoked sausage may be added if you wish.

12 medium-size new potatoes
½ cup white wine vinegar
3 medium carrots
1 medium sweet onion
1 medium apple
3 tablespoons capers, chopped
1 cup frozen peas
½ bunch fresh parsley
4 hard-boiled eggs
6 large dill pickles
1 cup mayonnaise
4 tablespoons Dijon mustard
¼ cup lemon juice
salt and freshly ground black pepper
2 medium tomatoes, cut into wedges or slices
2 lemons, cut into wedges

Boil the potatoes in their jackets in salted water until just tender, drain, and let cool slightly. Peel the potatoes and slice them medium-thick into a very large salad or mixing bowl. Sprinkle them with a little vinegar to absorb flavor and so they do not discolor.

Peel the carrots and grate them into the potatoes. Chop the onion fine and add. Peel the apple and grate it into the mix. Add the chopped capers. Parboil the peas for 2 minutes in salted water, drain, cool, and add. Chop 3 or 4 tablespoons of the parsley and add this to the salad. Take 2 of the boiled eggs, finely chop these, and add. Take 3 of the pickles, chop these fine, and add. To dress the salad, add the mayonnaise, mustard, remaining vinegar, lemon juice, and a good quantity of salt and pepper. Mix well. Taste for seasonings and add more mayonnaise and vinegar if the salad is a little dry.

Turn the salad into the bowl in which you will serve it and smooth over its surface. To decorate it, select some nice sprigs of fresh parsley, tomato wedges, and lemon wedges, cut the remaining 2 eggs into quarters, and slice the 3 remaining pickles. Now, using your imagination, lay these ingredients on top of the salad in a nice pattern. Cover the salad with foil or plastic and cool in the refrigerator for at least 1 hour before serving.

SERVES 8.

Baked Carp Salad

For this salad, a fresh, good-tasting fish is roasted in butter and then mixed with a few vegetables and dressed in a vinaigrette. Although carp is the fish of choice for Czechs, this dish is very good made with pickerel, trout, or bass. The concept is simple and may easily be varied: substitute celeriac for the peas, for example, or change the oil and vinegar for a mayonnaise dressing.

1 pound carp fillets
salt and freshly ground black pepper
4 tablespoons (½ stick) butter, melted
½ small sweet onion, finely chopped
1 large dill pickle, chopped
1 medium carrot, grated
2 tablespoons chopped fresh parsley
½ cup frozen peas
4 tablespoons vegetable oil
2 tablespoons white wine vinegar
1 tablespoon lemon juice

Preheat the oven to 350°F degrees.

Season the fish fillets with salt and pepper. Place in an oven dish, and pour on the melted butter. Bake in the oven until just tender or 10 minutes per inch of thickness. Remove the fish from the oven and let cool slightly.

Using two forks, tear the fillets into bite-size pieces into a small salad bowl or deep plate. Add the chopped onion, chopped pickle, grated carrot, and chopped parsley. Parboil the peas in boiling, salted water for 2 minutes, drain, and cool. Add the peas to the salad.

To dress the salad, pour on the oil, vinegar, and lemon juice, season with additional salt and pepper, and mix well. This salad may be served when the fish is still a little warm or after it has cooled.

SERVES 4.

Pickerel and Potato Salad

As with many fish dishes, the choice of fish is largely up to you and here any freshwater species, such as carp, trout, or perch, may be used instead of pickerel. In this recipe, the fish is poached instead of baked and more substantive vegetables are incorporated with it in a mayonnaise dressing.

- ¾ pound pickerel fillets
- salt and freshly ground black pepper
- 2 tablespoons butter
- 4 tablespoons white wine vinegar
- 8 whole black peppercorns
- 1 bay leaf
- 3 medium new potatoes
- 1 medium carrot
- ½ small celeriac
- ½ small sweet onion
- 2 tablespoons chopped fresh parsley
- 2 tablespoons lemon juice
- 4 tablespoons vegetable oil
- 1 lemon, cut into wedges

Season the fillets with salt and pepper. Melt the butter in a large pan, add 2 tablespoons of vinegar, ¼ cup water, the whole peppercorns, and the bay leaf. Bring to a boil. Add the fillets, cover, and poach for about 10 minutes or until tender. Remove the fish from the liquid and let cool.

Boil the potatoes in salted water until done. Remove, let cool, peel and dice. Peel the carrot and celeriac, dice them, and parboil in boiling salted water until just tender, about 10 minutes. Drain and cool. Finely chop the onion.

Using two forks, tear the fish into bite-size pieces into a salad bowl. Add the potatoes, carrots, celeriac, and onion. Sprinkle on the chopped parsley. Add the remaining 2 tablespoons vinegar, lemon juice, and vegetable oil, season with additional salt and pepper, and mix well. Cool in the refrigerator for 1 hour before serving. Serve with lemon wedges.

SERVES 4.

Smoked Trout Salad

Any smoked fish will do for this salad, though trout is especially nice. A smoked fish salad is a lovely starter to a meal but may also be a main lunch course.

- ¾ pound smoked trout
- 1 small endive
- ½ small sweet onion
- 2 medium tomatoes
- ½ English cucumber
- 2 tablespoons chopped fresh parsley
- 3 tablespoons vegetable or olive oil
- 3 tablespoons lemon juice
- salt and freshly ground black pepper

Using two forks, tear the trout into bite-size pieces into a salad bowl. Clean the endive well, dry, and tear each leaf into 2 or 3 pieces. Finely slice the onion. Cut each tomato into 8 pieces. Peel the cucumber and slice into fine rounds. Add the endive, onion, tomato, cucumber, and chopped parsley to the fish. Pour on the oil and lemon juice and season with salt and pepper. Mix well. Cool in the refrigerator for 30 minutes before serving.

SERVES 4.

Roast Beef Salad

All kinds of meat may be put in a salad. A favorite combination in Prague is roast veal and roast pork. Many smoked meats are also used. Just about anything may be added to the meat depending on your taste, either bound in with the dressing or placed on top of the salad as decoration. Try cheese, hot peppers, eggs, beets, potatoes, asparagus, peas, or apples.

Many good things may be done with leftover roast, including making a salad. While you may wind up roasting a small cut of beef especially for this preparation, a large chunk of yesterday's supper is perfect. Many Czechs prefer their meat cooked well-done, but this salad is even better, in my mind, when the beef is rare. Combining meat and salad allows for almost endless permutations. To vary the recipe below, change the vegetables, try a creamy yogurt or mayonnaise dressing instead of the vinaigrette, or use a different meat such as roast or smoked pork.

½ small head romaine lettuce
1 small endive
1 clove garlic
½ pound cooked roast beef
½ small sweet onion
2 medium tomatoes
½ English cucumber
4 tablespoons olive oil
2 tablespoons red wine vinegar
1 teaspoon Dijon mustard
salt and freshly ground black pepper
2 tablespoons chopped fresh parsley

Wash the lettuce and endive well, dry the leaves, and tear each into bite-size pieces. Place in a salad bowl that has been rubbed with the clove of garlic.

Cut the roast beef into fairly thin strips about 2 inches long. Add to the lettuce. Finely slice the onion and add. Dice the tomato and add. Peel the cucumber, slice into thin rounds, and add this to the salad.

To make the vinaigrette, whisk together the oil, vinegar, and mustard until they are well blended. Season with salt and pepper. Sprinkle the chopped parsley on the salad, then dress it with the vinaigrette, mixing well. Serve within 30 minutes.

SERVES 4.

Beef and Bean Salad

Instead of lettuce, this meat salad uses dried white beans for its main vegetable. Fresh green beans, boiled until just tender, are also very nice. The dressing is made from yogurt and sour cream, though a vinaigrette would also work well. While you may want to prepare some beef exclusively for this salad, a leftover roast or some beef boiled for stock or soup would also do fine.

1 cup dried white beans
½ teaspoon baking soda (optional)
salt
10 whole black peppercorns
1 strip bacon
2 bay leaves
2 medium carrots
½ small celeriac
½ pound cooked roast beef
½ small sweet onion
2 tablespoons chopped fresh parsley
1 clove garlic
½ cup plain yogurt
2 tablespoons sour cream
2 tablespoons white wine vinegar
freshly ground black pepper

The day before you wish to serve the salad, soak the beans in plenty of water with baking soda, if you have it, to help tenderize the beans.

The next day, drain the beans, place in a pot, cover with water, and add salt, whole peppercorns, bacon, and the bay leaves. Bring to a boil, cover, reduce heat, and simmer until done, about 1½ hours. When the beans are tender, drain them, discarding the bacon, peppercorns, and bay leaf.

Peel the carrots and celeriac, cut them into thin strips, and boil in salted water until just tender, about 5 minutes. Drain.

Place the beans in a salad bowl. Add the carrots and celeriac. Cut the beef into fine strips about 2 inches long. Add the beef to the beans. Finely slice the onion and add. Add the chopped parsley.

To make the dressing, mince or crush the garlic, then mix in the yogurt, sour cream, and vinegar. Mix well. Season with salt and pepper. Add to the salad, mix well, and refrigerate for at least 1 hour before serving.

SERVES 4.

Tongue Salad

For this recipe I recommend a freshly boiled beef tongue, though smoked tongue is also good. Use a small leftover piece from a previous dinner. If you have never tried tongue, try to get over the queasy associations; this meat has a very rich and fine texture.

- ½ pound boiled beef tongue, peeled
- 4 medium tomatoes
- ½ small sweet onion
- 1 tablespoon capers
- 2 tablespoons chopped fresh dill
- ¼ cup mayonnaise
- ¼ cup yogurt
- 4 tablespoons white wine vinegar
- salt and freshly ground black pepper

Cut the boiled tongue into fine strips about 2 inches long. Place in a salad bowl. Cut each tomato into 8 slices and add. Finely slice the onion and add. If using large capers, chop these a little, while small capers may be left whole. Add the capers to the salad. Sprinkle on the chopped dill.

Make the dressing by mixing together the mayonnaise, yogurt, and vinegar, then seasoning this with salt and pepper. Add the dressing to the salad, mix well, and cool in the refrigerator for at least 30 minutes before serving.

SERVES 4.

Roast Pork and Zucchini Salad

The vegetables are lightly cooked for this salad and then bound with the meat in a vinaigrette. Select the smallest, youngest zucchini you can find as these have the most delicate flavor.

- 2 small leeks
- 3 small zucchini
- 1 small red bell pepper
- 6 tablespoons olive oil
- ½ teaspoon dried thyme
- ½ pound cooked roast pork
- 1 tablespoon red wine vinegar
- 1 tablespoon lemon juice
- salt and freshly ground black pepper
- 2 tablespoons chopped fresh parsley

Wash the leeks well, dry them, and cut off the green parts. Slice the remaining white leeks into fine rounds. Wash the zucchini and cut them thinly into half rounds. Core the pepper, cut into quarters, and then slice thinly.

Heat 2 tablespoons oil in a frying pan on medium-low heat. Add the leeks and sauté for 3 or 4 minutes. Add the zucchini and red pepper and sprinkle on the thyme. Fry, stirring occasionally, until the zucchini are just a little wilted, about 5 minutes. Take off the heat and let cool.

Cut the roast pork into thin strips about 2 inches long. Place in a salad bowl. Add the zucchini mixture.

Make the vinaigrette by whisking together the remaining 4 tablespoons oil, the vinegar, and lemon juice. Season the dressing with salt and pepper. Sprinkle the parsley on the salad, pour on the vinaigrette, and mix well. Cool in the refrigerator for at least 30 minutes before serving.

SERVES 4.

Chicken and Celeriac Salad

Leftover roast chicken or a couple of freshly sautéed or poached chicken breasts make for a tasty and substantial salad. The apple in this recipe makes for a slightly sweet taste that complements the celeriac well. Rabbit is an excellent substitute for chicken.

1 medium celeriac
½ pound cooked chicken, skinless and boneless
1 small apple
½ small sweet onion
1 tablespoon chopped fresh dill
2 tablespoons vegetable or olive oil
2 tablespoons lemon juice
1 teaspoon Dijon mustard
salt and freshly ground black pepper

Peel the celeriac and cut into thin strips about 2 inches long. Boil in salted water until tender, about 5 minutes. Drain and cool.

Cut the chicken into thin strips and place in a salad bowl. Add the cooked celeriac. Peel the apple and then grate it into the salad. Finely slice the onion and add. Mix in the chopped dill.

To make the vinaigrette, whisk together the oil, lemon juice, and mustard until well blended. Season with salt and pepper. Pour the vinaigrette on the salad, mix well, and then cool in the refrigerator for at least 30 minutes before serving.

SERVES 4.

4

FISH

Czechs have no border with the sea and so freshwater fish predominate in the cuisine: carp, perch, bass, trout, salmon, pickerel, tench, pike, smelts, and eel. Of all these species, carp is undoubtedly the favorite. Carp is fried or baked with a little butter and lemon for a quick lunch, or its head is made into soup and its fillets breaded and fried for Christmas Eve supper. Carp is a rich, oily fish that dwells on the bottom of lakes and rivers. It is usually sold still alive and for a good reason: since it is a bottom feeder, keeping it in some fresh water for a few days before it is used cleans it out. To make sure the carp you purchase will have a tasty and delicate flesh, avoid older and heavier fish; a small, young carp of 3 to 4 pounds is ideal. A young carp's flesh is dense and flavorful, reminiscent of catfish or a good mackerel.

While many of the dishes below feature carp, they are just as good made with pickerel, trout, catfish, or bass, for example. As a rule for fish recipes, if the specified fish is not available or does not look fresh, don't hesitate to substitute another. Fish cook and taste differently depending on whether they come from salt or fresh water, whether they are dark or light in flesh color, and whether their meat is dense or falls into larger flakes. As you become more familiar with different species you will quickly pick up their family resemblances.

The crucial thing about a successful fish dish is freshness. Since most of the recipes below are quite simple, don't worry about the availability of a particular kind of fish before setting off to the market or fishmonger's. What you most want is a fresh fish that tastes good. The way in which you proceed to cook it will complement its basic flavor, but if you start off with something bad, nothing you do will get you around this. It matters little, then, if you come home with a pickerel or a bass, or even a cod for that matter. If you can find good carp, use them if you like them; otherwise, trout and pickerel are two excellent freshwater fish that may be used in all kinds of ways in the kitchen. The only freshwater fish that I would be careful about using indiscriminately is salmon since its taste and color are quite distinctive.

Choosing a fresh fish is not that difficult. For whole fish there are many different signs: glistening skin resistant to the touch, scales that do not rub off easily, translucent eyes that have not sunk down into their sockets, and bloody-red gills. For fillets or steaks, you have fewer clues: basically, avoid a dried-out appearance. Above all, whatever fish you are thinking about buying, it should not smell too "fishy." A developed fishy smell means it is old and unsuitable for eating. If you are having trouble finding fresh fish, use frozen fish instead and you may not even notice the difference.

I prefer simple preparations for fish that feature their distinctive flavors rather than masking them under all types of other ingredients. Fish cook quickly and need only some lemon, butter, salt, and pepper to taste good. As long as the fish is fresh and is not cooked too long the result will be a fine meal that did not take you very much time to prepare. As a general rule, cook a fish for 10 minutes per inch of thickness at its thickest point. This means, for example, that a thin ½-inch trout fillet would take no more than 5 minutes, while a whole pickerel 4 inches thick at the center would bake for 40 minutes. This rule applies for a fairly high heat. When cooking a whole fish, you may want to make a few cuts into the thickest part of the fish and then cook it a little less. Cutting the flesh makes it easier for the heat to penetrate and allows the thinner and thicker parts of the fish to cook the same amount of time.

Fish tastes good lightly seasoned on its own, with vegetables, covered with a sauce, fried, poached, roasted, or baked. Any nice fillet or small whole fish may be given the simplest treatment. To make it on top of the stove, season it with salt and pepper, lightly cover it in some flour, and melt some butter in a frying pan; when the butter is hot, put in the fish and fry until golden on both sides and tender in the middle; sprinkle on some fresh parsley and squeeze on some lemon juice, and serve. That's all that's needed. To roast fish in the oven, season it, dot with butter, put in a medium-high temperature oven, and when it's done, again add parsley and lemon. These simple methods may be used for any of the fish mentioned above. They are ideal for fish that have a fine taste and texture, such as carp, pickerel, or trout, while blander fish, such as perch, benefit from more complex treatments. As you can see from the recipes below, adding a little something to the coating of the fish or some vegetables to the roasting pan transforms these ordinary methods into more complex dishes.

Pan-Fried Whole Trout

Trout are often available live at your fishmonger's or supermarket to assure you of a fresh fish for your meal. Cooking the trout whole, intact with its head, makes for a pretty and very tasty dish. If you prefer, a little white wine and some more butter may be added along with the lemon juice and reduced to make a simple sauce. Serve this trout with new potatoes and a green salad or some peas or fresh asparagus.

2 small trout (1 pound each)
salt and freshly ground black pepper
3 tablespoons flour
4 tablespoons (½ stick) butter
2 tablespoons chopped fresh parsley
1 lemon

Clean and gut the fish if it has not already been prepared. Wash the fish in cold water and then dry it with paper towels. Season the trout with salt and pepper and cover with flour.

Melt 3 tablespoons of the butter on medium-high heat in a large frying pan. When the butter has melted and is quite hot, shake off the excess flour from the trout and put them into the pan. Fry them until lightly golden on one side, 4 or 5 minutes, shaking the pan occasionally to make sure the fish does not stick. Turn the trout over, add the remaining 1 tablespoon butter, and fry until golden on the other side. Add the parsley and juice from half the lemon. Cook for another few seconds. Serve with additional parsley and lemon wedges.

SERVES 2.

Pan-Fried Fish Fillets

Trout, pickerel, carp, or, indeed, just about any type of fresh- or salt-water fish may be cooked in this manner. You may vary the recipe by adding some white wine and more butter toward the end to make a sauce, or frying a little chopped onion and garlic before the fish is put into the pan.

4 medium fish fillets, e.g. pickerel, carp, salmon
salt and freshly ground black pepper
¼ cup flour
4 tablespoons (½ stick) butter
2 tablespoons chopped fresh parsley
1 lemon

Wash the fillets gently in cold water and dry with paper towels. Season them with salt and pepper and dredge in flour.

Melt the butter in a large pan on medium-high heat. When the butter is hot, shake the excess flour off the fillets and put them in the pan. Cook for 2 to 3 minutes depending on the thickness of the fillets, shaking the pan occasionally to make sure the fish does not stick. Turn the fillets over and fry until lightly golden on the other side. Add most of the parsley and the juice of ½ a lemon and cook for a few more seconds. Serve with fresh parsley sprinkled on top and lemon wedges on the side.

SERVES 4.

Fish Fillets in a Light Batter

Coating fish in batter provides slightly bland species like perch with an interesting texture and a medium to soak up other flavors. Try this method with flaky fish like cod. The batter may be varied by substituting white wine or beer for the milk.

4 fish fillets, e.g., perch, cod, or whitefish
salt and freshly ground black pepper
¼ cup milk
2 eggs
½ cup flour
1 cup vegetable oil
1 lemon, cut into wedges

Wash the fillets gently in cold water, dry them with paper towels, and season with salt and freshly ground black pepper.

Make the batter by mixing together the milk and eggs with some salt and pepper, then adding the flour, just enough to make a medium-thick batter.

Heat the oil in a large frying pan on medium-high heat. When the oil is hot, coat each fillet in the batter and then place in the frying pan. Fry the fish for 3 to 4 minutes per side until golden brown, depending on their thickness. Remove and drain on paper towels. Serve with lemon wedges.

SERVES 4.

Fried Carp

For this dish the fish is coated with flour, egg, and bread crumbs and then fried. Use any type of white-fleshed fillet this way. Carp done in this manner is traditionally served on Christmas Eve with a fancy potato salad.

- 4 carp fillets
- salt and freshly ground black pepper
- ½ cup flour
- 2 eggs, beaten
- 1 cup fine bread crumbs
- 2 tablespoons butter
- 2 tablespoons vegetable oil
- 2 tablespoons chopped fresh parsley
- 1 lemon, cut into wedges

Wash the fillets gently in cold water, dry with paper towels, and season with salt and pepper.

Arrange 3 deep plates before you: place the flour in the first, the eggs in the second, and the bread crumbs in the third. Take a fillet, cover it with flour, then put it in the beaten eggs and coat well. Finally, cover well in bread crumbs.

When the fillets are breaded, melt the butter and oil in a large frying pan on medium heat. Add the fillets and fry until golden brown on each side, 3 to 4 minutes per side. Serve with chopped parsley and lemon wedges.

SERVES 4.

Bass Broiled with Parsley Butter

These bass fillets are cooked quickly in a hot oven with a little flavored butter. The same method may be used with carp, trout, pickerel, pike, salmon, etc. Try using fresh chives or dill instead of the parsley, or mix some anchovies with the butter.

4 bass fillets
salt and freshly ground black pepper
4 tablespoons (½ stick) butter
2 tablespoons chopped fresh parsley
1 lemon, cut into wedges

Preheat the broiler in your oven. Wash the fillets gently in cold water, dry with paper towels, and season with salt and pepper. Mash the butter with the parsley until well blended. Place the fish on a buttered baking sheet and dot with the herb butter. Broil the fish until golden brown, about 8 minutes, and serve with lemon wedges.

SERVES 4.

Broiled Salmon

In this dish the salmon is marinated in oil and lemon and then broiled. Make sure you do not overcook this fish since it loses its flavor when it dries out.

4 salmon steaks, each 1 inch thick
salt and freshly ground black pepper
4 tablespoons olive oil
2 lemons
2 tablespoons chopped fresh dill
4 shallots, finely chopped
2 cloves garlic, crushed

Wash the salmon steaks gently in cold water, then dry with paper towels. Season them with salt and freshly ground black pepper. Place the steaks in a glass dish. Pour on the oil and juice from 1 lemon, then add the dill, shallots, and garlic. Leave the salmon to marinate in the refrigerator, covered, for about 1 hour.

Preheat the broiler in your oven. Place the fillets on a baking sheet and put some of the marinade on top of each. Broil for 10 minutes until golden. Cut the remaining lemon into wedges and serve with the fish.

SERVES 4.

Roast Pickerel

Pickerel is a very fine tasting fish that may be cooked whole or in fillets. I use chives to flavor the dish, though fresh parsley or dill would also be good.

4 pickerel fillets
salt and freshly ground black pepper
4 tablespoons (½ stick) butter
2 tablespoons chopped fresh chives
2 lemons
2 tablespoons white wine

Wash the pickerel fillets gently in cold water, then dry with paper towels. Season with salt and pepper.

Preheat the oven to 450°F.

Place the fillets in a buttered baking dish, spot with butter, sprinkle on the chopped chives, and then pour on the juice from 1 lemon and the white wine. Roast in the oven for 8 to 10 minutes depending on thickness. Cut the remaining lemon into wedges and serve with the fish.

SERVES 4.

Roast Carp with Sour Cream

Rather than oil or butter, this dish uses sour cream to moisten the fish and add richness. Try mixing the sour cream with some yogurt for a lighter variation. I prefer to use shallots in recipes like this since they are milder than onions, but the latter will do fine as well.

4 carp fillets
salt and freshly ground black pepper
1 tablespoon butter
4 shallots, finely sliced
2 tablespoons chopped fresh dill
½ cup sour cream
2 lemons

Preheat the oven to 450°F.

Wash the fish fillets gently in cold water, then dry with paper towels. Season with salt and pepper. Place the fillets in a buttered baking dish, lay on the sliced shallots and chopped dill, and cover each with sour cream. Pour on the juice from 1 lemon. Put the fish in the oven and roast for about 10 minutes until tender. Cut the remaining lemon into wedges and serve with the fish.

SERVES 4.

Roast Mackerel with Vegetables

The rich, dense, and slightly oily taste of mackerel appeals to some more than others, though I find this cheap fish unjustly maligned. Mackerel benefits from other flavors and the wine, nutmeg, and vegetables work well in this recipe.

2 small parsnips, diced
2 medium carrots, diced
4 mackerel fillets
salt and freshly ground black pepper
1 medium onion, chopped
2 tablespoons chopped fresh parsley
1 bay leaf
grated nutmeg
2 tablespoons olive oil
1 cup dry white wine
2 lemons
2 tablespoons bread crumbs (optional)

Preheat the oven to 450°F.

Bring a pot of salted water to a boil and add the parsnips and carrots. Simmer for 5 minutes, remove, and drain.

Wash the mackerel fillets gently in cold water and dry with paper towels. Season with salt and pepper. Place the fish in a baking dish. Add the onion, parsnips, carrots, parsley, and bay leaf. Grate on a little nutmeg. Pour on the olive oil, white wine, and the juice of 1 lemon.

Bake for 10 minutes. If the sauce needs thickening, sprinkle on the bread crumbs and bake for a couple more minutes. Cut the remaining lemon into wedges. Serve the mackerel with the vegetables on the side, covered with the sauce, and accompanied by lemon wedges.

SERVES 4.

Trout Poached in Red Wine

While white wine is typically used in fish recipes, this combination is not an absolute rule. I use fillets in this recipe, though it may be modified for small, whole trout. A large, whole pickerel may be poached in the same way.

- 8 trout fillets
- salt and freshly ground black pepper
- 6 shallots, finely chopped
- 2 cloves garlic, crushed
- 2 tablespoons chopped fresh parsley
- 1 bay leaf
- ½ bottle dry red wine
- 4 tablespoons (½ stick) butter
- 1 lemon, cut into wedges

Wash the fish gently in cold water and dry with paper towels. Season with salt and pepper.

Place the fish fillets in a large pot so all the trout fit together on the bottom. Add the shallots, garlic, most of the parsley, and bay leaf. Pour on the red wine. Bring slowly to a boil, reduce the heat, and simmer, uncovered, for about 10 minutes until the fish is just done. Carefully remove the trout from the pot and keep warm in the oven.

Turn the heat up high under the wine and cook it vigorously, uncovered, shaking the pot occasionally, until it is reduced by about half. Whisk in the butter to make a thin sauce.

Serve the trout with a little sauce, sprinkled with the remaining parsley and with lemon wedges on the side.

SERVES 4.

Trout Cooked Blue

(Pstruzi Na Modro)

For this dish, small, whole trout are subjected to hot vinegar so as to curl them, then they are poached with root vegetables, and served sprinkled with lemon juice and butter. "Na Modro" or "cooked blue" is a traditional method of curing the fish with vinegar so that it "curls." Carp fillets may also be cooked in this manner for a fine effect.

- 4 small whole trout, 1 pound each
- ½ cup white wine vinegar
- 2 medium carrots, diced
- 2 small parsnips, diced
- ½ small celeriac, diced
- 1 small onion, chopped
- 2 cloves garlic, sliced
- 8 whole black peppercorns
- 4 pieces allspice
- 1 bay leaf
- salt and freshly ground black pepper
- 4 tablespoons (½ stick) butter, melted
- 2 lemons
- 2 tablespoons chopped fresh parsley

Wash the trout in cold water and dry with paper towels.

Place the trout in a large dish. Heat up the vinegar until almost boiling, then pour it onto the fish. Let stand 15 minutes.

Into a large pot that will hold the trout, place the carrots, parsnips, celeriac, onion, garlic, peppercorns, allspice, bay leaf, and salt and pepper. Add the vinegar from the fish and enough water to half fill the pot. Bring to a boil, reduce the heat, cover, and simmer for 10 minutes. Add the fish and cook until done, about 10 minutes.

Remove the fish and place on serving plates. Combine the melted butter, juice of 1 lemon, and additional salt and pepper. Pour the lemon-butter sauce on the fish, sprinkle on the parsley. Cut the remaining lemon into wedges and serve alongside the fish.

SERVES 4.

Carp Poached with Vegetables

When cooking trout or carp "na modro" *or "to the blue," root vegetables are used only to flavor the poaching broth. Here the carp is poached with carrots, celeriac, and parsnips and then served alongside the vegetables. I use water along with vinegar and lemon juice to poach the fish, but substituting white wine for the water adds even more flavor.*

1 small onion, finely chopped
2 medium carrots, diced
2 small parsnips, diced
½ small celeriac, diced
8 whole black peppercorns
4 pieces allspice
1 bay leaf
2 tablespoons chopped fresh parsley
salt and freshly ground black pepper
2 lemons
¼ cup white wine vinegar
4 carp fillets
3 tablespoons butter, melted

Into a large casserole dish or pot, place the onion, carrots, parsnips, celeriac, peppercorns, allspice, bay leaf, 1 tablespoon of the parsley, and salt and pepper. Add the juice of ½ a lemon, the vinegar, and about 4 cups water. Bring to a boil, reduce the heat, cover, and simmer for 15 minutes.

Add the carp fillets to the vegetables and broth and poach, covered, until done, about 10 minutes. Remove the fillets and place on serving plates. Drain the vegetables and place around the fish. Pour the melted butter and juice of ½ a lemon on the carp, and sprinkle on the remaining 1 tablespoon parsley. Cut the remaining lemon into wedges and serve with the fish.

SERVES 4.

Carp Poached with Caraway

This dish of carp poached in white wine gets a distinctive flavor from crushed caraway seeds and fresh chives.

4 carp fillets
salt and freshly ground black pepper
1 tablespoon caraway seeds, crushed
1 small onion, finely sliced
2 tablespoons chopped fresh chives
4 tablespoons (½ stick) butter
2 lemons
1 cup dry white wine

Preheat the oven to 200°F.

Wash the carp fillets gently in cold water and dry with paper towels. Season with salt, pepper, and the crushed caraway seeds.

Place the fillets in a large frying pan or pot, add the sliced onion and 1 tablespoon chives. Dot with 2 tablespoons butter and pour on the juice of 1 lemon and the white wine. Bring slowly to a boil, reduce the heat, and simmer, uncovered, until done, about 10 minutes.

Remove the fish to a serving platter and keep warm in the oven. Raise the heat under the poaching liquid and reduce a little. Whisk in the remaining 2 tablespoons butter and adjust the seasonings. Cut the remaining lemon into wedges. Pour the sauce over the fish, sprinkle on the remaining 1 tablespoon chives, and serve with lemon wedges on the side.

SERVES 4.

Carp Poached with Paprika

This dish combines fish with tomatoes and paprika and then finishes off with a thickening of sour cream for a colorful and rich meal.

4 carp fillets
salt and freshly ground black pepper
1 small onion, finely chopped
2 tablespoons butter
2 medium tomatoes, diced
1 tablespoon paprika
2 lemons
1 cup dry white wine (optional)
½ cup sour cream
1 tablespoons chopped fresh parsley

Wash the carp fillets gently in cold water and dry with paper towels. Season with salt and pepper.

Fry the onion in the butter on low heat until golden. Add the diced tomatoes and the paprika and fry for 5 minutes on medium-low heat. Add the juice of 1 lemon and the white wine or an equal quantity of water. Place the fish in the broth, bring slowly to a boil, and simmer until done, about 10 minutes. Mix in the sour cream and cook for another minute. Cut remaining lemon into wedges. Serve sprinkled with fresh parsley and lemon wedges on the side.

SERVES 4.

Carp in Black Sauce

(Kapr na Černo)

If you cannot find carp for this dish, use a firm-textured fairly heavy fish such as catfish. The sauce is a very rich sweet-and-sour combination and anything too delicate will be overcome by it. The fish is cooked with root vegetables, dried fruits, and nuts. It is really up to you as to which fruits and nuts to use. I suggest combining prunes, raisins, almonds, and hazelnuts, but all of these are not necessary. The "black" sauce comes from the use of dark beer, dark bread, and a little sugar caramelized in butter. This dish is just as good or, perhaps, better served reheated the day after, with dumplings.

4 tablespoons (½ stick) butter
1 medium onion, chopped
2 medium carrots, diced
2 medium parsnips, diced
½ small celeriac, diced
2 lemons
½ cup red wine vinegar
1 bottle (12 ounces) dark ale
8 whole black peppercorns
4 pieces allspice
1 bay leaf
1 teaspoon thyme
½-inch piece ginger
1 tablespoon grated lemon zest
salt and freshly ground black pepper
3 slices dark pumpernickel bread
1 tablespoon sugar
2 tablespoons flour
6 prunes, roughly chopped
¼ cup raisins
2 tablespoons sliced, peeled almonds
2 tablespoons sliced, peeled hazelnuts
4 carp steaks

In a large pot or casserole dish, melt 2 tablespoons butter on low heat. When hot, add the chopped onion and fry until almost golden, stirring occasionally. Add the carrots, parsnips, and celeriac and fry for 5 minutes. Add the juice from 1 lemon, the vinegar, and the dark ale. Add water if needed to cover the vegetables. Mix in the peppercorns, allspice, bay leaf, thyme, ginger, and lemon zest. Season with salt and pepper. If the bread is a little hard, grate it; otherwise, chop it fine; then add to the vegetables. Bring the liquid to a slow boil, cover, and simmer for 15 minutes.

To make the dark roux, melt the remaining 2 tablespoons butter in a small frying pan on medium-low heat. Add the sugar and cook until it caramelizes a little, about 5 minutes, stirring well. Add the flour and cook until quite dark, about 10 minutes, stirring often. Mix the roux into the vegetables and cook for a couple of minutes. Add the prunes, raisins, almonds, and hazelnuts. Mix well. Lay the carp steaks into the sauce, cover the pot, and cook for 12 to 15 minutes or until done.

Remove the fish to a serving dish, then drain the sauce from the vegetable-fruit-nut mixture into a small pot. Arrange the vegetable mixture around the fish. If needed, reduce the sauce a little by boiling it quickly, uncovered. Pour the sauce on top of the fish. Cut the remaining lemon into wedges. Serve with lemon wedges and dumplings.

SERVES 4.

Gypsy Carp

(Kapr Po Cikánsku)

This fish is cooked very simply with a good deal of potatoes and onions and flavored with paprika and caraway. The resulting dish is fragrant and hearty. Just about any firm-fleshed fish will taste good made this way.

8 medium potatoes
6 tablespoons olive oil
2 medium onions, sliced
4 cloves garlic, chopped
4 carp steaks
2 tablespoons flour
1 tablespoon paprika
1 tablespoon caraway seeds, crushed
salt and freshly ground black pepper
2 lemons
1 tablespoon chopped fresh parsley

Boil the potatoes in their skins in salted water until done,15 to 20 minutes. Remove the potatoes, let cool a little, then peel them. Slice the potatoes into thick rounds.

Preheat the oven to 450°F.

Take a large casserole dish and oil the bottom with a little of the olive oil. Put in the potatoes.

Heat 2 tablespoons olive oil in a frying pan on low heat, then add the onions and garlic. Fry the onion until it is almost golden, stirring occasionally. Add this mixture to the potatoes.

Wash the carp steaks gently in cold water and dry with paper towels. Dredge them in the flour.

Heat 2 tablespoons olive oil on medium heat in a large frying pan. When hot, add the carp steaks and fry until slightly golden on both sides, about 2 minutes per side.

Sprinkle the potatoes and onions with the paprika, caraway, and salt and pepper to taste. Place the carp steaks on top. Pour on the remaining 2 tablespoons olive oil and the juice of 1 lemon. Put the dish in the oven and bake until done,10 to 12 minutes. Cut remaining lemon into wedges. Serve sprinkled with parsley and with lemon wedges on the side.

SERVES 4.

Salt Cod with Potatoes

Dried, salted cod takes some time to prepare but is worth it for the unique, creamy flavor that some people prefer over any fresh fish. Remember to start this dish the day ahead for the salt cod needs to be soaked for several hours.

1 pound salt cod
6 medium potatoes
6 tablespoons olive oil
1 medium onion, finely sliced
2 cloves garlic, crushed
2 lemons
2 tablespoons chopped fresh parsley
freshly ground black pepper

Put the salt cod in a good quantity of cold water and soak overnight. The next day, rub the fish with a fork to loosen the salt and its flakes. Drain the water and put to soak in fresh cold water. Repeat after a couple of hours.

Put the fish in a fresh pot of water, bring slowly to a boil, and cook until tender, about 1 hour.

Boil the potatoes in their skins in salted water until tender, about 15 to 20 minutes. Peel them and then finely slice them.

Heat the oil in a frying pan on low heat. Add the onion and garlic and cook for a few minutes, stirring occasionally, until almost golden.

Put the cooked fish in a large bowl. Using two forks, flake the fish into small pieces. Mix in the boiled potato slices. Pour on the onions and garlic and their cooking oil. Pour on the juice from 1 lemon. Sprinkle on the chopped parsley and season with pepper. Mix well. Cut remaining lemon into wedges and serve with the fish.

SERVES 4.

5

POULTRY

Chicken is popular in the Czech Republic and yet it in no way monopolizes the category of poultry. Duck, both domesticated and wild, and goose are used just as much and are even tastier. While wild duck is difficult to find in North America unless you hunt for it yourself, excellent domestic ducks and geese are readily available and sometimes are quite cheap. These birds may be a little more difficult to carve at first, since their joints are not exactly in the same place as a chicken's, but the practice is worth it. Both ducks and geese have less meat on their bones than chickens, so a bigger bird will be needed if you are cooking for three or more. But stay away from huge, old birds as they will be tough. Turkeys also make an appearance in Czech cooking and are usually stuffed and roasted.

If your poultry ideal is the breast of a young hen, then this chapter may disappoint. Chicken breasts have unduly cornered the restaurant, recipe, and shelf market. They are the most expensive part of the bird, especially when deboned, a procedure that takes about three cuts with a knife and 15 seconds. They are also the most likely portions to turn dry and tasteless. Try cooking with whole legs or thighs and you will see juicier flesh and less cash output. But when it comes to spending a bit more to get grain-fed free-range poultry, do put out. You can actually taste this meat and its color is not a washed out white.

While there is a danger in drying out breast meat when cooked separately, poultry in general may be cooked somewhat longer than is often thought with little damage and often improved taste. Apart from duck, which is good done medium or rare as well as well done, poultry should never be undercooked. If you carve into a roast chicken or split a goose thigh and see a hint of pink on the bone, this is all right, but if the juice runs red then stick it back on the heat.

The sight of a crisp, golden roasted bird is truly beautiful. Much poultry is cooked whole for this purpose and also to keep the flesh juicy. Dishes made with carved birds are also very good, especially when there is plenty of sauce or broth to add flavor. Chicken, being quite mild in flavor, can take a variety of ingredients in its preparation, such as onions, garlic, various herbs, and wine.

Ducks and geese are delicious made simply, with vegetables and other savory additions, and also with sweet accompaniments such as fruit or tangy sauces of vinegar or citrus. Their meats are darker and more flavorful. On occasion a duck or goose may be fatty but this excess grease can easily be discarded during the cooking process. A couple of hints: prick the bird all over with a fork to let the fat escape through the skin, and degrease the basting liquid or sauce with a spoon. But don't throw away the grease. Chicken fat should always be reserved in a jar in the fridge. It is excellent for frying. Duck and goose fats are even better and are often quite prized.

One last point: when buying a whole bird, don't look down upon the innards if you're lucky enough to find them packaged and stuck inside the bird. Chicken livers are excellent in their own right and help a stuffing when crushed in with other ingredients. The neck, heart, and kidneys are also liked by some and may always be used for making broth. When it comes to duck and goose, their livers may be even more precious than the birds themselves. Fried quickly on high heat in butter, they make one of the tastiest meals in any cuisine.

Roast Chicken

Perhaps one of the most elegant and satisfying meals to prepare is a roast bird. As in any recipe that features one thing purely and simply made, the quality of the chief ingredient is crucial. Choose a small to medium-size bird, preferably free range, with some yellow color in the skin and flesh. A little salt and pepper, some garlic and lemon, an herb, and that's all there is to it. Just let the chicken roast until it is tender, basting occasionally and leaving the skin to crisp.

1 (3½- to 4-pound) chicken
salt and freshly ground black pepper
2 cloves garlic
1 teaspoon thyme
2 tablespoons chopped fresh parsley
juice of 1 lemon
1 tablespoon olive or vegetable oil
2 tablespoons flour

Preheat the oven to 400°F.

Dry the chicken and rub all over, inside and out, with salt and pepper. Take 1 garlic clove and cut it into fine slivers. Stick several of these in between the skin and the flesh of the breast and legs. Put the chicken breast side up in a roasting pan a little larger than the bird. Chop up the remaining garlic and throw it around the chicken. Sprinkle on the thyme and 1 tablespoon of the parsley. Pour on the juice from the lemon. Drizzle a little oil on top of the bird. Pour about ½ cup of water into the pan. Place the chicken in the oven.

After 15 minutes, baste the bird with some of its juices and move it to and fro in the pan to make sure it is not sticking to the bottom. Reduce the oven heat to 350°F. Keep roasting the bird until it is done, about another 1¼ hours or until the juices run clear when you prick the thigh. Baste every 15 or 20 minutes, adding a little water if needed.

If the breast skin is not absolutely crisp when the chicken is done, just raise the heat in the oven in the last few minutes of cooking.

Remove the chicken to a carving platter. To make the gravy, degrease the cooking juices with a spoon. Add ½ cup water or chicken broth if you have it, and bring to a low boil. Add the remaining 1 tablespoon parsley. In a small cup, mix the flour with a little water until well blended. Add a couple of spoonfuls of the hot liquid to the flour mixture and mix. Then pour this thickener into the gravy, mixing continuously, and bring to a boil. Taste for salt and pepper, then pour into a gravy boat. Take the bird to the table and carve. Boiled, roasted, or mashed potatoes go well with this dish, as do dumplings, plus a green salad or some green beans or carrots.

SERVES 4.

Roast Stuffed Chicken

Just about anything can be put inside a chicken to make a tasty stuffing, from a simple bread-based filling or a mixture of vegetables to a combination of other meats or fruits or nuts. I have chosen here a fairly easy bread stuffing with parsnips and leeks. Other vegetables, such as carrots or mushrooms, may be substituted. Use the chicken liver if you have it, otherwise omit without worry.

2 small parsnips
1 small leek
3 strips bacon
1 small onion, finely chopped
2 cloves garlic, crushed
2 French rolls or 4 slices of white bread
¼ cup milk
2 tablespoons chopped fresh parsley
1 tablespoon marjoram
salt and freshly ground black pepper
nutmeg
1 egg
1 (3½- to 4-pound) chicken, with its liver (finely chop livers and reserve)
1 tablespoon vegetable oil
1 cup dry red wine
2 tablespoons flour

To make the stuffing, peel and wash the parsnips, dice them, and then parboil them in salted, boiling water for 5 minutes. Drain and reserve. Wash the leek very well, chop off and discard the green tops, then slice finely.

Slice the bacon fairly fine and fry until almost crisp in a frying pan on medium heat. Add the onion and fry for a few minutes, stirring occasionally, until almost golden. Add the chopped chicken livers and fry for a couple of minutes. Add the garlic and cook for another couple of minutes. Add the leeks and cook for 2 more minutes. Take the pan off the heat. Mix in the cooked parsnips.

Dice or tear the bread into smallish pieces and soak them quickly in the milk, then add to the vegetables. Mix in the parsley, marjoram, and salt and pepper to taste. Grate in a little nutmeg. Mix in the egg.

Preheat the oven to 400°F.

Dry the chicken and rub on salt and pepper inside and out. Then stuff as much of the stuffing as will fit into the bird's cavity. Once done, it is best to secure the opening of the cavity with some string or a couple of toothpicks, but this is not necessary. Place the chicken breast side up in a roasting pan. If there is stuffing remaining this may be wrapped in foil and put in to roast with the chicken. Sprinkle the oil on top of the bird and pour the wine around it. Place in the oven.

After 15 minutes, baste the bird and reduce the oven temperature to 375°F. Keep roasting, basting occasionally, adding water if necessary. The chicken will be done in about another 1¼ hours or when the juice from the thigh runs clear. If the skin isn't quite crisp enough, raise the oven temperature at the end of the cooking time.

Remove the bird from the pan onto a carving platter. To make a gravy, degrease the cooking juices with a spoon and place on medium heat on top of the stove. Add a little water or broth. Mix flour with an equal amount of water in a small cup. Add to this some of the hot liquid, then pour the flour mixture into the gravy, mixing continuously. Cook for a couple of minutes, making sure the gravy has reached a boil and thickened. Season and serve with the chicken and stuffing. Roasted or mashed potatoes plus a green salad are nice accompaniments.

SERVES 4 TO 5.

Roast Chicken with Mushrooms

This chicken is roasted with a good deal of mushrooms, permeating the meat with flavor. Ordinary fresh white mushrooms do well here, but use a tastier fungus, such as portobellos or dried porcinis, if available and affordable. The sauce prospers from alcohol, either white wine as suggested here, or a smaller quantity of brandy. The sour cream may be omitted in favor of a flour-water thickening (see previous recipe) or a roux.

3 tablespoons lard or vegetable oil
1 (3½-to 4-pound) chicken
1 medium yellow onion, finely chopped
2 ribs celery, diced
2 cloves garlic, crushed
¾ pound fresh mushrooms, sliced
1 cup dry white wine
juice of 1 lemon
2 tablespoons chopped fresh parsley
1 teaspoon thyme
salt and freshly ground black pepper
1 cup chicken broth or water
½ cup sour cream (optional)

Preheat the oven to 375°F.

Heat the lard or oil in a roasting pan on top of the stove on medium-high heat. Put in the bird and brown on both sides. Remove the chicken and turn the heat down to medium. Put the chopped onion in the pan and fry, stirring occasionally, until almost golden. Add the diced celery and the garlic. Cook for 3 or 4 minutes. Add the mushrooms and cook for another 3 or 4 minutes.

Put the chicken back in the pan. Pour on the white wine and the lemon juice. Sprinkle on the parsley and thyme. Season with salt and pepper. Put in the oven. Baste the chicken every 15 minutes or so, adding some broth or water if the liquid dries out. The meat should be tender and the skin crisp after 1½ hours or less.

Once the chicken is done, remove it to a platter and put the pan with its vegetables and liquid on top of the stove on medium heat. Add some broth or water if needed for a good quantity of sauce. Add sour cream and heat through, blending well with a whisk.

Serve the bird surrounded with mushroom sauce. This dish is good with dumplings, rice, or potatoes, and a simple green vegetable such as asparagus or green beans.

SERVES 4.

Capon Cooked in Red Wine

If cooking for more than four people, a medium-size capon is a good idea. The flesh is tasty though it needs more cooking time than a young roasting chicken. If you cannot find a capon use a larger size hen. In this recipe the bird is simmered in red wine, a treatment close to the French Coq au Vin. One whole bottle of a cheaper dry red wine is just about optimal, though half a bottle and some water will do fine. Adding brandy to the dish makes it even richer, but it may be omitted without worry.

1 (5-pound) capon
8 tablespoons flour
4 strips bacon, sliced fine
1 medium yellow onion, chopped thick
2 cloves garlic, crushed
½ cup brandy (optional)
1 bottle (25.4 ounce) dry red wine
1 teaspoon thyme
2 tablespoons chopped fresh parsley
salt and freshly ground black pepper
½ pound mushrooms, sliced fine

Cut up the capon into 8 or 10 serving pieces (the breast may be halved on a big bird). Dust the chicken with some of the flour. Heat a large frying pan on medium heat and add the bacon. Fry the bacon until almost crisp. Turn down the heat to medium-low and add the chopped onion. Fry until almost golden, stirring occasionally. Add the garlic and cook for another couple of minutes. Remove the onion mixture from the pan and place in a large pot or casserole dish.

Turn up the heat under the frying pan to medium-high. Add a little oil if needed, then put in as many of the chicken pieces as will fit into the pot without crowding. Fry the chicken, moving it around occasionally, until the pieces are golden brown on both sides. When the chicken is browned, transfer it to the casserole dish. Put your frying pan aside for use in a few minutes.

Turn the heat under the casserole dish to medium. Add the brandy, if using it, and heat for 3 or 4 minutes. Then, using a match, carefully light the chicken pieces to burn off the alcohol. (If this does not work, don't worry about it, and continue on to the next step.) Once the flame has gone down, pour in the red wine and, if needed, enough water to just cover the chicken. Mix in the thyme, parsley, and salt and pepper to taste. Turn the heat down to medium and leave uncovered.

Now go back to your frying pan. Remove some of the grease from it, leaving a couple of tablespoons. Place it on a high heat. Add the sliced mushrooms. Fry until golden brown. Turn the heat down and sprinkle on 3 or 4 tablespoons of the remaining flour. Cook for a couple of minutes, then mix this roux into your casserole.

Leave the chicken to cook on a light simmer, partially covered, for about 1 hour, though if your guests are late, cooking it twice as long will do little harm. Serve with dumplings, new potatoes, rice, or a good bread, and a green salad.

SERVES 6.

Chicken Paprikash

For this recipe you may use a whole chicken cut up into serving pieces, or an assortment of thighs or breasts, whichever you prefer. One method of making this dish begins by boiling the meat with some root vegetables for 15 or 20 minutes. I prefer to fry the meat, as below, though if you don't have any chicken stock sitting around you may want to choose the boiling method. This will give you enough broth for the recipe and for some soup as well.

2 tablespoons lard or vegetable oil
1 medium onion, finely chopped
1 tablespoon good quality paprika
1 small (3½-pound) chicken, cut into serving portions
2 tablespoons flour
3 cups chicken stock
salt and freshly ground black pepper
1 cup sour cream
juice of ½ a lemon

Choose a large frying pan with high sides which will hold all your meat and a good quantity of sauce—if none is available, use a large pot that is good for frying. Heat up the lard or oil over medium-low heat. Add the chopped onion and fry, stirring occasionally, until almost golden. Sprinkle on the paprika and cook, stirring occasionally, for a couple of minutes.

Turn up the heat to medium. Add the chicken portions. Sauté the chicken until it is lightly browned on both sides. Turn the heat down again to low and then throw in the flour. Cook for 2 minutes, stirring well. Pour in the chicken stock, stirring constantly. Raise the heat and bring to a low boil. Season with salt and pepper to taste. Simmer, partially covered, until the chicken is tender, about 40 minutes.

A few minutes before serving, take the pan off the heat and stir in the sour cream and lemon juice until well blended. Serve with dumplings, potatoes, or rice, and a cucumber salad.

SERVES 4.

Chicken with Lemons

Citrus does wonders for vegetables, fish, and meat. Lemon juice and a whole, sliced lemon are used here to flavor chicken. If you have no chicken broth, substitute some water instead. Your own collection of chicken breasts or thighs will do fine instead of the whole bird.

3 tablespoons vegetable oil
1 medium onion, finely sliced
1 (3½- to 4-pound) chicken, cut into serving portions
2 lemons
2 cups chicken stock
2 bay leaves
1 teaspoon thyme
1 teaspoon sugar
salt and freshly ground black pepper
2 tablespoons flour
2 tablespoons chopped fresh parsley

Heat the oil in a large frying pan or pot on medium-high heat. Add the onion and sauté until tender. Put in as many of the chicken pieces as will fit comfortably and fry them, stirring occasionally, until golden brown on both sides.

Repeat until all the chicken is fried, then return all the chicken to the pan.

Pour in the juice of 1 lemon and cook for a few minutes. Turn the heat down to medium and pour in the chicken stock. Slice the remaining lemon with the peel, and add. Add bay leaves, thyme, sugar, and salt and pepper to taste. Bring to a rolling boil and simmer, partially covered, until the chicken is tender, about 40 minutes.

Before serving, check for seasonings and tartness. You may want to add a little more sugar if the sauce is on the bitter side. To thicken the sauce, combine flour with some water and some of the hot liquid from the chicken. Mix together, and then pour this in with the chicken, stirring constantly. Lightly boil for 2 minutes to let the flour cook. Sprinkle with parsley and serve with dumplings or rice, and green beans or asparagus.

SERVES 4.

Chicken with Peppers

Chunks of chicken or larger serving portions may be cooked equally well in this way, finished either on top of the stove or in the oven. If red bell peppers are too pricey, green ones alone will do. Add sour cream for richness if you want, but the dish is also good without it.

- 2 strips bacon
- 1 green bell pepper
- 1 red bell pepper
- 1 medium onion, finely chopped
- 1 clove garlic, crushed
- oil (optional)
- 2 chicken legs, cut in half
- 1 tablespoon paprika
- ½ teaspoon thyme
- salt and freshly ground black pepper
- juice of ½ a lemon
- ¾ cup chicken broth or water
- ½ cup sour cream (optional)

Slice the bacon into fine strips. Core the peppers, wash them, and then cut them into strips.

Heat a large, ovenproof frying pan on medium-high heat. Fry the bacon until almost crisp. Add the onion and fry, stirring occasionally, until almost golden. Add the peppers and garlic and cook for 5 minutes. Remove all this from the pan and reserve.

Put the pan on high heat and add some oil if necessary. When the pan is quite hot, put in the chicken. Brown the meat on both sides, stirring occasionally.

Put the vegetables and bacon in with the chicken. Sprinkle on the paprika and thyme and season with salt and pepper. Pour in the lemon juice and the broth. You may continue cooking the chicken, uncovered, on top of the stove on medium heat, or put it in a 400°F oven. Either way, the dish will be done in about 30 minutes. If you wish, the sauce may be thickened with sour cream just before serving: simply mix in the sour cream and heat through for 2 minutes. Serve with rice and a green salad.

SERVES 2.

Chicken with Wild Mushrooms and Garlic

Mushrooms and garlic are beautiful together, but when the mushrooms are wild and have been dried to intensify their flavor, the combination is sublime. Dried mushrooms need to be soaked in warm water before use. Don't throw out their soaking liquid—strain it through cheesecloth to remove any dirt and use the liquid in the sauce.

1 ounce dried porcini mushrooms
3 tablespoons lard or vegetable oil
4 chicken breasts or legs
1 medium onion, finely chopped
3 cloves garlic, crushed
1 cup dry white wine
juice of ½ a lemon
2 tablespoons chopped fresh parsley
1 teaspoon marjoram
salt and freshly ground black pepper
2 tablespoons flour

Soak the dried mushrooms in 1 cup of warm water for 15 minutes. Remove the mushrooms and save the liquid. If there is dirt on the mushrooms, rub it off and strain the liquid through cheesecloth. Chop the mushrooms roughly.

Heat the lard on medium-high heat in a large frying pan or casserole dish. Add the chicken portions and brown on both sides, stirring occasionally. Add the chopped onion and garlic. Fry for 4 to 5 minutes. Add the white wine, the liquid from the mushrooms, and the lemon juice. Add the mushrooms. Sprinkle on the parsley and marjoram. Season with salt and pepper. Bring the liquid to a low boil and then simmer, partially covered, for 30 minutes, turning the chicken once or twice.

To thicken the sauce, mix the flour with a few tablespoons of water in a small cup. Mix in some of the cooking juice and then stir the thickener into the sauce. Cook for 2 to 3 minutes. Serve with dumplings or rice, and either some parsnips or carrots.

SERVES 4.

Chicken with Onions

Onions cooked slowly will sweeten and lose their sharpness, so don't be afraid of their quantity in this recipe. Use sweet white or red onions if you wish, though yellow cooking onions will do just fine.

2 tablespoons lard or vegetable oil
8 chicken thighs
2 large sweet white onions
1 teaspoon grated fresh ginger
1 clove garlic, crushed
1 teaspoon thyme
2 bay leaves
salt and freshly ground black pepper
2 tablespoons chopped fresh parsley
1½ cups chicken broth
2 tablespoons red wine vinegar

Heat the lard or oil on medium-high heat in a large frying pan or casserole dish. Put in the thighs and fry until golden-brown on both sides.

Slice the onions fairly thin in semicircles. Add to the chicken. Turn the heat down to medium. Cook for about 10 minutes or until the onions are golden and beginning to fall apart.

Add the ginger and garlic. Mix well. Add the thyme, bay leaves, and salt and pepper. Sprinkle on the parsley and pour on the chicken broth and vinegar. Bring to a low boil, cover, and simmer for 45 minutes.

If the sauce needs thickening, cook the dish on a higher temperature, uncovered, for a few minutes to reduce the liquid.

Serve with rice or potatoes.

Serves 4.

Chicken with Sauerkraut

A traditional combination of meat with sauerkraut is spiced with caraway seeds and enriched with bacon. Serve with dumplings on a cold winter day.

- 3 strips bacon
- 1 medium onion, finely chopped
- 4 chicken legs
- 2 tablespoons flour
- 1½ cups chicken broth
- 1 pound sauerkraut
- 1 tablespoon caraway seeds, crushed
- salt and freshly ground black pepper

Heat a large frying pan or casserole dish on medium heat. Slice the bacon fine. Put the bacon in the pan and fry until almost crisp. Add the chopped onion and fry, stirring occasionally, until almost cooked through. Add the chicken legs and fry until golden brown on both sides.

Sprinkle on the flour and mix well. Cook for 2 minutes. Pour in the chicken broth and cook, stirring well, for a few minutes. Add the sauerkraut and crushed caraway seeds. Season with salt and pepper. Bring to a low boil, cover, and simmer until done, about 45 minutes. Serve with potatoes or dumplings.

SERVES 4.

Chicken with Beans

Chicken legs are cooked with broad white beans, bacon, paprika, and parsley for a tasty and inexpensive meal. Omit the sour cream if you wish—if the sauce needs thickening, which it may not, simply reduce the liquid by boiling it, uncovered, over high heat for a few minutes before serving.

1½ cups dried white beans
3 strips bacon, finely sliced
1 medium onion, finely chopped
4 chicken legs
1 large green pepper, diced
2 tablespoons flour
1 cup chicken broth or water
1 cup canned tomatoes
1 tablespoon paprika
2 tablespoons chopped fresh parsley
salt and freshly ground black pepper
½ cup sour cream

The night before you wish to make this dish, put the dried beans in 4 or 5 cups of water and leave to soak.

The next day, drain the beans, put them in a medium-size pot, cover with water, and bring to a boil. Lower the heat, cover the pot, and simmer until the beans are tender, about 1 hour. Drain the beans and reserve.

In a large frying pot or casserole dish, fry the bacon on medium heat until almost crisp. Add the chopped onion and fry, stirring occasionally, until golden. Add the chicken legs, raise the heat, and fry them until golden brown on both sides. Add the diced green pepper and fry for another 2 minutes.

Sprinkle the flour on the chicken and cook, stirring well, for 2 minutes. Pour in the chicken broth and tomatoes. Add the beans. Mix well.

Add the paprika, parsley, salt, and pepper. Bring to a low boil, cover, and simmer until done, about 45 minutes.

Just before serving, stir in the sour cream and heat through. Serve with potatoes and a green salad.

Serves 4.

Roast Duck with Red Cabbage

A classic combination that should be tried as an alternative to the typical sweet duck-with-fruit renditions of this delicious and versatile bird. Served with dumplings this makes a popular and satisfying Czech meal.

½ medium red cabbage
1 cup red wine vinegar
2 tablespoons caraway seeds
salt and freshly ground black pepper
1 large (5-pound) duck
2 cloves garlic, halved

Wash the cabbage and then shred it very finely, either with a knife or grater. Put the cabbage in a large pot, add ½ cup water, 1 tablespoon caraway seeds, and salt and pepper. Turn the heat on medium-low, cover, and cook 30 minutes, stirring occasionally. Add ½ cup vinegar and cook 15 minutes.

Preheat the oven to 400°F.

Wash the duck inside and out and dry with a cloth or paper towels. Prick the skin all over with a fork. Rub the duck with the garlic. Season the bird inside and out with salt, pepper, and the remaining caraway seeds.

Choose a large roasting dish and place the cooked cabbage evenly across the bottom. Place the duck on top, breast side up. Pour the remaining ½ cup vinegar on the duck. Put the dish in the oven.

After 15 minutes, baste the bird with some of the pan juices, adding a little water if necessary. Reduce the temperature to 350°F. Baste the bird every 15 to 20 minutes, skimming off any excess fat as you go along. The duck and the cabbage should be tender after 2 hours in the oven. Serve with bread or potato dumplings, and a green salad.

SERVES 4.

Roast Duck Stuffed with Prunes and Hazelnuts

Like chicken, ducks may be stuffed with almost anything, be it bread, rice, meat, or vegetables. This dish enhances a basic bread stuffing with dried plums and hazelnuts. The dark, rich fruit goes very well with the dense texture of duck.

- 1 cup prunes, chopped
- 1 cup dry red wine
- 2 strips bacon, finely sliced
- 1 small onion, chopped
- 2 cloves garlic, crushed
- 2 French rolls
- ¼ cup milk
- ½ cup peeled hazelnuts
- 2 tablespoons chopped fresh parsley
- 1 tablespoon marjoram
- salt and freshly ground black pepper
- 1 to 2 eggs
- 1 large (5-pound) duck

Put the chopped prunes into the red wine to soak for 30 minutes. Fry the sliced bacon in a frying pan on medium-high heat until almost crisp. Add the onion and garlic and stir well, reduce the heat to medium-low, and fry for another 5 minutes or until the onion is almost golden. Remove from heat and cool.

Break up the rolls into smallish bits with your fingers, place in a medium-size bowl, and pour on the milk. Let the bread soak up the milk for a few minutes. Then mix in the bacon and onion. Remove the prunes from the wine and add them, reserving the wine for later. Clean the hazelnuts of all skin, chop them roughly, and mix them into the stuffing. Season with parsley, marjoram, and salt and pepper. Break the egg into the stuffing and mix it in well. If the stuffing is still loose, add another egg to bind it better.

Preheat the oven to 400°F.

Wash the duck and trim off any excess fat. Dry it with a cloth or paper towels. To let the fat escape from the bird during roasting, prick the skin of the duck with a fork all over. Season the bird inside and out with salt and pepper. Fill the cavity of the bird with stuffing, putting any excess in foil to cook alongside. Close the opening of the cavity with toothpicks or string.

Put the duck on top of a broiling pan with a rack, so that when it cooks, the juice and fat collect underneath and the duck does not sit in the liquid. If you don't have a broiling pan, simply skim the fat off as you baste. Pour the wine in which you soaked the prunes on top of the duck. Put the bird in the oven.

After 15 minutes, baste the bird and reduce the heat to 350°F. Continue roasting and basting until the duck is tender, about 2 hours. Serve with potatoes and a green vegetable such as asparagus, green beans, or kale.

SERVES 4.

Roast Duck with Sauerkraut and Apples

The sauerkraut mixed with grated apple goes outside and inside the duck, developing two slightly different flavors and providing plenty of stuffing for all.

4 large apples (tasty but not too sweet)
1 pound sauerkraut
salt and freshly ground black pepper
1 large (5-pound) duck
1 tablespoon paprika
2 bay leaves
1 cup dry white wine

Preheat the oven to 400°F.

Peel and core the apples, then grate them, but not too finely. Mix together the grated apple and the sauerkraut. Season with salt and pepper.

Wash and dry the duck, and prick it all over with a fork. Rub it inside and out with paprika; season with salt and pepper. Stuff the duck with as much of the sauerkraut-apple mixture as will fit, and then secure the cavity opening with toothpicks or string.

Choose a fairly large roasting pan. Spread the remainder of the sauerkraut on the bottom of the pan then place the duck on top. Insert the bay leaves into the sauerkraut. Pour the wine onto the duck. Put the duck into the oven.

After 15 minutes, baste the duck and then reduce the temperature to 350°F. Baste every 15 minutes, skimming off any excess fat and adding a little water if necessary. The duck should be tender and ready to eat in 2 hours. Serve with dumplings.

SERVES 4.

Duck with Garlic

Roasting is a wonderful way to treat duck though this method may be a problem if you are serving more than two people and only small ducks are available. Roasting two birds in one oven may not always be feasible. Carving one or two birds into portions and then cooking them may be easier and also offers new possibilities for preparing the meat. This dish roasts a portioned bird with a good deal of garlic. The result is a rich sauce and tender, juicy meat.

1 small (4-pound) duck
1 tablespoon paprika
salt and freshly ground black pepper
2 tablespoons vegetable oil
2 cups beef or veal broth
4 cloves garlic, crushed
1 teaspoon marjoram
2 tablespoons flour

Preheat the oven to 375°F.

Wash and dry the duck, then cut it into serving portions (two breast halves and two legs). Cut off any excess fat. Rub the duck with paprika. Season it with salt and pepper. Choose a large, ovenproof frying pan or roasting dish. Pour in the vegetable oil and put on high heat. Once the oil is quite hot, almost smoking, put in the duck pieces. Fry them, stirring once or twice, until one side is golden brown, then turn them over and brown the other side. Pour off excess fat.

Once the duck has been browned, pour in the broth. Mix in the garlic and sprinkle on the marjoram. Season with additional salt and pepper. Roast in the oven, uncovered, for 45 minutes (if you like duck rare, reduce the cooking time). Baste once or twice.

When the duck is ready, remove it from the sauce and keep it warm in the oven. Thicken the sauce by mixing the flour with some water in a small cup, adding some of the hot gravy, then whisking the thickener back into the sauce and boiling for a couple of minutes. Serve with dumplings and a green vegetable such as asparagus or green beans.

SERVES 2.

Braised Duck in Red Wine

A good quantity of dry red wine provides the sauce for this traditional combination of duck and root vegetables. Choose a wine that is fit to drink since much of the taste here is derived from this central ingredient. Wine maintains much of its character even after cooking.

- 2 small ducks (4 pounds each)
- 4 tablespoons vegetable oil
- 2 medium onions, chopped
- 2 cloves garlic, crushed
- 2 medium carrots, diced
- 2 small parsnips, diced
- ½ small celeriac, diced
- ½ bottle (12.7-ounce) dry red wine
- 2 bay leaves
- 1 teaspoon thyme
- ½ teaspoon ground cloves
- salt and freshly ground black pepper
- 2 tablespoons flour
- 1 tablespoon chopped fresh parsley

Cut the ducks up into serving portions. Heat 2 tablespoons oil in a large casserole dish on high heat. When quite hot, put in half the duck pieces. Fry, stirring occasionally, until golden brown on both sides. Pour off excess fat. Remove the browned duck and brown the remaining pieces, then remove these as well.

Turn down the heat under the casserole dish to medium-low. Add the onions and fry until translucent, about 5 minutes, stirring occasionally. Add the garlic and cook another couple of minutes. Add the carrots, parsnips, and celeriac and fry them for 4 to 5 minutes, stirring occasionally.

Put the duck pieces back into the casserole. Pour in the wine. If more liquid is needed to just cover the meat and vegetables, add some water. Add the bay leaves, thyme, and ground cloves. Season with salt and pepper. Cover the casserole and simmer, on top of the stove, stirring occasionally, until the duck is tender, about 1 hour.

Mix the flour with some cold water in a small cup. Add to this 2 tablespoons of the hot cooking liquid and mix together. Then pour this thickener into the casserole dish, mixing well. Cook for 3 to 4 minutes, allowing the sauce to boil and thicken. Sprinkle in the parsley and mix well.

Serve with dumplings or rice.

SERVES 4 TO 6.

Braised Duck with Celeriac and Peas

If peas or celeriac are not available or don't look nice in the store, substitute any other vegetables that you think might go well, paying attention to the color that each adds to the dish.

1 small (4-pound) duck
salt and freshly ground black pepper
2 strips bacon, sliced
1 large onion, chopped
2 medium carrots, diced
½ small celeriac, diced
2 cups beef broth or water
⅓ cup red wine vinegar
2 bay leaves
1 teaspoon savory
2 tablespoons flour
1 cup frozen peas
2 tablespoons chopped fresh parsley

Cut up the duck into serving portions. Trim off any excess fat and prick all over with a fork. Season each piece with salt and pepper.

Put a large casserole dish on medium-high heat. Add the sliced bacon and fry until almost crisp. Remove the bacon and reserve it. Turn up the heat to high. Put the duck pieces into the hot bacon fat and fry them until golden brown on both sides.

Reduce the heat to medium. Remove any excess grease from the casserole dish. Add the chopped onion to the duck. Fry the onion, stirring occasionally, until almost golden. Add the carrots and celeriac. Cook for 3 to 4 minutes. Return the bacon to the casserole. Add the broth or water, vinegar, bay leaves, and savory. Season with additional salt and pepper. Partially cover, reduce the heat, and let simmer until the duck is tender, about 1 hour.

To thicken the sauce, mix the flour with some cold water in a small cup, then add some of the hot cooking liquid. Mix this thickener into the sauce, stirring well, and let cook for a couple of minutes. Stir the frozen peas and the parsley into the sauce and simmer for 2 to 3 minutes or until the peas are just heated through. Serve with potatoes, dumplings, or rice.

SERVES 2 TO 4.

Duck in the Wild Style

(Kachna Na Ďivoko)

A combination of wine, vinegar, and herbs and spices makes for a wonderfully rich sauce that is meant to imitate the gamey flavor of wild duck.

1 large (5-pound) duck
2 strips bacon, sliced
salt and freshly ground black pepper
4 tablespoons (½ stick) butter
1 large onion, chopped
2 medium carrots, diced
2 medium parsnips, diced
½ small celeriac, diced
1 cup dry red wine
2 cups beef broth or water
⅓ cup red wine vinegar
1 lemon
2 bay leaves
½ teaspoon grated nutmeg
½ teaspoon ground allspice
1 teaspoon thyme
2 tablespoons flour
½ teaspoon sugar

Cut the duck into serving portions, getting rid of any excess fat as you go. Using a small paring knife, make 3 or 4 small incisions in each duck piece just large enough to slide in a small slice of bacon. Once you have larded all the duck pieces in this way, season the meat with salt and pepper. Let the meat sit in a cool place for about 1 hour.

Melt 2 tablespoons butter on medium-high heat in a large casserole dish. Once the bubbles have subsided but before the butter begins to brown, add the duck pieces. Fry the duck until it is golden brown on both sides, then remove it from the casserole. Turn the heat down to medium and skim off any excess grease.

Preheat the oven to 375°F.

Add the onion to the casserole and fry it until almost golden, stirring occasionally. Add carrots, parsnips, and celeriac and fry, stirring occasionally, for 5 minutes. Return the duck to the dish. Add the red wine, beef broth, and vinegar.

Pare off a few thin strips of the lemon's peel. Slice the peel fine and add to the casserole. Squeeze the juice of the lemon into the dish. Add the bay leaves, nutmeg, allspice, and thyme. Season well with additional salt and pepper.

Once the liquid has reached a low boil, cover the casserole and put it in the oven. Basting occasionally, let the meat braise for about 1 hour or until tender.

Once the meat is done, prepare a roux to thicken the sauce: melt the remaining 2 tablespoons butter in a frying pan on medium heat, mix in the flour and sugar, and fry for 2 to 3 minutes, stirring well.

Mix the roux into the casserole and let bubble, uncovered, in the oven for another 5 minutes. Serve with dumplings or potatoes.

SERVES 4.

Roast Goose Stuffed with Apples

Goose, like duck, may be a little fatty, but if cooked right this is no problem. Indeed, goose fat itself is quite prized—it is wonderful for frying. Keep a jar of it in the fridge so that it won't spoil. Any type of traditional stuffing will suit a goose. Apples, though, are a favorite and they are combined here with raisins and almonds. If the liver is provided with the goose, fry this gently and then mash it into the stuffing.

1 (7-pound) goose
salt and freshly ground black pepper
2 cloves garlic, cut in half
2 strips bacon, sliced
1 medium onion, chopped
2 French rolls
⅓ cup milk
½ cup raisins
2 cups dry white wine
4 tart apples, such as Granny Smith
¼ cup slivered almonds
2 tablespoons chopped fresh parsley
¼ teaspoon ground allspice
¼ teaspoon ground cloves
½ teaspoon thyme
2 eggs
2 tablespoons flour

Wash and dry the goose and cut off any excess fat. Season it well, inside and out, with salt and a good deal of pepper. Rub the goose with garlic halves. Save the garlic for use in the stuffing. Prick the goose all over with a fork.

Preheat the oven to 400°F.

Fry the sliced bacon on medium heat in a pan until almost crisp.

Add the chopped onion and fry, stirring occasionally, until almost golden. Chop up the garlic cloves with which you rubbed the goose. Add these to the onions, cook a couple of minutes, then take the pan off the heat.

In a medium-size bowl, break up the rolls into ½-inch pieces. Pour the milk onto the bread and let it soak for a few minutes. Put the raisins into the wine and let these soak as well. Peel and core the apples, then cut them up into cubes. Add the apples to the bread. Chop up the almonds a little and add these to the stuffing. Mix in the onions and bacon. Take the raisins out of the wine, reserving the liquid. Add the raisins to the stuffing, then mix in the parsley, allspice, cloves, and thyme. Season well with additional salt and pepper. Break the eggs into the stuffing and mix them in well.

Put as much of the stuffing into the goose as you can, wrapping the remainder in aluminum foil to cook alongside. Put the goose, breast-side up, on a broiling pan rack, preferably the type which collects the cooking juice and fat below the surface on which the meat sits. Pour a little of the white wine on the goose, then place it in the oven. After 15 minutes, baste the goose with some more wine and turn the temperature down to 350°F. Continue roasting until the meat is tender, about 2½ hours, basting occasionally.

When the goose is done, take it out of the oven and let sit on a platter for 10 minutes. Meanwhile, skim the fat off the cooking liquid, reserving it for other uses. Put the remaining juices on medium heat on top of the stove. Mix the flour with some water in a small cup, stir in some of the hot cooking liquid, then mix the thickener back into the sauce. Cook the gravy a couple of minutes, then season with salt and pepper.

Serve with dumplings or potatoes, and either green beans or carrots.

SERVES 4.

Goose with Barley and Peas

In this dish, the goose, dried green peas, and barley are all precooked separately, then combined to braise in the oven. The result is a hearty and tasty winter meal complete in itself or with some good bread.

1 cup dried green peas
1 cup barley
1 (6- to 7-pound) goose
salt and freshly ground black pepper
2 strips bacon, sliced
1 large onion, chopped
1 clove garlic, crushed
2 cups chicken broth
2 bay leaves
1 teaspoon marjoram
2 tablespoons chopped fresh parsley

Several hours before you wish to serve this dish, or the night before, put the peas and barley to soak, separately, in good deals of cold water.

Cut up the goose into serving portions, trimming off any excess fat. Prick the goose pieces all over with a fork and then season with salt and pepper. Heat a large casserole dish on medium heat and then throw in the bacon pieces. Fry the bacon until almost crisp, then remove and reserve. Turn the heat up to high, then place the goose pieces in the pot. Fry the goose until golden brown on both sides.

Turn the heat down to medium. Skim off any excess fat and reserve for another use. Add the onion to the casserole and fry, stirring occasionally, for 5 minutes. Add the garlic and the fried bacon. Cook for 2 more minutes, then pour in the chicken broth. Season with additional salt and pepper, and add the bay leaves. Once the broth reaches a low boil, cover the pan and turn the heat down to medium-low. Continue cooking until the meat is almost tender, about 45 minutes.

Meanwhile, drain the peas from their soaking water, place in a medium-size pot, and pour on more than enough water to cover. Do the same with the barley in a separate pot. Bring both pots to a boil, then cover them and let simmer, on low heat, until almost tender, about 45 minutes. Drain.

Preheat oven to 350°F.

Once the peas and barley are ready, mix them into the goose casserole. Mix in, as well, the marjoram and parsley. Season with salt and pepper. Bake, covered, in the oven for 30 minutes. Check occasionally to see if there is enough liquid in the pot: if not, pour on some more broth or water. Serve with bread.

SERVES 4 TO 6.

Roast Goose Marinated in Vegetables

A similar treatment of beef, with the addition of cream, yields the classic Czech svíčková. *The idea is simple and very tasty: leave meat to marinate in the fridge for one or two days with the vegetables in which it will cook. The marinade brings out the flavor of the vegetables and the meat has plenty of time to soak it up.*

- 1 (6- to 7-pound) goose
- 2 strips bacon, sliced
- salt and freshly ground black pepper
- 2 large onions, quartered and finely sliced
- 4 medium carrots, finely sliced
- 4 small parsnips, finely sliced
- ½ small celeriac, finely sliced
- 1 cup dry red wine vinegar
- 2 tablespoons vegetable oil
- 1 teaspoon thyme
- 1 tablespoon chopped fresh parsley
- ½ teaspoon grated nutmeg
- ½ teaspoon allspice
- 2 tablespoons flour

One or two days before you wish to serve this dish, cut the goose up into serving portions, trim off any excess fat, and prick the pieces all over with a fork. Using a small paring knife, cut 3 or 4 incisions into each portion and then stick a piece of bacon in each. Season with salt and pepper.

Choose a large casserole dish, preferably a stockpot, that has a lid. Put half of the onions, carrots, parsnips, and celeriac on the bottom of the pot. Next, place the goose pieces on top. Now cover the goose with the remaining vegetables. Season well with additional salt and pepper. Pour on the vinegar. Cover the pot and place in the refrigerator to marinate. Check after a few hours to baste the meat and stir around the vegetables. If more liquid is needed to wet the ingredients, add some vinegar mixed with water. Allow the goose to marinate in this way for 1 to 2 days.

Once the goose is marinated, separate the meat, vegetables, and the liquid. Dry the goose pieces with paper towel. Heat the oil in a large frying pan on high heat. When quite hot, put in the goose and fry until golden brown on both sides.

Preheat the oven to 350°F.

Take the pan off the heat, remove the goose to the casserole dish, and skim any excess fat from the frying pan, reserving it for later use. Turn the heat down to medium, then add the vegetables to the frying pan. Cook for about 5 minutes, then transfer the vegetables to the casserole dish. Mix in the thyme, parsley, nutmeg, and allspice.

Place the goose pieces on top of the vegetables in the casserole, pour on the reserved marinating liquid, then place, uncovered, in the oven. Roast, basting occasionally until the meat is tender, about 2 hours.

When the meat is done, take it out of the casserole and keep it warm in the oven. Take the vegetables and the cooking liquid and purée them, either in a food processor or by mashing them through a sieve.

Heat 2 tablespoons of the reserved goose fat in a frying pan, then stir in the flour and fry for a couple of minutes, stirring well. Pour in the puréed vegetables and heat through (adding some water if the sauce is too thick). Check the seasonings for salt and pepper. Serve the goose with dumplings, all covered in sauce.

SERVES 4.

Roast Turkey with Chestnut Stuffing

Chestnuts are exquisite in stuffings and the temptation to use them above all other kinds of nuts for any poultry is hard to resist. I often use fresh chestnuts, when they are in season, and go through the tedious process of boiling and peeling them, scorching my fingers as I go along. My obsession with fresh ingredients may be misplaced here—a can of chestnut purée will do fine, though you won't have any nuts leftover for roasting in the fireplace.

1 (10-pound) turkey
salt and freshly ground black pepper
3 strips bacon, sliced
1 large onion, chopped
2 celery stalks, diced
1 clove garlic, crushed
3 French rolls
½ cup milk
1 can (8 ounces) chestnut purée
1 teaspoon sage
2 tablespoons chopped fresh parsley
2 eggs
8 tablespoons (1 stick) butter
2 tablespoons flour

Wash and dry the turkey, then season it inside and out with salt and pepper. Preheat the oven to 375°F.

Heat a frying pan on medium heat, then add the sliced bacon. Fry the bacon until almost crisp. Add the onion and fry, stirring occasionally, until almost golden. Add the celery and the garlic and cook for 3 to 4 minutes, stirring occasionally. Take off the heat.

In a large bowl, break up the French rolls into ½-inch pieces. Pour on the milk and let the bread soak for a few minutes. Then mix in the onions and celery. Add the chestnut purée and mix well. Add the sage and parsley. Season well with salt and pepper. Break in the eggs and mix well.

Fill the cavity of the bird with the stuffing and then secure the opening with toothpicks or string. Place the turkey in a large roasting pan, breast-side up. Put 6 tablespoons butter on top of the bird and pour about ½ cup water around it. Place in the oven. Roast for 3½ hours, basting occasionally, until done.

When the turkey is ready, transfer it to a serving platter. Remove the excess grease from the pan juices. Melt the remaining 2 tablespoons butter in a frying pan then add the flour. Fry for a couple of minutes, stirring well, then add the pan juices and a little broth or water if needed. Let boil for 2 to 3 minutes. Season the gravy with salt and pepper.

Serve with dumplings or potatoes.

SERVES 8.

6

Beef and Veal

Red meat is the focal point of Czech cuisine and beef is perhaps the favorite. Almost every part of the cow is used in an infinite number of ways. Traditional cuts, such as steak and roast, share equal billing with tripe, heart, tongue, liver, and brains. Beef is fried, grilled, roasted, braised, boiled, stuffed, marinated, larded, sauced, and made into sausage. Beef is served as a main dish or starter, or made into soups and salads. The same goes for veal. Beef is served simply, quickly fried in butter and oil and accompanied by fried potatoes, as well as elaborately, as in *svíčková*, perhaps the most famous Czech treatment of beef. For this dish, the choicest cut of beef, the tenderloin, is marinated for at least a day with root vegetables, wine vinegar, and herbs, then roasted and served with a sauce made from a purée of the vegetables enhanced by cream.

A myriad of sauces have been concocted to accent the taste of beef, from simple gravies to cream sauces featuring various herbs, such as dill and marjoram. Many Czechs prefer their meat well-done and often even the best cut is boiled in the manner of a pot roast and then sauced. I prefer to save such recipes for blade or chuck roasts and suggest cooking finer cuts for a shorter period of time and grilling and roasting rather than boiling.

All types of stews are made with beef and the most popular are the various kinds of *guláš* (or goulash for simplicity's sake). Goulash basically means a stew flavored, at least in part, with paprika. Given the centrality of this ingredient, try and find a good quality paprika since they range from a rather tasteless red powder that will do little but color your dish to a fragrant, distinctive, and at times hot, spice. The most basic goulash has little more in it than beef, onions, and paprika, while the more complex feature several vegetables, a combination of meats, or as in *segedínsky guláš*, a heavy sauerkraut base.

One piece of kitchen equipment that is used frequently in Czech meat cooking is the mallet or tenderizer. If you do not have one and are not familiar with its use, it is not essential to any of the recipes but you may want to acquire one eventually. A meat mallet is good for pounding meat, such as a steak, to a desired thickness and for breaking down some of the tougher muscles in the flesh. If you are making beef birds, for example, you need rather thin strips of meat to attain the right result. You may have a butcher who will provide beef as thin as is needed, but if not, you will need a mallet back at home.

Pounding meat is quite simple. All you need to be careful of is taking your frustrations out on the meat. Too heavy a stroke may break through or tear the meat. Use a gentle motion and move the meat around between strokes so that it does not stick to the surface of your cutting board.

Finally, a note about innards. There are many more Czech recipes for organs than I have included here. I have been selective because many people have a distaste for anything but the fleshiest flesh. This is a shame since some organs, such as the brain and tongue, are, in my mind, the tastiest part of the animal and, furthermore, there are so many interesting preparations for them. If organs make you queasy, there is nothing I can say to convince you to try these recipes. But if you are curious, I urge you to experiment, for the fluffiness of brains fried in fresh butter or the texture of a boiled tongue sauced in mustard cannot be topped. And I have yet to point out sweetbreads, for which a mention is more than sufficient to whet the appetite.

Steaks Fried in Butter

The simplest and perhaps most common way of serving beef is to season it with salt and pepper and fry it in butter. Nothing else is needed and very little else is as good. Nevertheless, performing this simple task has its hazards: you need the right cut of meat, the right temperature, and the right amount of time. Steaks cooked this way can easily be jazzed up. Try rubbing the meat with a little garlic before cooking. A popular Czech variant, served at lunch or dinner and not just at breakfast, is to serve each steak with a fried egg on top. While you may find a thick sirloin or T-bone on occasion, Czechs prefer their steaks on the thinner side and steaks are often pounded a little to get them this way. The best cuts for this are thinner sirloins, rib-eyes, or slices of tenderloin.

2 sirloin or rib-eye steaks
salt and freshly ground black pepper
1 tablespoon vegetable or olive oil
2 tablespoons butter
1 tablespoon chopped fresh parsley

Using a metal or wooden meat mallet, lightly pound each steak on both sides until it is about ½ inch thick. Season with salt and pepper.

Heat the oil in a large frying pan on medium-high heat. Add the butter and let it bubble for a few seconds. The pan should be hot enough to sear the steaks as soon as you put them in. Cook the steaks until golden brown on each side and to the desired doneness (2 to 3 minutes for rare, 4 for medium, 5 to 6 for well-done). Sprinkle on the parsley. Serve with fried potatoes and a salad or green vegetable.

Serves 2.

Steaks with Mushrooms and Wine

By reducing wine on high heat and whisking in some butter, you can make a rich and thick sauce without adding flour. Mushrooms and a little garlic add even more flavor to this classic treatment.

- 2 sirloin or rib-eye steaks
- 1 clove garlic
- salt and freshly ground black pepper
- 2 tablespoons vegetable or olive oil
- ⅓ pound white mushrooms, sliced
- ½ cup dry red wine
- 2 tablespoons butter
- 1 tablespoon chopped fresh parsley

Sightly pound the steaks on both sides with a meat mallet until about ½ inch thick. Cut the garlic clove in half and rub the garlic onto both sides of the steaks. Season them with salt and pepper.

Heat the oil in a large frying pan on medium-high heat. Once the oil is almost smoking, put in the steaks. Sear them to a golden brown on both sides. Add the sliced mushrooms and brown them quickly. Pour in the red wine and let it bubble rapidly for a couple of minutes. Mix in the butter. If you like your steaks closer to well done, let them simmer in the sauce for a couple more minutes. Sprinkle on the parsley. Serve with new potatoes and a green salad.

SERVES 2.

Steaks with Peppers and Tomatoes

Fresh tomatoes simmered quickly for a few minutes make for a light and tasty sauce for steaks. If nice tomatoes are not available, canned ones will do the trick as well. The addition of green bell peppers enhances both color and flavor.

2 sirloin or rib-eye steaks
salt and freshly ground black pepper
2 tablespoons olive oil
2 strips bacon, diced
1 small onion, chopped
1 green bell pepper, sliced
1 clove garlic, crushed
3 medium tomatoes, chopped
1 teaspoon oregano
1 tablespoon chopped fresh parsley

Pound the steaks lightly with a meat mallet on both sides until they are about ½ inch thick. Season them with salt and pepper and trim off any excess fat.

Heat the oil in a large frying pan on medium-high heat. When the oil is almost smoking, put the steaks in the pan and fry them for about 2 minutes per side or golden brown. Remove them from the pan.

Turn the heat down to medium heat. Add the bacon and fry until almost crisp. Remove any excess grease. Add the onion and fry, stirring occasionally, until almost golden. Add the peppers and garlic and cook for 5 minutes. Add the chopped tomatoes and bring to a boil. Season with salt, pepper, oregano, and parsley.

Put the steaks back in the pan and heat them through for about 2 minutes (for well-done meat, keep them in a few minutes longer). Serve with new potatoes.

SERVES 2.

Gypsy Steaks

These steaks may be made mild or quite hot, depending on how much cayenne pepper you put in the sauce.

2 sirloin steaks
salt and freshly ground black pepper
2 tablespoons lard
2 strips bacon, sliced
1 large yellow or sweet white onion, finely sliced
1 tablespoon paprika
pinch of cayenne pepper
2 tablespoons flour
1 cup beef broth or water
1 tablespoon chopped fresh parsley

Trim the steaks of excess fat. Pound them lightly with a meat mallet until about ½ inch thick. Season with salt and pepper.

Heat the lard in a large frying pan on medium-high heat. When quite hot, put in the steaks and brown them on each side for 2 minutes. Remove and turn the heat down to medium heat.

Add the bacon to the pan and fry until almost crisp. Add the sliced onion and fry, stirring occasionally, until almost golden. Add the paprika and cayenne to taste. Cook for 2 minutes. Add the flour and cook, stirring occasionally, for another 2 minutes. Pour in the broth, season with additional salt and pepper, and bring to a light boil.

Put the steaks back in the pan and heat them through, or cook for a few minutes longer for more well-done meat. Mix in the parsley and serve with boiled or fried potatoes.

SERVES 2.

Breaded Veal Cutlets

Veal should be pounded quite thin so that it needs only a minute or two to cook—frying it longer will toughen the flesh. Cutlets may be coated simply in flour, or flour and egg, or, as here, in bread crumbs as well. While store-bought crumbs will do, a freshly grated French roll provides a subtler texture.

¾ pound veal cutlets
salt and freshly ground black or white pepper
½ cup flour
2 eggs, beaten
½ cup fine bread crumbs
3 tablespoons butter
1 tablespoon chopped fresh parsley
1 lemon, quartered

Lightly pound the cutlets on both sides until they are as thin as you can get them without tearing. Season them with salt and pepper. Taking one cutlet at a time, dredge it in flour, dip it in the beaten eggs, then cover it with bread crumbs.

Once all the cutlets have been breaded, heat the butter in a large frying pan on medium heat. Once the butter bubbles have begun to subside, put in as much of the veal as will fit without crowding the pan. Fry the veal quickly, 1 minute per side, until all the cutlets are done.

Sprinkle the cutlets with parsley and arrange the lemon wedges around them. Serve with fried or boiled potatoes and a green vegetable, such as asparagus or green beans.

Serves 4.

Veal Cutlets with White Wine and Garlic

For this dish thin veal slices are fried and then simmered briefly in a simple sauce of white wine, lemon juice, onion, and garlic.

¾ pound veal cutlets
salt and freshly ground black pepper
½ cup flour
3 tablespoons butter
1 small onion, very finely chopped
3 cloves garlic, crushed
1 cup dry white wine
1 lemon
½ teaspoon marjoram
1 tablespoon chopped fresh parsley

Lightly pound the veal with a mallet on both sides until it is as thin as you can get it without tearing. Season the cutlets with salt and pepper. Dredge them in flour; reserve the excess flour for later use.

Melt the butter on medium heat in a large frying pan. Once the butter bubbles have begun to subside, put in as much veal as will fit without crowding the pan and fry for 1 minute per side. Cook all the veal this way then remove it from the pan.

Add the onion to the pan and fry, stirring occasionally, until translucent, 3 to 4 minutes. Add the garlic and cook for 2 minutes. Mix in 1 tablespoon of the dredging flour and cook for another 2 minutes. Stir in the white wine. Grate some of the zest of the lemon into the sauce, then add its juice. Add the marjoram and parsley and season with additional salt and pepper.

Bring to a low boil, then return the veal cutlets to the pan. Heat the meat through for about 2 minutes. Serve with new potatoes or rice and a delicate vegetable such as asparagus.

SERVES 4.

Veal Cutlets in Mustard and White Wine

Mustard may be added to a sauce or, as here, spread on meat before it is fried. The subtle taste of veal needs very little else to make a fine dish.

¾ pound veal cutlets
salt and freshly ground black pepper
2 tablespoons good quality mustard
2 tablespoons lard or butter
1 tablespoon flour
1 cup dry white wine
½ teaspoon thyme
1 tablespoon chopped fresh parsley

Lightly pound the cutlets on both sides with a meat mallet until they are as thin as you can get them without tearing. Season them with salt and pepper. Spread the mustard thinly on both sides.

Melt the lard or butter in a large frying pan on medium heat. When quite hot, add as many cutlets as will fit without crowding the pan and fry for 1 minute per side. Cook all the veal this way then remove from the pan.

Sprinkle the flour into the pan and cook for 2 minutes, stirring occasionally. Pour in the wine and bring to a low boil. Mix in the thyme and parsley and season with additional salt and pepper. Return the veal and heat through.

Serve with boiled potatoes or rice and a green vegetable such as spinach or kale.

SERVES 4.

Veal Cutlets with Horseradish Sauce

The mild taste of veal goes well with a single sharp ingredient, such as lemon juice or mustard or, as in this dish, horseradish.

- ¾ pound veal cutlets
- salt and freshly ground black pepper
- ½ cup flour
- 2 tablespoons lard or butter
- 1 cup beef broth
- 1 tablespoon horseradish
- 1 tablespoon lemon juice
- ½ cup sour cream

Lightly pound the veal on both sides with a meat mallet until it is as thin as you can get it without tearing. Season the meat with salt and pepper. Dredge the cutlets in flour, reserving excess flour for later use.

Heat the lard or butter in a large frying pan on medium heat. When quite hot, put in as many cutlets as will fit without crowding the pan. Fry on each side for 1 minute. Cook all the veal this way then remove it from the pan.

Sprinkle 2 tablespoons of the dredging flour into the pan and, stirring occasionally, fry for 2 minutes. Pour the broth into the pan and bring to a low boil, stirring well. Mix in the horseradish and lemon juice. Season with additional salt and pepper. Cook for a few minutes, until the sauce has thickened a little. Mix in the sour cream. Return the veal to the pan and heat through.

Serve with potatoes or dumplings and a vegetable such as green beans.

SERVES 4.

Veal Cutlets with Wild Mushrooms

Fresh wild mushrooms will go well with veal though this recipe uses dried porcinis, makes sauce out of their soaking liquid, and supplements them with some fresh white mushrooms.

1 ounce dried porcini mushrooms
¾ pound veal cutlets
salt and freshly ground black pepper
½ cup flour
3 tablespoons lard or butter
⅓ pound white mushrooms, sliced
1 cup beef broth
1 tablespoon lemon juice
zest of 1 lemon
½ teaspoon marjoram
2 tablespoons chopped fresh parsley

Soak the dried mushrooms in some hot water for about 20 minutes. Drain them, reserving the liquid, and brush off any dirt. Chop them roughly.

Lightly pound the veal on both sides with a meat mallet until as thin as possible without tearing. Season the cutlets with salt and pepper. Dredge the cutlets in flour.

Heat 1 tablespoon of the lard or butter on high heat in a large frying pan. When very hot, throw in the fresh mushrooms and brown them quickly. Remove them from the pan and turn the heat down to medium heat.

Add the remaining 2 tablespoons lard or butter to the pan and when hot, put in as much of the veal as will fit comfortably. Cook on each side for 1 minute and then remove. Do the same with the rest of the veal.

Add 1 tablespoon of the dredging flour to the pan and, stirring occasionally, fry for 2 minutes. Mix in the dried mushrooms and stir in the broth. Add the lemon juice, lemon zest, and marjoram and season with additional salt and pepper.

Bring to a low boil. Return the cutlets and fresh mushrooms to the pan and heat through. Sprinkle on the parsley. Serve with potatoes or dumplings.

SERVES 4.

Veal Cutlets Stuffed with Spinach

Veal is often pounded and then rolled around a stuffing but even a thin cutlet may be sliced almost in half with a sharp knife and filled with a tablespoon of this or that, in this case spinach cooked in butter, garlic, and lemon.

- 1 pound fresh spinach
- salt and freshly ground black pepper
- 2 lemons
- 2 cloves garlic, crushed
- 1 tablespoon chopped fresh parsley
- 4 tablespoons (½ stick) butter
- ¾ pound veal cutlets
- ½ cup flour
- 2 eggs, beaten

Wash the spinach very well then put it in a pot with some salt and pepper. Put on medium heat, cover, and cook until the spinach wilts, about 5 minutes. Squeeze out all the excess liquid from the greens with a spoon. Add the juice of 1 lemon, garlic, parsley, and 2 tablespoons butter. Cook for 2 to 3 minutes.

Using a sharp knife, cut a slit lengthwise into each cutlet. Spoon a little of the spinach mixture into each pocket. Season the veal with additional salt and pepper and dredge in flour.

Heat the remaining 2 tablespoons butter in a large frying pan on medium heat. Dip the cutlets in the beaten egg. When the butter is quite hot, put the veal in the pan. Cook for 2 minutes per side. Cut the remaining lemon into wedges and serve with the veal, along with boiled or fried potatoes and a green salad.

SERVES 4.

Roast Beef

A good roast of beef is easy to make and impressive to serve, and little else is as satisfying. For a quick roast, that is, a meat that you want to serve just when it is done to your liking (rare, medium, or medium-well, etc.), choose a high quality cut such as rump, sirloin-tip, or loin; cheaper cuts such as chuck or rib roast work better if they are roasted longer with more liquid.

- 1 (3- to 4-pound) sirloin-tip roast
- 2 strips bacon, sliced fine
- salt and freshly ground black pepper
- 1 tablespoon marjoram
- 2 tablespoons vegetable oil or lard
- 1 cup dry red wine or water
- 1 cup broth or water
- 2 tablespoons flour
- 2 tablespoons chopped fresh parsley

Using a small paring knife, make an incision into the roast and insert a piece of sliced bacon. Continue doing this until the meat is well larded (this may be done a few hours ahead of cooking).

Preheat the oven to 400°F.

Season the beef well with salt and pepper. Rub on the marjoram. Place the meat in a roasting pan. Pour the oil or spread lard on top of the roast and pour the wine or water around it.

Put in the oven and cook for 15 minutes. Baste the roast and turn the temperature down to 350°F. Cook until done, basting occasionally. You may need to add some water or wine at some point. For a medium roast, 18 minutes per pound is about right.

When the roast is done, remove it to a serving platter. Remove the excess grease from the pan juices, then set them on medium heat on top of the stove. Add broth or water. Mix the flour with some water in a small cup, add some of the hot pan juices, then mix this thickener into the gravy. Bring the sauce to a low boil, season with additional salt and pepper, and stir in the parsley.

Serve the roast with its gravy with dumplings or boiled or roasted potatoes and a green vegetable or salad.

SERVES 4 TO 6.

Roast Beef with Mushrooms and Wine

Just about any vegetable may be cooked along with a roast: potatoes, carrots, parsnips, celeriac, or green beans. Simply add the vegetable to the pan when the roast is almost done but there is time remaining to cook the new ingredient. Mushrooms work well because they will not disintegrate no matter how long they cook and their flavor will permeate the meat.

- 1 (3- to 4-pound) rump roast
- 2 cloves garlic, sliced fine
- salt and freshly ground black pepper
- 1 teaspoon thyme
- 2 tablespoons vegetable oil
- 2 cups beef broth or water
- ½ pound mushrooms
- 2 tablespoons flour
- 2 tablespoons chopped fresh parsley

Using a small paring knife, cut incisions into the beef and insert a slice of garlic into each (this may be done a few hours before cooking). Season the meat well with salt and pepper. Rub the beef with thyme.

Preheat the oven to 400°F.

Place the beef in a roasting pan. Pour the oil on top of the meat. Pour ½ cup broth or water around the roast. Put in the oven and cook for 15 minutes. Baste the meat, add the whole mushrooms, and turn the heat down to 350°F. Continue cooking, basting occasionally and adding more liquid if needed, until the meat is done (about 18 minutes per pound for medium).

When the beef is done, put it and the mushrooms on a serving platter. Skim the excess fat from the pan juices and add the remaining broth or water. Bring to a low boil on medium heat on top of the stove.

Mix the flour with some water in a small cup, stir in some of the hot pan juices, then mix this thickener back into the gravy. Cook for a couple of minutes. Stir in the fresh parsley.

Serve with dumplings or potatoes, roasted or mashed, and a vegetable such as kale, Swiss chard, or green beans.

SERVES 4 TO 6.

Roast Beef, Gypsy Style

Roasted for a long time, onions basically dissolve into a thick and slightly sweet sauce. Paprika and cayenne serve to give the gravy a piquant flavor, while allspice and cloves accentuate the sweetness of the onions.

- 4-pound loin roast
- 2 strips bacon, sliced fine
- salt and freshly ground black pepper
- 2 large yellow onions, chopped fine
- 1 tablespoon paprika
- pinch of cayenne
- ½ teaspoon ground allspice
- ½ teaspoon ground cloves
- 2 cups beef broth or water
- 6 tablespoons (¾ stick) butter

Preheat the oven to 400°F.

Using a small paring knife, cut incisions into the beef and stick a slice of bacon in each. Season the meat well with salt and pepper. Place the beef in a large roasting pan. Put the chopped onions around it. Sprinkle them and the roast with the paprika, cayenne, allspice, and cloves. Pour about 1 cup of broth or water into the pan. Arrange pieces of the butter on top of the meat.

Put the roast in the oven. After 15 minutes, baste the meat and reduce the temperature to 350°F. Cook, basting occasionally and adding more broth if needed, for a total of 2 hours (about 30 minutes per pound).

Remove the roast to a serving platter. The sauce should be quite thick. You may want to increase its volume by adding some more broth and boiling it quickly on top of the stove.

Serve with dumplings or potatoes and a vegetable such as cauliflower or carrots.

SERVES 6.

Roast Beef Marinated in Vegetables

(Svíčková)

This classic of Czech cuisine calls for the finest cut of beef, tenderloin, though the same treatment of marinating and roasting meat with vegetables and vinegar will also work well with less expensive cuts. A good quality, strong wine vinegar is essential for the marinade. Though an unorthodox choice, you may want to try Italian balsamic vinegar for its sweetness and long-lasting character. This dish must be served with dumplings.

- 1 beef tenderloin (2 pounds)
- 1 strip bacon, sliced fine
- salt and freshly ground black pepper
- 1 medium onion, chopped
- 2 medium carrots, chopped
- 2 medium parsnips, chopped
- ½ small celeriac, diced
- 1 teaspoon thyme
- ½ teaspoon allspice
- 2 tablespoons chopped fresh parsley
- 2 bay leaves
- 1 cup red wine vinegar
- 4 tablespoons vegetable oil
- 4 tablespoons (½ stick) butter or lard
- juice of 1 lemon
- ½ teaspoon sugar
- ½ cup sour cream

A day before you wish to serve this dish, you need to lard and marinate the beef. First, using a small paring knife make incisions into the tenderloin and stick a piece of bacon into each. Season it well with salt and plenty of pepper.

To marinate the meat, place it in a fairly large glass or ceramic pan (do not use metal). Cover and surround it with onion, carrots, parsnips, and celeriac. Sprinkle on the thyme, allspice, and parsley. Season with additional salt and pepper. Put in the bay leaves. Pour on the vinegar and 2 tablespoons of oil. The vegetables will let off some juice to increase the liquid, but if you think more is needed, add some more vinegar or a little water. Cover the pan and leave in the refrigerator until the next day, turning the meat over once and basting occasionally.

Preheat the oven to 350°F.

To roast the meat, take the tenderloin out of the marinade and pat it dry with a paper towel. Heat the remaining 2 tablespoons of oil on high heat in a pan large enough to hold the tenderloin. When quite hot, put in the meat and sear it all over. Remove the beef to a roasting pan.

Pour a ½ cup water into the frying pan, and boil it rapidly for 1 to 2 minutes, then pour these juices onto the roast. Put all the vegetables and the marinating liquid around the roast. Place pieces of the butter or lard on top of the meat. Put in the oven and roast, basting occasionally, until done, about 1½ hours.

When the meat is tender, take it out of the oven and reduce the oven temperature to warm. Take the meat out of the pan, then pour out all the liquid and vegetables into a bowl. Put the meat back in the pan and return it to the oven. Now purée the vegetables and liquid, either using a food processor or by pressing them through a fine sieve.

To make the sauce, pour the vegetable purée into a medium-size pot and heat it to a low boil on medium heat. Season it with salt and pepper. Add the lemon juice and sugar. If the sauce needs to be thinned, add some water or beef broth. Just before serving, stir the sour cream into the sauce and heat it through.

Serve slices of the tenderloin with dumplings, both covered in sauce.

SERVES 4.

Roast Beef in Dill Sauce

Czechs often boil beef and then douse it with sauce like this one flavored with dill. Roasting the meat is nicer for texture and taste, for which the dill sauce is still a wonderful accompaniment.

1 (3- to 4-pound) sirloin-tip roast
2 strips bacon, sliced fine
salt and freshly ground black pepper
6 tablespoons (¾ stick) butter
1 cup dry white wine
2 tablespoons flour
zest of 1 lemon
3 tablespoons chopped fresh dill
1 cup heavy cream

Preheat the oven to 400°F.

Using a small paring knife, cut incisions in the beef and insert a piece of bacon in each. Season the meat well with salt and pepper. Put the beef in a roasting pan, place 3 tablespoons of butter on top, and pour on the white wine. Put in the oven and roast 15 minutes. Baste and turn the oven down to 350°F. Continue roasting, basting occasionally and adding some water if necessary, until tender, about another 1½ hours.

Transfer the roast to a serving platter. Skim off any excess fat from the pan juices and add some water to make a cup of liquid. Melt the remaining 3 tablespoons butter in a frying pan on medium heat, then stir in the flour and fry for 2 minutes. Stir in the pan juices. Bring to a low boil on top of the stove. Add the lemon zest and dill, and season with additional salt and pepper. Cook for another 2 minutes. Stir in the cream and heat through. Serve with dumplings and a green salad.

SERVES 4 TO 6.

Roast Beef Stuffed with Vegetables

To stuff a beef roast you may simply cut a pocket into it or, as here, slice and then pound the meat to create a large sheet, which is then rolled around the stuffing. Just about anything can go inside, from fresh or pickled vegetables to other meats and eggs, depending on your taste. This roast is also excellent cold.

- 1 (2- to 3-pound) round roast
- salt and freshly ground black pepper
- ¼ pound green beans
- 2 strips bacon, sliced fine
- 1 medium onion, chopped
- ⅓ pound white mushrooms, sliced
- 2 medium carrots, diced
- 1 teaspoon marjoram
- 2 tablespoons chopped fresh parsley
- 2 tablespoons lard or vegetable oil
- 1 cup dry red wine (optional)
- 3 tablespoons flour

Slice the roast almost all the way through and flatten it out. Using a meat mallet, lightly pound it on both sides until it is about ½ inch thick. Season it well with salt and pepper.

Bring a small pot of salted water to a boil and throw in the green beans. Let them boil for 2 to 3 minutes then remove and drain.

Fry the bacon until almost crisp in a frying pan on medium heat. Add the onion and, stirring occasionally, fry until almost golden. Add the mushrooms and brown these for a few minutes. Add the carrots and cook, stirring occasionally, for 5 minutes.

Take the pan off the heat. Mix in the green beans, marjoram, and parsley. Season with additional salt and pepper.

Preheat the oven to 350°F.

Lay the stuffing down on one side of the beef then carefully roll up the roast. Tie the roll with string. Heat the oil or lard in a frying pan large enough to hold the roast. When quite hot, put in the roast and brown it on all sides.

Transfer the meat to a deep roasting pan. Pour on the wine, if using, and enough water to reach halfway up the roll. Put in the oven and roast, basting occasionally, for 2 hours.

Once the meat is tender, place it on a serving platter. Bring the cooking liquid to a low boil on top of the stove. Mix the flour with some water in a small cup, stir in some of the hot cooking liquid, then mix the thickener back into the sauce. Season with salt and pepper. Let boil 1 to 2 minutes.

Serve slices of the stuffed beef with dumplings or potatoes.

SERVES 4.

Pot Roast of Beef

The advantage of a pot roast is that it turns a cheaper cut of beef into an extremely tender dish with a good deal of sauce. Any combination of vegetables may be joined with the meat, just watch out that you put them in at the right time so they do not disintegrate.

1 (3- to 4-pound) rib, chuck, or round roast
salt and freshly ground black pepper
2 tablespoons lard or vegetable oil
1 cup dry red wine
1 teaspoon marjoram
2 bay leaves
8 medium potatoes, skins on
4 carrots, sliced thick
½ medium cauliflower, in florets
3 tablespoons butter
4 tablespoons flour
2 tablespoons chopped fresh parsley

Trim off any excess fat from the beef, then season well with salt and pepper.

Preheat the oven to 350°F.

Heat the lard or oil in a frying pan large enough to hold the roast. When quite hot, put in the roast and brown it on all sides. Transfer the roast to a large ovenproof pot. Add the wine and enough water to just cover the meat. Add the marjoram and bay leaves and season with additional salt and pepper. Cover the pot and put it in the oven.

After 1½ hours, turn the meat over and add the whole potatoes and sliced carrots. Cover, and continue cooking.

After another 30 minutes, put in the cauliflower. As soon as the cauliflower is cooked, about 20 minutes, take the pot out of the oven.

Transfer the beef and vegetables to a serving platter and keep warm. Put the sauce on medium heat.

Melt the butter in a frying pan, then stir in the flour and fry for 2 minutes. Add a little of the warm sauce. Mix this thickener into the sauce and let boil for 2 minutes. Stir in the parsley.

Serve slices of the pot roast accompanied by the vegetables and a good deal of gravy.

SERVES 4.

Roast Veal with Wild Mushrooms and Garlic

Rolled loins of veal are not too expensive and, when roasted, make a fine textured and tasty dish. I use dried porcini mushrooms for this roast, though fresh wild mushrooms would be excellent instead.

1 ounce dried porcini mushrooms
1 (3-pound) rolled veal loin
2 cloves garlic, sliced thin
salt and freshly ground black pepper
1 teaspoon marjoram
2 tablespoons vegetable oil
1 cup dry white wine
4 tablespoons (½ stick) butter
2 tablespoons flour
2 tablespoons chopped fresh parsley

Put the dried mushrooms in 1 cup warm water to soak for 20 minutes. Drain, reserving the liquid, and brush off any pieces of dirt. Roughly chop the mushrooms and strain and reserve their liquid.

Preheat the oven to 350°F.

Using a small paring knife, cut incisions into the roast and insert a sliver of garlic into each. Season the veal well with salt and pepper. Rub in the marjoram.

Heat the oil in a large frying pan on medium-high heat. When quite hot, put in the veal and brown well all over.

Put the veal in a small roasting pan and pour the wine around it. Add the mushrooms and their liquid. Put 2 tablespoons of the butter on top of the meat. Place the roast in the oven. Cook, basting occasionally, for 2 hours.

Remove the veal to a serving platter. Skim off any excess fat from the pan juices. Melt the remaining 2 tablespoons butter in a frying pan, then stir in the flour and fry for 3 minutes. Add the pan juices. Let boil, stirring well, for 2 minutes. Season with additional salt and pepper and mix in the fresh parsley.

Serve with dumplings or potatoes and a vegetable such as spinach, asparagus, or green beans.

SERVES 4.

Roast Veal Stuffed with Sausage

Rolled loins of veal are perfect for stuffing. Simply untie the roast, unroll the meat, spread the stuffing over it, and put it together again. I use here a traditional meat stuffing made from sausage. Use a tasty fresh or smoked sausage and avoid distinctive spicing such as fennel seeds or hot peppers.

2 strips bacon, sliced fine
1 medium onion, chopped
2 cloves garlic, crushed
¼ pound sausage meat, removed from its casing
⅓ pound white mushrooms, sliced
salt and freshly ground black pepper
1 teaspoon marjoram
2 tablespoons chopped fresh parsley
¼ teaspoon grated nutmeg
2 eggs
1 (3-pound) rolled loin of veal
2 tablespoons lard or vegetable oil
2 cups broth or water
juice of 1 lemon
2 tablespoons flour

Fry the bacon in a frying pan on medium heat until it is almost crisp. Add the chopped onion and garlic and fry, stirring occasionally, until almost golden. Mix in the sausage meat and fry until it is golden brown. Add the mushrooms and cook another 5 minutes. Take the pan off the heat.

Season the stuffing well with salt and pepper. Mix in the marjoram, parsley, and nutmeg. Break the eggs into the stuffing and mix well.

Preheat the oven to 350°F.

Untie and unroll the roast. Spread the stuffing on the meat, then roll the roast up again and tie it secure. Season the meat with additional salt and pepper.

Heat the lard or oil on medium-high heat in a large frying pan. When quite hot, put in the roast and brown it on all sides. Transfer the meat to a roasting pan and pour a cup of broth or water around it. Put it in the oven. Roast, basting occasionally and adding more broth if needed, for 2 hours.

Put the roast on a serving platter. Skim off any excess fat from the pan juices, add the remaining broth and the lemon juice, and bring to a low boil on top of the stove. Mix the flour with some water in a small cup, stir in a few tablespoons of the hot liquid, then mix this thickener back into the sauce. Season with additional salt and pepper and cook for 2 minutes.

Serve with dumplings or potatoes and a vegetable such as carrots, beets, or spinach.

Serves 4.

Beef Stew

Stew is another of those dishes for which, once you have the basic idea and technique, a recipe is more a restriction than an aid—just about anything can go in it, depending on what is in your refrigerator or what you picked up in the market or store. A good stew comes from a selection of complementary ingredients cooked slowly and for a fair amount of time. Any cheaper cut of beef may be used and many butchers sell cubes of what they call "stewing beef." This is fine, though I prefer to use beef shank when available. The meat falls into bite-size portions and the marrow and bone enhance the stock. If using beef shank, remove the bones before serving (the meat should fall right off them).

2 tablespoons lard or vegetable oil
1½ pounds beef shank
1 medium onion, chopped
1 clove garlic, crushed
2 small leeks, sliced
1 cup dry red wine (optional)
2 bay leaves
2 tablespoons tomato purée
salt and freshly ground black pepper
3 medium carrots, sliced
½ small celeriac, diced
3 medium potatoes, diced
½ teaspoon thyme
½ teaspoon marjoram
2 tablespoons chopped fresh parsley
2 tablespoons flour

Heat the lard or oil in large pot and when quite hot, put in the beef. Brown the meat all over. Add the onions and fry, stirring occasionally, until almost golden. Add the garlic and leeks and cook for 2 to 3 more minutes. Add about 8 cups water and the red wine, if using it. Add the bay leaves. Mix in the tomato purée. Add some salt and pepper. Put on medium heat and cover.

Once the liquid has reached a low boil, lower the heat a little and let cook for 1½ hours. Once the meat is almost tender, add the carrots, celeriac, potatoes, thyme, marjoram, and parsley. Cook on a low boil, uncovered, until tender.

Thicken the sauce a little by mixing the flour with some water in a small cup, adding some of the hot liquid, then mixing this thickener back into the stew. Boil for a couple more minutes. Check the seasonings for salt and pepper.

Serve with rice or bread and a green salad.

Serves 4 to 6.

Beef Birds

(Hovézí Ptáčky)

A stew of sorts, this dish stuffs thin slices of beef with various vegetables and then braises them in broth or water.

- 2 pounds sirloin
- salt and freshly ground black pepper
- ¼ cup mustard
- 2 medium carrots
- 2 medium parsnips
- 4 tablespoons lard or vegetable oil
- 1 medium onion, chopped
- 2 pickles, finely chopped
- 2 tablespoons chopped fresh parsley
- ½ teaspoon marjoram
- 1 egg
- 2 hard-boiled eggs, sliced
- 2 cups dry red wine
- 2 cups beef broth or water
- 2 tablespoons flour

Trim any excess fat from the sirloin, then using a meat mallet lightly pound the meat on both sides until it is about ⅛ inch thick. Cut the meat into squares with sides about 3 inches in length. Season with salt and pepper. Spread about 1 teaspoon mustard on each meat square.

Cut the carrots and parsnips into thin strips about 2 inches long.

Heat 2 tablespoons lard or oil in a frying pan. Add the onion and fry, stirring occasionally, until almost golden. Add the carrots and parsnips and cook for 3 to 4 minutes. Take off the heat. Mix in the pickles, parsley, and marjoram. Season with additional salt and pepper. Break in the raw egg and mix well.

Take a square of beef and put 1 to 2 tablespoons of the vegetable mixture on one side. Add a slice of the boiled egg. Now roll up the "bird" and secure the flap with a toothpick. Fill all the beef rolls this way.

Heat the remaining 2 tablespoons lard or oil on medium-high heat in a large pot. When quite hot, add as many of the birds as will fit without crowding the pan and brown them all over. Brown all the birds this way.

Put all the beef rolls back in the pot and pour in the wine and the broth or water. Season with salt and pepper. Bring to a low boil, reduce the heat, partially cover, and let simmer until tender, about 1 hour.

To thicken the sauce, mix the flour with some water in a small cup, add some of the hot liquid, then stir this thickener back into the sauce and let it boil for a couple of minutes. Serve with dumplings, potatoes, or rice and a green salad.

Serves 4.

Veal Stew with Mushrooms

This stew is lighter than the beef version, using white wine instead of red and omitting tomatoes. It is rich nevertheless, due in part to the sour cream mixed in at the end. Ordinary white mushrooms will do well for this dish, though a tastier fungus such as the chanterelle or porcini would be even better.

2 tablespoons lard or vegetable oil
1½ pounds cubed stewing veal
1 medium onion, chopped
2 cloves garlic, crushed
¾ pound mushrooms, sliced thick
1 cup dry white wine
juice of 1 lemon
½ teaspoon marjoram
2 tablespoons chopped fresh parsley
salt and freshly ground black pepper
2 tablespoons flour
½ cup sour cream

Heat the lard or oil in a large pot on medium high heat. When quite hot, put in the veal and lightly brown it all over. Add the chopped onion and the garlic and fry, stirring occasionally, until almost golden. Add the mushrooms and brown them. Add the white wine, lemon juice, and about 4 cups water. Mix in the marjoram and parsley and season well with salt and pepper. Cover the pot and bring to a low boil. Reduce the heat and simmer until the meat is tender, about 1½ hours.

To thicken the sauce, mix the flour with some water in a small cup, add a little of the hot liquid, then stir this thickener back into the sauce. Let boil for 2 minutes. Just before serving, stir in the sour cream.

Serve with dumplings, potatoes, or rice and a green salad.

SERVES 4.

Bratislavsky Goulash

Quite similar to a traditional stew, this combination of beef and root vegetables is seasoned with bay leaves, thyme, and paprika, cooked in white wine, and intensified by the addition of mustard and sour cream.

- 2 tablespoons lard or vegetable oil
- 1½ pounds stewing beef
- 1 medium onion, chopped
- 1 cup dry white wine
- juice of 1 lemon
- 2 bay leaves
- ½ teaspoon thyme
- 1 tablespoon paprika
- salt and freshly ground black pepper
- 2 medium carrots, sliced
- 2 medium parsnips, sliced
- ½ small celeriac, diced
- 2 tablespoons chopped fresh parsley
- 2 tablespoons flour
- 1 tablespoon mustard
- ½ cup sour cream

Heat the lard or oil on medium-high heat in a large pot. When quite hot, put in the cubed beef and brown it all over. Add the chopped onion and fry, stirring occasionally, until almost golden. Pour in the white wine, lemon juice, and about 5 cups water. Add the bay leaves, thyme, and paprika and season well with salt and pepper. Bring to a boil, cover, reduce the heat and simmer until the meat is tender, about 1½ hours.

Add the carrots, parsnips, celeriac, and parsley to the pot. Continue cooking on a low boil, uncovered, until the vegetables are tender, about 20 minutes.

To thicken the stew, mix the flour with some water in a small cup, add some of the hot liquid, then stir this thickener back into the sauce. Let boil 2 minutes. Just before serving, stir in the mustard and the sour cream and let the sauce heat through.

Serve with potatoes, dumplings, or bread and a green salad.

SERVES 4 TO 6.

Pražsky Goulash

This is a simple, meat intensive stew that combines beef with good-quality frankfurters, plenty of onions and paprika and caraway.

2 tablespoons lard or vegetable oil
1½ pounds stewing beef
2 large onions, chopped
2 cloves garlic, crushed
1 tablespoon paprika
2 tablespoons tomato purée
½ teaspoon marjoram
1 tablespoon caraway seeds, crushed
salt and freshly ground black pepper
4 frankfurters, sliced thick
2 tablespoons butter
2 tablespoons flour

Heat the lard or oil in a large pot on medium-high heat. When quite hot, put in the beef and brown it all over. Add the onions and garlic and fry, stirring occasionally, until almost golden. Sprinkle on the paprika and fry for another couple of minutes. Add about 5 cups water. Stir in the tomato purée. Mix in the marjoram and caraway seeds and season well with salt and pepper. Bring to a boil, cover, reduce the heat, and let simmer until tender, about 1½ hours.

A few minutes before serving, add the frankfurters and heat through. To thicken the sauce, make a roux by melting the butter in a frying pan, then adding the flour and frying for 3 to 4 minutes; add a little of the hot liquid, then stir the roux into the stew and cook for a couple of minutes.

Serve with bread, potatoes, or dumplings and a green salad.

SERVES 4 TO 6.

Goulash with Peppers

Plenty of green bell peppers and tomatoes make this goulash colorful and tasty. Putting potatoes into the stew makes this a meal in itself.

- 2 tablespoons lard or vegetable oil
- 1½ pounds stewing beef
- 1 large onion, chopped
- 2 cloves garlic, crushed
- 1 tablespoon paprika
- 2 large green bell peppers, sliced
- 1 tablespoon caraway seeds, crushed
- ½ teaspoon marjoram
- 1 can (28 ounces) tomatoes
- salt and freshly ground black pepper
- 3 large potatoes, diced
- 2 tablespoons butter
- 2 tablespoons flour
- juice of 1 lemon

Heat the lard or oil on medium-high heat in a large pot. When quite hot, put in the beef and brown all over. Add the chopped onion and the garlic and fry, stirring occasionally, until almost golden. Sprinkle on the paprika and fry for a couple of minutes. Add the green bell peppers and fry for another couple of minutes. Add about 5 cups water, then mix in the caraway seeds, marjoram, and the tomatoes. Season well with salt and pepper. Bring to a boil, cover, reduce the heat, and let simmer until tender, about 1½ hours.

Add the potatoes and cook until tender, about 20 minutes. To thicken the sauce, make a roux by melting the butter in a frying pan, then adding the flour and frying for 3 to 4 minutes; add a little of the hot sauce, then stir the roux into the stew and cook for a couple of minutes. Stir in the lemon juice and check the seasonings for salt and pepper.

Serve with bread and a green salad.

SERVES 4 TO 6.

Beef with Celeriac

Better quality cuts of beef such as sirloin are excellent when sliced, browned, and then cooked in a sauce with one or two vegetables. Combining beef with julienned celeriac in a light dill sauce, for example, makes a nice change from steak and feeds more people.

- 1½ pounds sirloin
- salt and freshly ground black pepper
- 2 tablespoons lard or vegetable oil
- 1 medium onion, chopped
- 2 cups beef broth
- ½ small celeriac, cut into fine strips
- 2 tablespoons chopped fresh dill
- 2 tablespoons butter
- 2 tablespoons flour
- ½ cup sour cream

Trim the fat from the sirloin and then slice the meat across the grain into strips about ¼ inch thick. Season the beef with salt and pepper.

Heat the lard or vegetable oil on medium-high heat in a large frying pan. When quite hot, put in the beef and brown it. Add the onion and fry, stirring occasionally, until almost golden. Add the broth and season with additional salt and pepper. Bring to a boil, reduce the heat, and simmer, uncovered, for about 20 minutes.

Meanwhile, bring a small pot of salted water to a brisk boil. Put in the celeriac and cook until tender, about 5 minutes. Drain. Add the celeriac to the beef. Stir in the chopped dill. To thicken the sauce, make a roux by melting the butter in a frying pan, then adding the flour and frying for 3 to 4 minutes; add a little hot sauce, then stir the roux into the beef and cook for a couple of minutes. Just before serving, mix the sour cream into the sauce and heat it through.

Serve with potatoes or egg noodles and a salad.

SERVES 4.

Beef Stroganoff

This classic combination of sliced beef and mushrooms in a sour cream-enhanced sauce should be served on egg noodles to people who crave a rich meal.

- 1½ pounds sirloin
- salt and freshly ground black pepper
- 3 tablespoons butter
- ½ pound mushrooms, sliced
- 1 small onion, chopped
- 1 clove garlic, crushed
- 2 cups dry white wine
- juice of 1 lemon
- 2 tablespoons chopped fresh dill
- ¾ cup sour cream

Trim the fat from the sirloin, then slice the steak across the grain into strips about ¼ inch thick. Season the meat well with salt and pepper.

Heat 1 tablespoon butter in a large frying pan on medium-high heat. When quite hot, throw in the mushrooms and brown them. Remove and reserve. Melt the remaining 2 tablespoons butter in the pan and add the beef. Brown the meat all over. Add the onion and garlic and fry, stirring occasionally, until almost golden. Pour in the white wine, bring to a low boil, and reduce the heat. Stir in the mushrooms, lemon juice, and dill. Season with additional salt and pepper. Simmer, uncovered, until tender, about 20 minutes.

A few minutes before serving, stir the sour cream into the sauce and heat through. Serve over egg noodles with a green salad.

SERVES 4.

Beef, Hunter's Style

For this dish, shanks of beef are browned, simmered with root vegetables, plenty of onions, and red wine, and then served with a sauce made from the purée of the poaching ingredients. If shanks of beef are not available, use cubed stewing beef or pieces of sirloin.

3 tablespoons butter
4 medium beef shanks
2 large onions, chopped
1 clove garlic, crushed
2 medium carrots, sliced
2 medium parsnips, sliced
½ small celeriac, diced
2 cups dry red wine
juice and zest of 1 lemon
2 bay leaves
½ teaspoon thyme
¼ teaspoon ground allspice
2 tablespoons chopped fresh parsley
salt and freshly ground black pepper

Melt the butter on medium-high heat in a large frying pan. When quite hot, put in the beef shanks and brown them on both sides. Add the onions and garlic and fry, stirring occasionally, until almost golden. Add the carrots, parsnips, and celeriac and cook, stirring occasionally, for 5 minutes. Pour in the red wine and some water, if needed, to just cover the meat. Add the lemon juice, lemon zest, bay leaves, thyme, allspice, and parsley. Season well with salt and pepper. Bring to a low boil, cover, reduce the heat, and simmer until the beef is tender, about 1½ hours.

Remove the beef from the pan. Remove the bay leaves and discard them. Purée the sauce either by using a food processor or by passing it through a fine sieve. Put the sauce back in the pan and bring to a low boil. Put the meat back in and heat through. Check the seasonings for salt and pepper.

Serve with dumplings, potatoes, or rice and a green salad.

SERVES 4.

Veal Paprikash

(Telecí Na Paprice)

Many seemingly complex dishes are in fact quite simple and gain their taste from one or two fine ingredients that go so well together they need nothing else. So it is with this combination of veal, paprika, and sour cream—quick and easy to make, rich and memorable to taste.

2 tablespoons butter
1½ pounds cubed veal
1 large onion, chopped very fine
2 tablespoons flour
1 tablespoon paprika
2 cups beef broth
salt and freshly ground black pepper
½ cup sour cream

Melt the butter in a large frying pan on medium heat. Put in the cubed veal and lightly brown on all sides. Add the chopped onion and fry, stirring occasionally, until almost golden. Sprinkle in the flour and paprika and cook for 2 minutes. Stir in the beef broth. Season well with salt and pepper. Bring to a low boil, reduce the heat, and simmer, partially covered, until the meat is tender, about 45 minutes.

Just before serving, check the seasonings for salt and pepper, then mix in the sour cream and heat through. Serve with dumplings, potatoes, or rice and a green salad.

SERVES 4.

Veal with Leeks

I always feel as if I don't use leeks enough in my kitchen. Leeks have a distinct though subtle taste that needs little else for accompaniment. Perhaps their only drawback is that they need thorough cleaning to get rid of the dirt hidden in their crevices.

- 4 small to medium leeks
- 3 tablespoons butter
- 1½ pounds cubed veal
- 1 clove garlic, crushed
- 2 tablespoons flour
- 2 cups beef broth or water
- juice of 1 lemon
- ½ teaspoon thyme
- salt and freshly ground black or white pepper
- ½ cup heavy cream

Cut the ends off the leeks, slice off their green parts, and cut them in half. Wash them well under running water, then slice them thinly.

Melt the butter in a large frying pan on medium heat. When quite hot, add the veal and lightly brown all over. Add the sliced leeks and the garlic and fry for 3 to 4 minutes, stirring occasionally. Stir in the flour and cook for a couple of minutes. Mix in the beef broth or water. Add the lemon juice and thyme. Season well with salt and pepper. Bring to a low boil, reduce the heat, partially cover, and simmer until tender, about 45 minutes.

Just before serving, stir in the heavy cream and heat through. Serve with dumplings, potatoes, or rice and a salad.

SERVES 4.

Veal with Peppers and Tomatoes

The excellent combination of green bell peppers and tomatoes is used here with cubes of veal to make a light and colorful dish.

2 tablespoons butter
1½ pounds cubed veal
1 medium onion, chopped
1 clove garlic, crushed
2 green bell peppers, cut in short strips
2 tablespoons flour
1 cup dry white wine
1 can (28 ounces) tomatoes
½ teaspoon thyme
2 tablespoons chopped fresh parsley
juice of 1 lemon
salt and freshly ground black pepper

Melt the butter in a large frying pan on medium-high heat. When quite hot, put in the veal and lightly brown it all over. Add the onion and garlic and fry, stirring occasionally, until almost golden. Add the green bell peppers and cook for 5 minutes. Sprinkle in the flour and cook another couple of minutes. Pour in the white wine and tomatoes. Add the thyme, parsley, and lemon juice. Season well with salt and pepper. Bring to a low boil, reduce the heat, partially cover, and simmer until tender, about 45 minutes.

If the sauce needs thickening, raise the heat and boil, uncovered, for a few minutes to reduce the liquid. Serve with rice or potatoes.

SERVES 4.

Veal Cooked in Rice

This dish is a complete meal in itself, with the meat and vegetables cooking with the rice all in one pan in the oven. The rice is infused with all the flavors from the meat and spices. The final pleasure: just one dish to wash.

- 2 strips bacon, sliced
- 1 pound cubed veal
- 1 medium onion, chopped
- 1 clove garlic, crushed
- ⅓ pound mushrooms, sliced
- ½ small celeriac, diced
- 2 cups white rice
- 4 cups beef broth or water
- ½ teaspoon thyme
- 2 tablespoons chopped fresh parsley
- juice of 1 lemon
- salt and freshly ground black pepper

Preheat the oven to 350°F.

Fry the bacon in a large casserole dish or ovenproof pot until almost crisp. Add the cubed veal and lightly brown it all over. Add the onion and garlic and fry, stirring occasionally, until almost golden. Add the mushrooms and brown them. Add the celeriac and cook for a couple of minutes. Add the rice and cook for another couple of minutes, stirring occasionally. Pour in the broth. Add the thyme, parsley, and lemon juice. Season well with salt and pepper.

Bring to a low boil, cover, and then put in the oven. Bake until the meat is tender and the rice is done, about 40 minutes. Serve with a green salad.

SERVES 4.

Meatloaf

(Sekaná)

The acme of comfort food, a good meatloaf is easy to make and pleases almost everyone. I mix beef with pork in the recipe below, but beef alone would also work well.

- 2 strips bacon, sliced
- 1 medium onion, chopped
- 1 clove garlic, crushed
- 2 French rolls
- ½ cup milk
- 1 pound ground beef
- 1 pound ground pork
- ½ teaspoon thyme
- 2 tablespoons chopped fresh parsley
- salt and freshly ground black pepper
- 2 eggs
- 2 tablespoons butter

Fry the bacon in a frying pan on medium heat until almost crisp. Add the onion and garlic and fry, stirring occasionally, until almost golden. Take off the heat.

Preheat the oven to 400°F.

In a large bowl, break the French rolls into fairly small pieces and pour in the milk. Let the bread soak up the liquid for 3 to 4 minutes. Add the ground beef, ground pork, and the onions and bacon and mix well. Sprinkle on the thyme and parsley. Season well with salt and pepper. Break in the eggs and mix everything together well.

Choose a small oven dish with high sides and butter it. Stuff in the meat mixture and smooth the top level. Put in the oven and bake for 1½ hours. Serve slices of the meatloaf with gravy, if you wish, and mashed potatoes and a vegetable such as carrots or spinach.

SERVES 4.

Beef Burgers
(Karbanátky)

Czech burgers or karbanátky *traditionally use bread soaked in milk or bread crumbs to supplement the ground beef and bind the ingredients with egg. The result is denser but also more flavorful than the North American hamburger.*

1 French roll
⅓ cup milk
1 pound ground beef
1 small onion, chopped very fine
1 clove garlic, crushed
½ teaspoon marjoram
2 tablespoons chopped fresh parsley
salt and freshly ground black pepper
1 egg
3 tablespoons lard or vegetable oil

In a medium-size bowl, tear the roll into fairly small pieces, pour on the milk, and let the bread soak for a few minutes. Mix in the ground beef, onion, and garlic. Sprinkle on the marjoram and parsley and season well with salt and pepper. Break in the egg and mix all the ingredients together well.

Using your hands, take a small handful of the meat mixture and form it into a round burger shape. Once all the patties have been made, heat half the lard or oil in a large frying pan on medium heat. When hot, put in as many of the burgers as will fit comfortably. Fry on both sides until golden brown and cooked all the way through, about 8 minutes per side. Repeat until all burgers are cooked. Serve with boiled potatoes and a vegetable such as green beans.

SERVES 4.

Calf's Liver with Onions and Bacon

Plenty of onions, fried slowly with bacon, are perfect for slices of tender calf's liver, fried until well-done or pink inside, depending on your pleasure.

- 1 pound calf's liver
- ½ cup flour
- 3 tablespoons butter
- 6 strips bacon, sliced
- 2 large onions, sliced
- salt and freshly ground black pepper
- 2 tablespoons chopped fresh parsley
- ½ teaspoon marjoram
- ¼ cup red wine vinegar

Wash and dry the calf's liver. Dredge it in flour, shaking off any excess. Melt the butter on medium heat in a large frying pan. When bubbling hot, put in the slices of liver and brown them well on both sides. Remove to a plate.

Add the bacon to the pan and cook, stirring occasionally, until almost crisp. Add the onions and fry, stirring occasionally, until golden. Put the liver back in the pan. Season with salt and pepper. Mix in the parsley and marjoram. Pour in the vinegar and a little water if needed to wet the pan. Simmer until the liver is done to your liking: only a few more minutes for medium or about 10 minutes for well-done.

Serve with boiled or mashed potatoes, or rice and a green salad.

SERVES 4.

Veal Tongue with Mustard and Capers

Tongue has one of the finest textures of all meats so it is a great shame that some shy away from this delectable organ. Tongue is easy to prepare and it tastes good on its own or with various added flavors, such as horseradish or, as below, mustard. Any leftovers will make wonderful sandwiches.

1 pound veal tongue
salt
2 tablespoons butter
1 small onion, finely chopped
2 tablespoons flour
2 cups beef broth
2 tablespoons mustard
1 teaspoon marjoram
1 tablespoon chopped fresh parsley
juice of 1 lemon
1 tablespoon capers
freshly ground black pepper

To prepare the tongue, wash it and then put it in a large pot. Cover with cold water and sprinkle in some salt. Bring to a boil and simmer, covered, until tender, about 1½ hours.

Remove the tongue from its liquid and let cool a little. Using a small paring knife, slit the skin of the tongue and peel it off carefully. At the base of the tongue you may need to cut off the skin. Put the tongue aside.

To make the sauce, melt the butter in a large frying pan on medium-low heat. Once it starts bubbling, add the onion and fry, stirring occasionally, until almost golden. Mix in the flour and fry for 2 minutes. Pour in the broth, mixing well, and bring to a low boil. Stir in the mustard. Add the marjoram, parsley, lemon juice, and capers. Season with salt and pepper.

Cut the tongue diagonally into ¼-inch slices. Add the slices to the sauce and heat them through for about 5 minutes.

Serve with rice or potatoes and either a green salad or a simple vegetable such as green beans or carrots.

SERVES 4.

Fried Calf's Brains

(Smaženy Telecí Mozek)

Organ meats have an incredible variety of textures, from the dense and flavorful tongue, on the one hand, to the light and ethereal brain. Use a wine reduction to sauce the meat, if so desired, or simply fry it in a little butter to enjoy the texture at its purest. Brains may also be coated with egg, as below, or in light bread crumbs.

- 2 sets calf's brains
- ½ cup flour
- salt and freshly ground black pepper
- 4 tablespoons (½ stick) butter
- 3 eggs, beaten
- 2 tablespoons chopped fresh parsley
- 1 lemon, sliced into thick wedges

Soak the brains in warm water for about 30 minutes. Remove their skin and any membranes. Separate the brains into halves. Dry the meat with paper towels. Dredge the brains in flour. Season with salt and pepper.

Heat the butter in a large frying pan on medium heat. Once it is bubbling, dip a portion of the brain in the egg, coating it well, then put in the frying pan. Do this with all the portions but do not crowd the pan. Fry the brains until lightly golden on the outside and tender inside, about 10 minutes. Sprinkle on the parsley and put on serving plates with lemon wedges.

Serve with boiled potatoes and a green salad or a vegetable such as carrots.

SERVES 4.

Fried Sweetbreads

(Smaženy Brzlík)

Sweetbreads are even more delectable than brains, if that is possible, and may be treated in similar ways. Simplicity is again the rule since you don't want to overpower the intrinsic taste of the meat.

2 sets sweetbreads
½ cup flour
salt and freshly ground black pepper
3 tablespoons butter
juice of 1 lemon
2 tablespoons chopped fresh parsley

Bring a pot of salted water to a boil. Wash the sweetbreads. Place them in the boiling water and cook them, gently, for about 5 minutes, then remove and drain. Separate the sweetbreads into quarters and remove their membranes. Dredge them in flour and season well with salt and pepper.

Melt the butter on medium heat in a large frying pan. When bubbling, put in the sweetbreads and fry them until golden on all sides and tender inside, 8 to 10 minutes. Pour on the lemon juice and sprinkle on the parsley. Place on plates.

Serve with boiled new potatoes and a green salad.

Serves 2.

Sweetbreads in Red Wine

A slightly more complicated way of cooking sweetbreads or brains begins by frying them in butter and then reducing red wine to sauce them. The richness of the sauce goes very well with the white, cloudy texture of the meat.

4 sets sweetbreads
¾ cup flour
salt and freshly ground black pepper
4 tablespoons (½ stick) butter
1 small onion, finely chopped
2 cups dry red wine
juice and zest of 1 lemon
2 tablespoons chopped fresh parsley

Bring a pot of salted water to a boil. Wash the sweetbreads, then put in the boiling water and cook gently for 5 minutes. Remove, drain, and cool slightly. Separate the sweetbreads into quarters and remove the membranes. Dredge in flour and season well with salt and pepper.

Melt the butter in a large frying pan on medium heat. When bubbling, put in the sweetbreads and lightly brown them on all sides for 3 to 4 minutes. Add the onion and cook a couple more minutes. Pour in the red wine and raise the heat so the liquid boils vigorously. Add the lemon juice and zest and the parsley. Season with additional salt and pepper. The dish is done when the sauce has thickened to the point that it coats a spoon, 5 to 6 minutes.

Serve with boiled new potatoes and either a green salad or a vegetable such as green beans or spinach.

SERVES 4.

Braised Tripe with Vegetables

(Zadělávané Dršťky)

Tripe needs to be cooked slowly in plenty of liquid for a long time. If these rules are followed, the meat will be highly flavored and will melt in your mouth. Precooked tripe is easily found, but if you cannot get it, then follow the tenderizing instructions as set out in the recipe for Tripe Soup (see page 49).

- ½ pound precooked tripe
- salt and freshly ground black pepper
- 3 tablespoons lard or vegetable oil
- 1 medium onion, chopped
- 1 cup red wine or beef broth
- juice of 1 lemon
- 1 tablespoon paprika
- ½ teaspoon thyme
- ½ teaspoon marjoram
- 2 medium carrots, diced
- ½ medium celeriac, diced
- 2 small parsnips, diced
- 2 tablespoons flour
- 2 tablespoons chopped fresh parsley

Wash and dry the precooked tripe, then cut it into fairly fine slivers. Season with salt and pepper.

Heat the lard or oil in a large pot on medium-high heat. Add the sliced tripe and fry for 2 minutes. Add the onion and cook another couple of minutes.

Pour on the red wine or broth and enough water to cover the meat well. Add the lemon juice. Stir in the paprika, thyme, and marjoram. Season with additional salt and pepper. Bring to a low boil, cover, and simmer until the meat is tender, about 2 hours.

Add the carrots, celeriac, and parsnips and cook until tender, about 30 minutes.

To thicken the sauce, mix the flour with some water in a small cup, add in a little of the hot liquid, then stir the thickener back into the dish. Cook for 2 to 3 minutes. Sprinkle with chopped parsley. Serve with rice or boiled potatoes and a green salad.

SERVES 4.

Beef Heart Stuffed and Braised
(Hovězí Srdce Nadívané)

Heart, like tripe, needs long, slow cooking and the reward is equally good: a tender and rich meat. Heart may be "shredded" like tripe and cooked this way, or you may stuff it with vegetables and/or meat as below.

1 medium beef heart
salt and freshly ground black pepper
2 strips bacon, sliced
1 medium onion, chopped
2 medium leeks
2 medium carrots, diced
2 small parsnips, diced
4 tablespoons chopped fresh parsley
½ teaspoon marjoram
½ teaspoon grated nutmeg
1 French roll, diced
⅓ cup milk
1 egg
3 tablespoons lard or vegetable oil
2 cups red wine or beef broth
3 tablespoons butter
3 tablespoons flour

Trim the fat off the heart and cut out the tubes on the inside to make the cavity bigger. Wash the heart and dry it with paper towels. Season with salt and pepper.

To make the stuffing, fry the bacon in a pan until almost crisp. Add the onion and fry, stirring occasionally, until almost golden. Meanwhile, wash the leeks well, trim off the green parts, and slice. Add the sliced leeks, and diced carrots and parsnips to the pan. Cook for 2 to 3 minutes. Take off the heat.

Mix 2 tablespoons parsley, the marjoram, and nutmeg into the vegetables. Soak the French roll in milk. Add to the vegetables. Season well with salt and pepper. Mix in the egg.

Stuff the heart with as much of the vegetable mixture as will fit, then sew the opening closed with some thread.

In a medium-size pot, heat the lard or oil on medium-high heat. When quite hot, put in the heart and brown well on all sides. Pour in the red wine or broth and enough water to cover the meat. Bring to a low boil. Season with additional salt and pepper. Cover, reduce the heat, and simmer for 2 hours. Remove the cover and continue cooking until tender, about another hour.

When the meat is tender, thicken the sauce by making a roux. Melt the butter in a small frying pan on medium-low heat. When bubbling, add the flour and cook, stirring constantly, for 4 to 5 minutes. Mix the roux into the sauce. Add the remaining 2 tablespoons chopped parsley and cook for a couple of minutes. Check the seasonings.

Slice the heart diagonally into ½-inch strips. Serve the heart slices covered with sauce alongside boiled potatoes or dumplings and a green salad.

SERVES 4.

7

Pork

Though it may be said that beef is the favorite meat among Czechs, some injustice is thereby done to pork. Pork is more versatile and ubiquitous than beef. Pork is found smoked as an appetizer, in soups and stews, roasted, and fried as cutlets. Drippings from bacon form the lard used to cook many other things or that is slathered on bread as a snack for the brave. Many of the same treatments for beef may be used on pork with equal satisfaction. Goulashes, for example, are commonly made from pork or a mixture of pork and beef. Roasting pork is a good idea, especially when accompanying it with cabbage and dumplings as in *vepřo-knedlo-zelo*, one of the best loved Czech meals. Pork has a more subtle taste than beef, is less fatty, and is usually served well-done. Serving pork pink should not frighten you anymore, though this is in no way as desirable as in the case of beef. The milder taste of pork calls out for tasty sauces and combinations, such as fruit, that one might not use with other meat.

Cured and smoked pork are also much appreciated and come in a large variety at the butcher or delicatessen, though in North America you may have to make do with hams and smoked pork hocks. The smoky taste of cured meat does not need such strong accompaniments as the fresh kind, though cured pork also benefits from sweet concoctions such as honey or fruit.

Breaded Pork Cutlets

(Řízky)

Like the German or Hungarian wiener schnitzel, *pork or veal cutlets are pounded thin with a meat mallet, then coated with flour, dipped in egg, and coated with bread crumbs. Cutlets may also be fried plain, sprinkled lightly with flour, or covered in an egg batter. If you do not have a meat mallet, ask your butcher for very thin, boneless cutlets. The breaded cutlets are fried quickly in hot oil and butter and served with lemon wedges.*

4 boneless, center-cut pork chops
salt and freshly ground black pepper
½ cup flour
3 eggs
2 tablespoons milk
1 cup fine bread crumbs
1 tablespoon oil
1 tablespoon butter
2 tablespoons chopped fresh parsley
1 lemon, quartered

Slice each of the pork chops lengthwise almost in half, so that it butterflies or opens up like a book. Using a meat mallet, gently pound the meat on both sides until it is quite thin, about 1/16 inch thick. Season the meat with salt and pepper.

Pour the flour onto a plate. Break the eggs into a large, shallow bowl, pour in the milk, and beat this mixture lightly until well mixed. Place the bowl beside the plate of flour. Pour the bread crumbs onto a plate and place it beside the bowl of eggs. Take one of the cutlets and coat it all over with flour, then dip it in the eggs and cover it well. Lift the cutlet out of the eggs, allowing any excess liquid to drip away, then place it on the bread crumbs. Cover the cutlet well with the crumbs, then remove. Repeat this procedure with all the cutlets. Now you are ready to start frying.

Preheat the oven to 200°F or warm.

Heat a large frying pan on medium-high heat (use two pans, if you can manage, to get the job done faster). Add oil and butter. When the oil is fairly hot, put in the cutlet. Fry quickly on one side until lightly golden, then turn over and complete the cooking. When the cutlet is golden on both sides, remove it to a platter and place in the oven to keep warm. Repeat this procedure with all the cutlets.

Serve the pork cutlets with a sprinkle of parsley and a quarter of lemon. Boiled potatoes or rice and a cucumber or beet salad go well.

SERVES 4.

Pork Cutlets Stuffed with Cheese

When choosing to cook with cheese, think about the consistency you want to achieve—some cheeses melt much better than others—and the flavors you are complementing. Milder cheeses are usually preferable. For this marriage with pork, an Edam, Emmenthal, or Gruyère does well.

- 4 boneless, center-cut pork chops
- salt and freshly ground black pepper
- 4 slices Gruyère cheese
- ½ cup flour
- 2 eggs
- ⅓ cup milk
- 1 cup fine bread crumbs
- vegetable oil for frying
- 1 tablespoon chopped fresh parsley
- 1 lemon, cut into wedges

If the chops are very thick, pound them lightly with a meat mallet until they are about ½ inch. Trim off any excess fat. Slice each of the cutlets lengthwise almost in half, leaving a hinge across one side. Season inside and out with salt and pepper.

Place one slice of cheese in each cutlet. Then arrange 3 bowls or plates beside each other, putting the flour in one, the eggs beaten with the milk in the next, and the bread crumbs in the last. Coat each cutlet in flour, dip well in the egg mixture, then cover with bread crumbs.

When all the cutlets are breaded, heat a few tablespoons of vegetable oil on medium-high heat in a large frying pan. When quite hot, add the cutlets. Fry the pork until golden brown on both sides, then reduce the heat and cook for a few more minutes until done.

Serve the cutlets sprinkled with parsley and a wedge of lemon, and either boiled potatoes or rice, and a green or tomato salad.

SERVES 4.

Pork Cutlets Stuffed with Sauerkraut

Just about anything can be used to stuff pork chops, from the common cheese or ham, to bacon, smoked meat, and various vegetables such as peas or spinach. Fillings may be secured with a toothpick or tied with thread, or one may rely on the batter to seal in the ingredients. In this case, the stuffing is loosely applied. Don't worry about the sauerkraut spilling out since the chops are cooked in more of the same.

4 boneless center-cut pork chops
salt and freshly ground black pepper
2 strips bacon, sliced fine
1 medium onion, chopped
2 cups sauerkraut
½ cup white wine
vegetable oil for frying
1 teaspoon paprika

Trim off any excess fat from the chops then slice them lengthwise almost in half. Season well with salt and pepper.

Fry the sliced bacon until golden brown on medium-high heat , then lower the heat and add the onion. Cook for a few more minutes, until the onion begins to turn golden. Add half the sauerkraut and the white wine. Mix well and cook for a few minutes to reduce the liquid.

Stuff as much of the sauerkraut mixture into the cutlets as possible. Secure them with a toothpick if you wish. Heat a few tablespoons of oil in a frying pan on medium-high heat. When quite hot, add the chops and brown them on both sides. Then add the remaining sauerkraut and sprinkle on the paprika. Leave to cook on medium heat for 10 to 15 minutes.

Serve with boiled potatoes or dumplings.

SERVES 4.

Pork Chops with Mushrooms

Either fresh or dried mushrooms may be used with pork to good advantage, or you may combine both to maximize quantity and flavor. Wild mushrooms such as Boletus *or chanterelles are best.*

- 4 pork chops
- salt and freshly ground black pepper
- 2 tablespoons mustard
- 2 tablespoons lard or oil
- 1 medium onion, chopped
- ½ pound fresh mushrooms, sliced
- 2 tablespoons chopped fresh parsley
- 1 teaspoon marjoram
- 1 cup white wine

Trim off any excess fat from the chops and season them well with salt and pepper. Spread the mustard over both sides of the chops.

Heat the lard or oil in a large frying pan on medium-high heat. When quite hot, put in the chops and brown them quickly on both sides. Add the onion and mushrooms and cook for a few more minutes, stirring well, until the mushrooms are golden. Reduce the heat and add the parsley, marjoram, and white wine. Season with additional salt and pepper and cook for about 10 minutes, until the chops are cooked through and the liquid has thickened slightly.

Serve with boiled potatoes or rice and a salad.

SERVES 4.

Pork Chops with Mustard and Capers

Mustard sauces are lovely with pork, veal, or tongue, and capers are a natural accompaniment. White wine is the sensible choice for the sauce, though a meat stock or water will do fine.

4 pork chops
salt and freshly ground black pepper
2 tablespoons vegetable oil
1 medium onion, chopped
1 cup white wine
4 tablespoons Dijon mustard
1 tablespoon chopped fresh parsley
1 teaspoon marjoram
2 tablespoons capers

Trim off any excess fat from the chops and season well with salt and pepper. Heat the oil in a large frying pan on medium-high heat. When quite hot, put in the chops and brown quickly on both sides. Reduce the heat to medium and add the chopped onion. Cook for 3 to 4 minutes, stirring occasionally.

Pour the wine into the pan, then stir in the mustard. Add the parsley, marjoram, and capers. Season with additional salt and pepper. Cook, uncovered, for about 10 minutes, so that the meat is done and the sauce has thickened a little.

Serve with rice and a vegetable such as spinach or green beans.

SERVES 4.

Pork Paprikash

You may make this dish with either cubes or julienne ("noodles") of pork cut from chops or a larger piece of meat. The rich, sour cream–thickened sauce is even tastier made with white wine.

2 tablespoons flour
2 pounds pork, cubed or sliced
2 tablespoons lard or vegetable oil
1 medium onion, chopped
1 cup dry white wine
juice of ½ lemon
1 tablespoon paprika
1 tablespoon chopped fresh parsley
salt and freshly ground black pepper
1 cup sour cream

Sprinkle the flour on the cubed or julienne pork.

Heat the lard or oil in a frying pan on medium-high heat. When quite hot, add the pork and brown on all sides. Reduce the heat to medium-low and add the chopped onion. Fry for a couple of minutes, stirring occasionally. Pour on the white wine and enough water to just cover the meat. Add the lemon juice, paprika, parsley, and salt and pepper to taste. Bring to a simmer, partially cover the pan, and let cook for 20 minutes, stirring occasionally and adding a little water if necessary.

Once the pork is cooked, check the sauce for seasonings. Then stir in the sour cream and heat the sauce for a couple of minutes.

Serve with egg noodles, rice, or potatoes and a green vegetable or salad.

SERVES 4.

Pork and Pepper Goulash

Any cut of pork may be used for this paprika-flavored stew, including the most tender loin, though such a fine cut should be simmered quite briefly, a half an hour and not much more. Cheaper cuts are almost preferable as they are likely to have a little more fat mixed with their lean, thus reducing the chances of a dried out meat.

3 tablespoons vegetable oil or lard
2 pounds pork, cubed
1 large onion, chopped
2 cloves garlic, crushed
2 medium green peppers, chopped
1 large sweet red pepper, chopped
2 tablespoons paprika
2 tablespoons chopped fresh parsley
1 teaspoon dried marjoram
2 bay leaves
1 tablespoon tomato paste
salt and freshly ground black pepper
4 potatoes, peeled and chopped
2 tablespoons butter
2 tablespoons flour

Heat 6 cups water in a large pot over medium heat.

Heat the oil or lard in a large frying pan on medium-high heat. Trim any excess fat off the pieces of pork. Put enough pork in the frying pan as will fit without crowding; brown the pork all over, then put it in the pot with water. Once all the meat has been browned, turn the heat down under the frying pan and add the onion and the garlic. Cook for a few minutes, stirring occasionally, until the onion is slightly transparent and golden. Add the onion to the pork. Raise the heat under the frying pan to medium and add the chopped peppers. Fry the peppers for a couple of minutes until they begin to brown. Now add these to the pork.

Add the paprika, parsley, marjoram, bay leaves, and tomato paste to the goulash. Add salt and pepper to taste. Bring to a boil, partially cover, and simmer for 45 minutes or so. Add the potato pieces, partially cover the pot again, and let simmer.

Melt the butter on low heat in a small pan or pot. Add the flour and, stirring constantly, cook this roux for a few minutes, until it begins to turn a light to medium brown. Mix the roux into the goulash. Let simmer for 5 minutes. Check the seasonings in the stew and test the potatoes to see if they are done.

Serve simply with bread and a small green or cucumber salad, or with rice.

SERVES 6.

Pork Roast

A well prepared roast of pork rivals a roast beef or leg of lamb for flavor, texture, and presentation spectaculars. A rack of loin chops, for example, looks and tastes magnificent. Use such a cut here, if you wish, and reduce the roasting time somewhat. A simpler and more affordable roast will use a rolled loin or some other cut for a similarly good meal, though minus some extravagance. Leave some of the fat on the roast as pork tends to be very lean and can dry out when cooking. If you have it, the pork skin may be scored with a knife and then roasted to make crackling.

2 cloves garlic
2 strips bacon
1 (4-pound) rolled loin of pork
1 teaspoon dried marjoram
freshly ground black pepper
3 tablespoons olive or vegetable oil
1 cup dry white wine
2 tablespoons butter
2 tablespoons flour
salt
2 tablespoons chopped fresh parsley

Preheat the oven to 400°F.

Peel the garlic and cut it and the bacon into thin strips. Using a small paring knife, make a small incision in the pork and, using the knife, insert a piece of garlic and bacon into the slit. Continue to so lard the roast until you have evenly covered the meat. Rub marjoram into the meat and then do the same with some pepper. Put the meat in an oven dish slightly larger than the meat itself. Pour on the oil and ½ cup water. Place in the oven and turn the heat down to 350°F.

After 15 minutes, check the roast—shake the pan to make sure the meat is not sticking to the bottom and baste it with some of its juices. Add the white wine and return the roast to the oven. Baste the roast every 15 to 20 minutes, adding some water as is necessary. The roast should be done 1½ hours after you first put it in the oven, though if you do not want any pink in the meat, leave it for another 10 to 15 minutes.

When the roast is almost done, melt the butter in a small pot or pan on low heat. Add the flour, stirring constantly. Cook for about 5 minutes until the roux begins to brown. When the pork is done, put it on a serving platter. Using a soup spoon, skim off any excess fat from the cooking liquid. Pour the roasting juices and some water (or a light broth, if you have it) into the roux, stirring well. Add pepper and salt to taste; make sure the sauce is neither too thick nor too thin (add water to thin it, reduce it on higher heat to thicken it). Sprinkle with chopped parsley.

Serve slices of the roast pork with sauce, roast potatoes, or rice, and a green vegetable such as broccoli or Swiss chard.

SERVES 6.

Pork Roast with Dried Apricots

Pork takes on other flavors very well, including fruity ones that would be out of place elsewhere. I have made this roast with a variety of different fresh and dried fruits, including prunes, apricots, apples, and figs. Use what you have or what you have not had in a while, or marry the fruit with a brandy or liqueur at hand: prunes with slivovice *(plum brandy), or apricots with* merunkovice *(apricot brandy). If you do not have any fancy liqueurs, don't worry, just use white wine or plain water instead.*

1 cup whole, dried apricots
1 cup dry white wine
2 cloves garlic
1-inch piece fresh ginger
1 (4-pound) rolled loin of pork
1 teaspoon marjoram
freshly ground black pepper
3 tablespoons olive or vegetable oil
2 tablespoons chopped fresh parsley
½ cup apricot or grape brandy (optional)
2 tablespoons butter
2 tablespoons flour
salt

Preheat the oven to 400°F. Put the dried apricots in the white wine and let sit for 30 minutes.

Peel the garlic and ginger and cut both into fine strips. Using a small paring knife, cut a small slit in the pork and then, using the knife, slide a piece of garlic and a piece of ginger into the slit. Dot the meat with garlic and ginger all around. Rub the meat with marjoram and pepper. Put the pork in a roasting pan with enough room to hold the meat and the apricots. Pour on the oil and add ½ cup water to the pan. Put the meat in the oven and reduce the heat to 350°F.

After 15 minutes, check the roast: shake the pan to make sure the meat has not stuck to the bottom and baste the meat with its juices. Add the parsley, apricot-wine mixture, and brandy (if using) to the pan and return to the oven. Baste the meat every 15 to 20 minutes, adding water as is necessary. The meat should be done after a total 1½ to 2 hours of roasting.

Once the meat is cooked, remove it and the apricots to a serving platter and keep warm. Skim any excess fat from the cooking liquid. Melt the butter on low heat in a small pot and add the flour, stirring constantly. Once the roux begins to brown a little, add the cooking liquid and some water. Bring the sauce to a boil, cook for a minute or two, season with salt and pepper. Reduce the sauce by boiling it if too thin or add a little water if too thick.

Serve slices of pork with apricots and sauce, together with roast potatoes or rice, and greens, asparagus, or a salad.

SERVES 6.

Roast Pork with Red Cabbage and Dumplings

(*Vepřo-knedlo-zelo*)

This is one of the classic dishes of Czech cuisine and it deserves a place of pride among comfort food. The pork is roasted simply until it is well done, then served sliced, with its sauce adorning slices of bread dumplings and large helpings of silky stewed red cabbage. Have seconds, stagger away from the table before any dessert is served, and digest several glasses of slivovice *(plum brandy) or* Becherovka.

1 (4-pound) rolled loin of pork
freshly ground black pepper
3 tablespoons vegetable oil or lard
1 tablespoon dried marjoram
2 tablespoons caraway seeds
2 tablespoons chopped fresh parsley
salt
2 bread dumplings (see page 78)
1 recipe Cabbage Poached in Vinegar (see page 313)

Preheat the oven to 400°F.

Trim the pork of any excess fat. Rub some pepper into the meat. Heat the oil or lard on medium-high in a large frying pan. When the oil is hot, put in the meat and brown on all sides. Put the meat in a roasting pan. Sprinkle on the marjoram, caraway seeds, and parsley. Add 1 cup water. Put in the oven and roast for 1½ to 2 hours, basting every 15 to 20 minutes and adding water as necessary.

When the meat is done, remove it to a serving platter. Skim any excess fat from the pan juices and add salt and pepper to taste. Serve slices of the pork with sliced dumplings and a heap of red cabbage, all covered with pan juices.

SERVES 6.

Roast Pork Tenderloin with Wild Mushrooms

The tenderloin is the finest cut of pork but it has to be handled well to bring out its distinction: if you overcook it, it will be dry and taste worse than a cheaper, fattier cut. So cook tenderloin briefly and put enough fat with it to bring out the taste of the very lean meat. Tenderloin is an expensive cut, but because it is so rich, less feeds more. This roast uses juniper and wild mushrooms to add flavor to the meat. Use fresh chanterelles or milk mushrooms, if you can find them, or mix together fresh button mushrooms with some dried wild ones.

2 tablespoons olive or vegetable oil
2 pork tenderloins (1½ pounds or so)
1 small onion, finely chopped
2 cloves garlic, crushed
½ pound fresh chanterelles or red milk mushrooms, sliced
1 dozen juniper berries, crushed
1 teaspoon dried marjoram
2 tablespoons chopped fresh parsley
freshly ground black pepper
1 cup dry white wine
2 tablespoons butter
2 tablespoons flour
salt

Preheat the oven to 350°F.

Heat the oil in a large frying pan on medium-high heat. When hot, add the tenderloins and sear on all sides until golden brown. Remove the meat to a large roasting pan. Reduce the heat under the frying pan and add the chopped onion. Fry for a couple of minutes, stirring occasionally. Add the garlic and cook another couple of minutes. Add the onion and garlic to the meat.

Raise the heat under the frying pan to medium, add a little oil if necessary, and then put in enough sliced mushrooms to cover the pan without crowding it. Sear the mushrooms on one side, then flip them over and cook for another couple of minutes. Add the mushrooms to the meat; repeat the procedure with the remaining mushrooms.

Add the crushed juniper berries, marjoram, parsley, and some pepper to the meat. Pour on the white wine and put the meat in the oven. Roast for 45 minutes, basting once or twice and adding water if necessary.

When the roast is almost done, melt the butter in a small pot on low heat. Add the flour and cook, stirring, for 5 minutes or until the roux begins to turn golden.

Remove the meat from the oven and transfer it to a serving platter. Skim any excess fat from the pan juices. Add the juices, the mushrooms, and some water to the roux and bring to a boil. Check the seasonings for salt and additional pepper. If the sauce is too thick, add more water; if too thin, reduce it by boiling.

Serve half a tenderloin per person, smothered with mushrooms and sauce, with boiled or roasted potatoes, or rice. Carrots, green beans, or a tomato salad are also good accompaniments.

SERVES 4.

Braised Ham

Hams are often quite imposing in size and are good saved for special occasions or for when you need ham sandwiches for the week to follow. They are quite easy to make though you need to start off with a quality piece of meat. Avoid canned hams or heavily smoked ones. The best ham I've ever had I transported in the trunk of my car to Newfoundland from Virginia. It was a hefty Virginia cured ham as tender as any meat I've tasted. I had three in my trunk and they served as good ballast on the slippery roads of Cape Breton. Quality hams of this sort need little adornment, though care should be taken to reduce the salt used in curing. Slathering ham with pints of honey may disguise a tasteless or bad ham, but is not a great idea for a good one. Use flavorings like cloves or honey in moderation.

1 (6-pound) boneless ham
8 whole cloves
4 tablespoons chopped fresh parsley
freshly ground black pepper
½ cup Dijon mustard

Follow any instructions that come with your ham in terms of soaking it, etc. to reduce salt (not doing so may ruin your dish).

Preheat the oven to 375°F.

Place the ham in a large roasting pan. Put in the cloves and sprinkle on parsley and pepper, but no salt. Spread the mustard on top of the ham. Pour in 2 cups water. Cover the roasting pan with a lid or aluminum foil. Put in the oven and roast for 2 hours, basting every 20 minutes and adding water as is necessary. After 2 hours, remove the lid or foil and cook the ham, uncovered, for another hour, basting occasionally.

When the ham is done, put it on a serving platter. Skim any fat from the braising liquid, then reduce it on high heat to make a relatively thin sauce. Discard the cloves. Check the seasonings.

Serve thin slices of ham with sauce, roasted or boiled potatoes, mustard, and a beet salad or green vegetable.

SERVES 8.

Braised Ham with Cabbage

Either red or green cabbage may be used to good effect in this recipe. Slow cooking the ham and cabbage in the oven makes vegetable and meat most tender and infuses flavor from one to the other. This is a simple, hearty dish for mid-winter.

1 small (4- to 5-pound) ham
freshly ground black pepper
1 small head red or green cabbage
2 tablespoons caraway seeds
½ cup red or white wine vinegar

Follow any instructions that come with your ham concerning soaking or reducing its salt content (ignore at your own and your guests' peril).

Preheat the oven to 350°F. Rub the ham all over with pepper and place it in a large roasting pan.

Remove the outside leaves from the cabbage, core it, then slice it thinly. Add the cabbage to the ham. Add the caraway seeds and 1 cup water. Cover the pan with a lid or foil and put it in the oven. Braise the ham in the oven for about 2½ hours. Baste every 30 minutes or so, adding water as is necessary. Mix in the vinegar during the last basting.

Serve slices of ham with dollops of cabbage alongside boiled potatoes and cucumber salad.

SERVES 6.

Braised Smoked Pork with Celeriac

A large smoked pork hock will do well-cooked this way, though portioning the meat may take a little more trouble than, say, with smoked pork chops. The smoked flavor of the pork is imparted into the root vegetables through slow cooking.

2 tablespoons vegetable oil or lard
1 medium onion, chopped
1 large clove garlic, crushed
3 pounds smoked pork hock or chops
1 medium celeriac, washed, peeled, and cut into strips
1 teaspoon dried marjoram
2 bay leaves
2 tablespoons chopped fresh parsley
freshly ground black pepper
1 cup dry white wine

Preheat the oven to 375°F.

Heat the oil or lard on medium-low heat in a small frying pan. When hot, add the onion and garlic and fry for a few minutes, until the onion becomes somewhat transparent and golden. Remove from heat.

Put the smoked hock or chops in a medium-size roasting pan. Add the strips of celeriac, marjoram, bay leaves, parsley, and pepper to taste, but no salt. Pour on the wine and enough water to cover the vegetables. Cover the pan with a lid or foil, and put it in the oven. Braise the pork for 2 hours, basting every 30 minutes and adding water as necessary.

Serve slices of pork with celeriac and pan juices, together with roasted or boiled potatoes and a green salad.

SERVES 4.

8

Lamb and Game

Lamb and game are perhaps an odd pairing of meats. Many Czechs have a lingering aversion for the former that can be traced to memories of thick-tasting old mutton, whereas the profusion of game meats have always been highly prized. From commonly available rabbit, venison, and duck, to wild boar and hare, the tastes and textures are exceedingly varied as is the likelihood of your success in cooking them, depending on the quality of the meat. When good, game exemplifies the best of meat, with high flavor and dense texture, but when inferior in grade, the dry results may be inedible.

I leave mutton aside and hope that the subtle taste of delicately prepared young lamb will win over at least a few converts. Only a small selection of the many forms of game and accompanying recipes are given below. In part this is because many of these meats are difficult to come by unless you are a hunter or have lots of money and happen to live in a fortunate location. But another reason is that the occasional nature of such dishes suggests simplicity. Most of us will not, for example, eat venison more than three or four times a year. If this is so, then a profusion of recipes is unnecessary. What you want to do is to bring out the full flavor of the meat and for this, fancy preparations are not required. As long as you know the method and length of time to cook it, with a few ingredients that are choice accompaniments, a few recipes will go a long way.

Lamb Chops with Mushrooms

Choice cuts of lamb, like beef, should be cooked pink in the center, though when well-done they are still very tasty. As with many distinctive tasting meats, an uncomplicated recipe is usually the best. Rubbing chops with a bit of garlic and then quickly grilling them or frying them in butter or oil makes a lovely meal. Adding some mushrooms and wine to this creates a splendid supper.

6 to 8 lamb chops, trimmed
salt and freshly ground black pepper
2 tablespoons lard or vegetable oil
1 small onion, chopped
2 cloves garlic, crushed
1/3 pound fresh mushrooms, sliced
1 cup dry red wine
1 teaspoon marjoram
1 tablespoon chopped fresh parsley
2 tablespoons butter

Season the chops well with salt and pepper. Heat the lard or oil in a large frying pan on medium-high heat. When quite hot, put in the chops and sear them on both sides until golden brown. Remove the chops to a warm plate.

Reduce the heat to low, remove any excess fat, and add the onion and garlic. Fry, stirring occasionally, until almost golden. Raise the heat to medium and throw in the mushrooms. Fry for about 5 minutes or golden brown.

Put the chops back in the pan, pour on the red wine, and sprinkle on the marjoram and parsley. Season with additional salt and pepper. Cook for a couple of minutes, until the sauce has thickened a bit. Then whisk in the butter.

Serve 3 to 4 chops per person, covered with mushrooms and sauce, alongside rice or boiled potatoes and a simple vegetable, such as green beans, or a green salad.

SERVES 2.

Roast Leg of Lamb

A roast may feel like a daunting prospect to novice cooks but it is in fact one of the most simple and elegant ways to prepare meat. A whole or half leg of lamb needs very little apart from some garlic and an herb such as marjoram or rosemary to produce an impressive dish. You may want to add some wine, either red or white, to the roasting pan to add more flavor to the gravy.

1 whole leg of lamb, trimmed
2 to 3 cloves garlic, cut in slivers
1 sprig fresh rosemary
salt and freshly ground black pepper
1 cup dry red wine
3 tablespoons flour
2 tablespoons chopped fresh parsley

Preheat the oven to 350°F.

Once most of the fat has been trimmed from the lamb, take a small paring knife and make incisions into the meat, putting a sliver of garlic and a leaf of rosemary into each. Season the meat well with salt and pepper.

Put the leg of lamb in a roasting pan, pour on some water and red wine, and place in the oven. Roast, basting occasionally and adding water or wine as needed, until done to your liking, about 20 minutes per pound for medium or 25 minutes for medium-well.

When the roast is done, remove from the roasting pan to a serving platter. Skim off any excess fat from the sauce and pour it into a small pan on the stove. Add some more water or wine if needed. Bring to a low boil. Mix the flour well with some water and a little of the hot sauce, then whisk into the sauce. Cook for a couple of minutes. Season with additional salt and pepper and add the fresh parsley.

Carve slices of the roast at the table and serve with gravy, boiled potatoes, and spinach, green beans, or carrots.

SERVES 4 TO 6.

Lamb Braised with Onions

The lamb is browned and then braised in a good deal of onions, which eventually dissolve into a fragrant and flavorful sauce. With long cooking the meat becomes very tender and infused with the cooking juices. Though most suitable for a cut that needs extended cooking, making a leg in this manner would not be unwise.

3 pound lamb shoulder
2 tablespoons lard or vegetable oil
3 large onions, finely chopped
2 cloves garlic, crushed
2 tablespoons flour
2 cups dry white wine
2 bay leaves
4 cloves
1 teaspoon marjoram
2 tablespoons chopped fresh parsley
2 tablespoons mustard
1 lemon
salt and freshly ground black pepper

Preheat the oven to 350°F.

Trim any excess fat from the meat. If the shoulder is not already tied with string, do so.

Heat the lard or oil in a large casserole dish on medium-high heat. When quite hot, put in the lamb and brown well on all sides. Skim off any excess fat. Remove the meat from the pot.

Add the onions to the pot and lower the heat to medium low. Fry the onions, stirring occasionally, until almost golden. Add the garlic and fry another couple of minutes. Sprinkle on the flour and cook another couple of minutes.

Place the meat back in the pot. Pour on the wine and about 2 cups water. Add the bay leaves, cloves, marjoram, parsley, and mustard. Grate the peel of the lemon into the sauce and then squeeze in the juice.

Season well with salt and pepper. Cover and place in the oven. Cook for about 2½ hours, turning the meat over once or twice.

Once the lamb is tender, the onions should be fairly well dissolved and the sauce not runny; if not, you may mash the onions with a fork or potato masher and thicken the sauce with a bit of flour mixed in water.

Serve slices of lamb covered in sauce with dumplings or rice and carrots, green beans, or cauliflower.

SERVES 4.

Lamb Braised with Turnips

Sometimes size matters, and sometimes it doesn't. With turnips, an increase in size transforms a delicate and crisp vegetable into an overpowering and cloying one. So choose small white turnips instead of large, yellow ones if you can. Shoulder of lamb is also good for this treatment since it benefits from a longer cooking time, but use your discretion with what is available.

1 (3-pound) shoulder of lamb
2 tablespoons lard or vegetable oil
1 medium onion, chopped
2 tablespoons chopped fresh parsley
1 teaspoon marjoram
salt and freshly ground black pepper
2 medium carrots, diced
3 small white turnips, diced
1 lemon
3 tablespoons flour

Preheat the oven to 350°F.

Trim any excess fat from the meat and tie with string if not already done so. Heat the lard or oil in a large casserole dish on medium-high. When quite hot, put in the meat and brown well on all sides.

Turn the heat down to medium and add the onions. Fry until almost golden, stirring occasionally. Add water to half cover the lamb. Add the parsley and marjoram. Season well with salt and pepper. Cover and place in the oven. Braise, turning the meat over once, for 1 hour.

After 1 hour, add the carrots and turnips to the lamb. Grate the lemon peel into the sauce and then squeeze in the juice. Cover, and cook for another 1 to 1½ hours.

When the meat is done, put the casserole dish on top of the stove on medium-high heat. Remove the lamb. Mix the flour with some water, add some of the hot liquid from the dish, then mix the flour back into the sauce. Cook for a couple of minutes.

Serve slices of the lamb, covered with sauce, alongside vegetables and dumplings, rice, or mashed potatoes.

SERVES 4.

Lamb Goulash with Tomatoes and Peppers

Lamb is wonderful for stewing: long braising makes a rich and tasty broth in which the meat almost falls apart. This paprika and tomato–infused stew comes with large chunks of tender green peppers.

- 2 pounds cubed lamb
- freshly ground black pepper
- 2 tablespoons lard or vegetable oil
- 1 large onion, chopped
- 1 clove garlic, crushed
- 3 large green peppers, cubed
- 1½ tablespoons paprika
- 1 can (28 ounces) tomatoes
- ½ teaspoon marjoram
- 1 tablespoon chopped fresh parsley
- salt
- 2 tablespoons flour

Trim any fat off the lamb and season with pepper. Heat the lard or oil in a large pot on medium-high. When quite hot, add the lamb and brown on all sides.

Reduce the heat to medium and add the onions. Fry for a few minutes, stirring well. Add the crushed garlic and cook for another couple of minutes. Add the green peppers and cook for another couple of minutes. Sprinkle on the paprika and stir well.

Add the canned tomatoes and enough water to just cover the meat. Season with marjoram, parsley, salt, and additional pepper. Bring to a low boil, partially cover, and cook until the lamb is tender, about 1½ hours.

Mix the flour with a little water, then stir in some of the gravy from the stew; mix this thickener into the stew and boil for a few more minutes to cook the flour.

Serve with rice, dumplings, or potatoes and a green salad.

SERVES 4.

Lamb Stew with Potatoes

A classic and simple stew, this combination of lamb and potatoes satisfies the heartiest of appetites and is hard to beat, especially on a cold and rainy day. Add other root vegetables, such as carrots or parsnips, if you wish.

2 pounds cubed lamb
2 tablespoons lard or vegetable oil
2 medium onions, chopped
½ pound mushrooms, sliced
½ teaspoon marjoram
2 tablespoons chopped fresh parsley
salt and freshly ground black pepper
8 medium potatoes, quartered
2 tablespoons flour

Trim any excess fat from the lamb. Heat the lard or oil in a large pot on medium-high. When quite hot, add the lamb and brown on all sides. Add the onions and fry, stirring occasionally, until almost golden. Add the sliced mushrooms and fry a few minutes longer.

Pour on about 8 cups water, more than enough to cover the meat. Bring to a low boil, then reduce the heat to medium-low. Season with marjoram, parsley, and salt and pepper. Partially cover and let simmer until the lamb is tender, about 1½ hours.

Add the potatoes to the stew and some more water to cover, if needed. Bring back to a boil, then simmer until the potatoes are done, about 20 minutes.

Mix the flour with some water, then add some of the broth from the stew; mixing well, incorporate this thickener into the stew and cook for a couple more minutes.

Serve with bread or rice and a green salad.

SERVES 4 TO 6.

Lamb Stew with Beans

Lamb is good stewed with just about any vegetable. Try substituting green beans or celeriac for the white beans. Canned white beans are fine, but dried beans have a nicer texture and a more defined taste.

- 1 cup dried white beans
- 2 pounds cubed lamb
- 2 tablespoons lard or vegetable oil
- 2 strips bacon, diced
- 1 large onion, chopped
- 1 clove garlic, crushed
- 1 bay leaf
- ½ teaspoon allspice
- ½ teaspoon marjoram
- 2 tablespoons chopped fresh parsley
- salt and freshly ground black pepper
- 4 medium carrots, sliced
- 2 large potatoes, cubed
- 2 tablespoons butter
- 2 tablespoons flour

The day before you wish to serve this dish, soak the beans in plenty of cold water.

The next day, drain the beans, put them in a medium pot, and cover with cold water. Bring the water to a boil, reduce the heat, partially cover, and simmer until almost tender, about 45 minutes. Drain and reserve.

Trim any excess fat from the lamb. Heat the lard or oil in a large pot on medium-high. When quite hot, add the lamb and brown on all sides. Reduce the heat to medium. Add the bacon and fry until almost crisp. Drain off any excess fat. Add the onion and fry for about 5 minutes. Add the garlic and fry a couple more minutes.

Pour on about 8 cups water. Throw in the bay leaf. Season with allspice, marjoram, parsley, and salt and pepper. Bring to a low boil, reduce the heat, partially cover, and simmer until the lamb is tender, about 1½ hours.

Add the drained beans, carrots, and potatoes, bring back to a boil, and cook until done, about 30 minutes.

To thicken the stew, if needed, make a roux by melting the butter in a frying pan, mixing in the flour, and cooking for a couple of minutes. Add a little hot stew, then stir the roux into the stew and heat through.

Serve with bread, rice, or potatoes and a green salad.

SERVES 4 TO 6.

Lamb Braised with Spinach

Lamb and spinach are a natural combination, and adding sour cream makes for a rich and creamy dish.

2 pounds cubed lamb
½ cup flour
2 tablespoons lard or vegetable oil
1 large onion, chopped
2 cloves garlic, crushed
1 teaspoon marjoram
salt and freshly ground black pepper
1 pound fresh spinach
¾ cup sour cream

Trim any excess fat from the lamb, then cover with flour, shaking off any excess. Heat the lard or oil in a large pot on medium-high. When quite hot, add the meat and brown on all sides.

Reduce the heat to medium and add the onion and garlic. Fry for about 5 minutes, stirring occasionally.

Barely cover the meat with cold water. Season with marjoram, salt, and pepper. Bring to a low boil, cover, and simmer.

While the lamb is braising, wash the spinach well and drain. Then add the spinach to the lamb and continue cooking until the meat is tender, about 1½ hours.

To finish the dish, uncover the pot and keep cooking, on medium heat, until much of the liquid has evaporated. Check the seasonings, then mix in the sour cream and heat through.

Serve with dumplings, potatoes, or rice and a vegetable such as carrots or parsnips.

SERVES 4.

Rabbit with Mustard Sauce and Capers

Rabbit is a delicate meat that needs a sharp or piquant sauce for best effect. The combination of mustard and capers is ideal. Use a good quality, fairly strong Dijon mustard and plenty of white wine. If you are unaccustomed to rabbit, ask your butcher to portion it for you, as the joints are not exactly where you might expect them.

3 tablespoons lard or vegetable oil
1 rabbit, cut in portions
1 small onion, finely chopped
1 clove garlic, crushed
3 cups dry white wine
2 tablespoons chopped fresh parsley
1 teaspoon marjoram
3 tablespoons Dijon mustard
salt and freshly ground black pepper
2 tablespoons capers

Heat the lard or oil on medium-high in a large frying pan or casserole. When quite hot, put in as many of the rabbit pieces as will fit without crowding the pan and fry them until golden brown on all sides. Repeat with the remaining rabbit portions, then return all the meat to the pan.

Reduce the heat to medium and add the onion. Fry for a few minutes until translucent. Add the garlic and fry for another couple of minutes.

Pour in the white wine. Add the parsley, marjoram, and mustard. Season with salt and pepper. Add the capers. Bring to a low boil, partially cover, and simmer until done, about 45 minutes. If the sauce needs thickening, remove the cover and reduce on high until you reach the desired consistency.

Serve with dumplings, rice, or potatoes and either carrots, green beans, or a green salad.

SERVES 2 TO 4.

Rabbit Marinated in Vegetables

Like svíčková, *here the meat is marinated for at least a day in a mixture of root vegetables, spices, and vinegar. The mild tasting rabbit will take on a rich flavor and will be very tender. The marinade is then puréed and thickened with cream to make a sauce.*

1 rabbit, cut in portions
1 medium onion, chopped
2 cloves garlic, crushed
2 small parsnips, diced
2 medium carrots, diced
½ small celeriac, diced
2 medium leeks, sliced
juice and zest of 1 lemon
1 cup red wine vinegar
1 teaspoon thyme
2 bay leaves
8 black peppercorns
4 allspice berries or cloves
1 teaspoon marjoram
salt and freshly ground black pepper
2 strips bacon, diced
½ cup heavy cream
2 tablespoons chopped fresh parsley

A day before serving, put the rabbit parts in a large glass dish with a cover. Add all the ingredients except the bacon, heavy cream, and parsley. The liquid should half cover the meat; if more is needed, add a little water. Season with salt and pepper. Leave covered in the refrigerator to marinate for about 24 hours, turning the meat over once or twice.

To prepare the dish, remove the rabbit from the marinade and dry it with a cloth or paper towels. Reserve the marinade. Fry the bacon on medium-high heat in a large frying pan or casserole dish. When almost crisp, add as many of the rabbit portions as will fit in the pan without crowding it. Fry the rabbit until golden brown on all sides. If necessary, remove the browned portions and fry the remaining rabbit. Put all the pieces back in the pan and turn the heat down to medium. Strain the liquid from the vegetables and reserve. Add the vegetables to the rabbit and fry for about 10 minutes, stirring occasionally. Pour in the marinade liquid and bring to a low boil. Partially cover and simmer until done, about 45 minutes.

Remove the rabbit from the pan and keep warm in the oven. Purée the vegetables and liquid in a food processor or by using a masher. Return to the pan and mix in the heavy cream and the parsley. Check the seasonings for salt and pepper. Add a little sugar if the sauce is too sour. Place the rabbit back into the pan and bring to a low boil.

Serve the rabbit with dumplings, rice, or potatoes and a green salad.

SERVES 4.

Venison Medallions in Red Wine

Venison is rich in taste and may be prepared very simply or with fancy sauces, often featuring fruit or wine. For this dish, tender medallions are browned and then simmered in red wine. Venison should be served medium or medium-rare, but it is also good well-done.

1½ pounds venison tenderloin
freshly ground black pepper
2 tablespoons lard or vegetable oil
1 small onion, finely chopped
2 cloves garlic, crushed
1 cup dry red wine
1 tablespoon chopped fresh parsley
2 tablespoons butter
salt

Slice the venison into medallions about ¾ inch thick and rub them with pepper. Heat the lard or oil in a frying pan on medium-high. When quite hot, add the medallions and fry them until golden brown on both sides.

Reduce the heat to medium and add the onion and garlic. Fry for a couple of minutes. Add the red wine and raise the heat to high. Boil quickly to reduce the sauce by about half. Add the parsley and whisk in the butter. Season with salt and more pepper.

Serve with potatoes and either peas, green beans, or a green salad.

SERVES 4.

Venison with Apples

Venison goes perfectly with sweet and sour flavors. Cooking it with fruit, such as apples, is a naturally good idea. You can also try this recipe with cherries or cranberries instead of apples.

- 1 (2- to 3-pound) venison roast
- 2 strips bacon, sliced
- 1 small onion, chopped
- ¼ celeriac, diced
- 2 cups dry red wine
- ¼ cup red wine vinegar
- 4 cloves
- 1 teaspoon thyme
- 2 bay leaves
- salt and freshly ground black pepper
- 4 sour apples, peeled, cored, and sliced ½ inch thick
- ¼ cup brandy

A few hours or a day before cooking, lard the roast with the slices of bacon by making incisions into the meat with a small paring knife and stuffing in the bacon. Leave covered in the fridge.

Preheat the oven to 400°F.

Put the venison in a medium roasting pan. Add the onion and celeriac. Pour on the red wine and the vinegar. Add the cloves, thyme, and bay leaves. Season with salt and pepper. Place in the oven and roast for 15 minutes. Baste the meat with the cooking liquid and reduce the heat to 350°F. Cook for another 15 minutes.

Add the apples and brandy to the pan, baste the meat, and roast until done, another 30 minutes for medium-rare, or 45 minutes for medium.

When the meat is done, remove it and the apples to a platter, then reduce the sauce on high heat on top of the stove until it is thickened slightly.

Serve with potatoes or rice and either green beans or a green salad.

SERVES 4.

Hare with Leeks and Mushrooms in Pastry

Z*ajic (hare) is hard to find these days in Europe, though it is all over the island of Newfoundland where I now live. The Arctic or Snowshoe hare found here is not identical to the European variety but quite a close match. Though similar in looks to rabbit, hare is much more of a typical game meat: darker with a rich flavor (whereas rabbit is lighter and more akin to chicken). The following dish is my favorite for this animal. In St. John's it now goes by the name* Lièvre en Feiulleté à la Bradley, *after a dinner party on Strawberry Marsh Road where it was created. This dish is best if started a day prior to serving so the meat has time to marinate and the broth to develop a rich taste, but it may all be done in three hours. The recipe for puff pastry is modified from Dione Lucas's* French Cooking.

- 1 brace/couple of hare
- 2 bay leaves
- whole black peppercorns
- 1 medium onion, finely chopped
- 3 cloves garlic, crushed
- 4 medium leeks, finely sliced
- 12 juniper berries, crushed
- 2 tablespoons chopped fresh parsley
- 1 teaspoon dried thyme
- 1 cup dry red wine
- ¼ cup balsamic or red wine vinegar
- 6 tablespoons olive or vegetable oil
- salt and freshly ground black pepper
- ½ pound mushrooms, sliced
- 1½ cups (3 sticks) plus 3 tablespoons salted butter
- 2 cups plus 3 tablespoons flour
- 2 egg whites
- 2 tablespoons milk

Debone the hare meat. Put the bones in a large pot, cover with water, add bay leaves and some peppercorns; bring to a boil and simmer, uncovered, for 1 to 2 hours to make a broth. (You may add other things to the broth if you wish, e.g., an onion, a couple of carrots, another piece of meat, etc., but this is not necessary.) Skim any scum from the surface of the broth. When the broth has finished cooking, discard the bones and other ingredients; strain and reserve the liquid.

While the broth is cooking, cut the meat into bite-size chunks and put into a container, preferably glass. Add the chopped onion, garlic, leeks, juniper berries, parsley, thyme, red wine, balsamic or wine vinegar, 2 tablespoons oil, and salt and pepper to taste. Mix all the ingredients together, cover the container, and put in the refrigerator to marinate (from 1 to 2 hours or overnight if possible). Baste the meat once or twice as it marinates.

Once you have finished marinating the meat and making the broth, you are ready to make the filling for the pastries. Drain the marinade from the meat and reserve. Separate the meat from the vegetables and other ingredients.

Heat 2 tablespoons of oil in a large frying pan on medium-high heat. When the oil is hot, put as much meat as will fit without crowding into the pan. Brown the meat all over, remove to a bowl, and repeat with the remainder of the meat. Add a little oil to the frying pan if needed, and fry the onion and leek mixture until it wilts and begins to turn transparent; mix the vegetables in with the meat. Add the remaining 2 tablespoons oil to the pan and add the sliced mushrooms; fry these until golden brown then mix in with the meat. To make the sauce for the meat, put the reserved marinade into a small pot together with 1 to 2 cups of the meat broth. Bring this liquid to a gentle boil.

Meanwhile, melt 3 tablespoons of the butter in another pot on low heat, then add 3 tablespoons flour; cook this roux for a few minutes, stirring constantly, until it begins to turn golden brown. Mix in 3 cups of the broth-marinade and bring to a boil, stirring while you do so. Check the sauce for seasonings, and let it simmer until it is just thick enough to coat the back of a spoon. Pour enough of the sauce on the meat mixture to wet all the ingredients. Save the rest of the sauce for serving with the pastries.

To make the puff pastry, mix together 2 cups flour with 1 teaspoon salt in a large bowl. Pour on ¾ cup very cold water and work this into the flour quickly until it forms a dough. Roll out the dough into a 12-inch square. Knead 1½ cups butter with your hands until it is a little soft and pliable. Shape the butter into a 4-inch square. Put the butter in the center of the dough, wrap the dough around it, wrap in a towel, and refrigerate for 30 minutes. On a floured board, roll out the dough to about a ¼-inch thickness; fold the two outside thirds or leaves of the dough into the center. Now roll the dough out again and fold it in thirds again. Wrap the dough in a cloth and refrigerate for another 30 minutes. Repeat the double rolling and folding operation two more times, so that the dough has been rolled and folded a minimum of six times.

Roll out your puff pastry until it is ¼ inch thick. Cut out 3-inch squares of pastry. Take a square of pastry and put in its center 3 to 4 tablespoons of the hare mixture. The pastries may be folded in different ways but perhaps the easiest is to bring the four corners of the square up to a central point, then crimp them and the sides together. Use a fork to make a tight and secure edge along the seams of the pastry. Fill and form all the pastries this way.

Preheat the oven to 350°F. Whisk together the egg whites and milk. Butter a large baking sheet and dust it with a little flour. Put the pastries on the sheet with an inch or two separating each. Brush them all over with the egg white mixture. Put in the oven and bake for 45 minutes or golden brown on top (you may need to broil them for a few minutes at the end to get the proper color, but watch them closely if you do this so they do not burn). When the pastries are almost done, heat up the remaining sauce.

Put a pastry per plate on top of its sauce, with asparagus and rice.

SERVES 6.

Hare Paprikash

I follow the previous rather fancy and time-consuming recipe for hare with a far simpler one where the taste of the meat is the heart of the dish. The hare may be left on the bone, in which case the meat is cooked longer, but some parts of the animal are quite fiddly, so I prefer de-boning it. Use a high quality hot or mild paprika; generic red powder will not do much to the taste of the cream or the meat.

4 tablespoons oil or lard
1 brace/couple of hare, deboned and cubed
1 medium onion, chopped
2 cloves garlic, sliced
2 tablespoons flour
1 teaspoon dried marjoram
2 tablespoons paprika
salt and freshly ground black pepper
1 to 2 cups beef broth or water
1 cup heavy cream
1 lemon, sliced
2 tablespoons chopped fresh parsley

Heat 2 tablespoons oil or lard in a large frying pan on medium-high. When quite hot, add as much of the cubed hare as will fit without crowding the pan. Brown the meat all over, remove to a bowl, and repeat with the remaining meat. When all the meat has been browned, reduce the heat to medium-low and add a little more oil if needed. Add the onion and garlic and cook for 3 to 4 minutes, stirring occasionally, until the onion begins to turn golden. Stir in the flour and cook for another few minutes. Return the meat to the pan, then sprinkle on the marjoram, paprika, and salt and pepper to taste. Stir in enough broth to cover the meat and bring to a gentle boil; partially cover the pan and let simmer for 45 minutes, stirring occasionally.

Check the meat for tenderness and the sauce for seasonings. If both are satisfactory or have been fixed (by a little more cooking or salt and pepper), stir the cream into the sauce and gently heat it through; do not boil vigorously.

Serve the hare paprikash on top of rice or egg noodles, with a slice of lemon and sprinkled with parsley. Accompany the paprikash with a cucumber or green salad and a vegetable such as carrots, green beans, or broccoli.

SERVES 4 TO 6.

Roast Caribou with Sour Berries

(*Dančy*)

*Caribou or reindeer is found in great herds in Newfoundland and makes for excellent game meat. The flesh is similar to venison (*srnčy*), though not quite as spectacularly tender. Unlike moose, however, caribou may be cooked very simply and for short periods. Steaks are very good, for example, and may be made like beef. This roast is made with local partridgeberries, which are very similar to cranberries and hence more sour than sweet. The berries may be fresh, frozen, or dried (if the latter, soak them in a little hot water or wine before adding to the roast.)*

1 (3- to 4-pound) caribou roast
2 cloves garlic
2 strips bacon
1 medium onion, finely chopped
1 teaspoon dried thyme
1 teaspoon dried marjoram
2 tablespoons chopped fresh parsley
salt and freshly ground black pepper
1 cup dry red wine
2 tablespoons olive or vegetable oil
1 cup partridgeberries or cranberries

Preheat the oven to 400°F.

Trim any excess fat from the roast. Peel the garlic cloves and slice them into slivers. Slice the bacon into thin strips. Using a small paring knife, cut a small incision into the roast, then use the knife to poke a sliver of garlic and a strip of bacon into the incision; lard the whole roast this way.

Put the meat into a roasting pan large enough to leave some room on all sides. Add the onion, thyme, marjoram, parsley, and salt and pepper to taste. Pour the wine and oil on top of the meat. Put the roast in the oven. After 15 to 20 minutes, baste the meat with its cooking liquid and add the berries to the pan; reduce the oven temperature to 350°F and return the meat to the oven. Continue to roast the meat, basting occasionally and adding water as necessary, for a little more than an hour, depending on the size of the roast and how rare you like the meat. Skim any excess fat from the sauce prior to serving.

Serves slices of the caribou covered with sauce, together with roasted potatoes and carrots.

SERVES 6.

Stuffed Moose Birds

The largest land animal found in Newfoundland is referred to here and elsewhere in Canada as moose, though in Europe it is known as elk. The meat is often considered tough, but as with most things, this depends on what you do with it. The following recipe uses a couple of different methods to tenderize the meat (slicing, pounding, slow cooking) and the result is fine and tender. The simple way to make moose most tender is to slice up your meat, trim it, pound it a little with a meat mallet, stuff each slice with something good, roll it up, secure it with a toothpick, brown it, and then stew it. Here's one more detailed and complex variation of this method, devised for my daughter Alexandra. Czechs call this dish "ptačky" because they look like little birds.

3 to 4 pounds moose
salt and freshly ground black pepper
4 strips bacon
2 onions, chopped
2 cloves garlic, chopped
2 stalks celery, sliced fine
⅓ cup pine nuts (or other chopped nuts)
4 slices white or brown bread
⅓ cup raisins
½ cup milk
1 bunch fresh parsley
oil
1 teaspoon dried oregano
2 teaspoons juniper berries, crushed
2 tablespoons butter
2 tablespoons flour
1 to 2 cups red wine (2 cups make a richer sauce)

Slice up the moose meat into small steaks, about ½ inch thick. Trim off any fat. Pound each steak lightly with a meat mallet until it is about half as thick. Season with salt and pepper.

Chop the bacon fine, then fry it in a large pan until almost crisp. Add half the chopped onion and half the chopped garlic clove and fry for a couple of minutes. Add the celery and fry another 2 minutes. Add the nuts and fry another 2 minutes. Take off the heat.

Soak the bread and raisins in the milk for 5 minutes. Break the bread up into bits. Mix the bread and raisins into the onions and bacon. Add 2 tablespoons of chopped parsley, and additional salt and pepper.

Take a piece of moose, put a tablespoon or so of stuffing on it, roll it up, and secure with a toothpick. Stuff all the moose this way.

Heat some oil on medium heat in a large frying pan. Put as many moose rolls in the pan as will fit comfortably and brown them gently all over. When browned, put moose rolls in a casserole dish. Add the oregano, crushed juniper berries, salt, pepper, and a couple of tablespoons of chopped parsley. Preheat the oven to 375°F.

Fry the remaining onion and garlic, and the butter, in the same frying pan you used for the meat. Add the flour and fry another 2 minutes. Pour in the red wine and cook, stirring, for 2 minutes. Pour onto the moose rolls. Add enough water to barely cover the meat. Put the casserole in the oven and bake for about 1 hour.

Serve moose with roasted or mashed potatoes and greens.

SERVES 6.

Breast of Grouse with Apricots

Grouse is a common woodland bird and its meat is similar to chicken. The breast is really the only edible part of the bird, but it is quite substantial for the size of the creature. Larding and marinating the meat, preferably overnight, helps to break up its rather dense texture. Similar treatment of partridge (krepelky) *and pheasant* (bažant) *does very well. As with much game, avoid drying out the meat while cooking and do not skimp on the fat, as the leanness of game needs some addition of fat for tenderness and flavor.*

1 brace/couple of grouse
2 strips bacon, sliced
2 garlic cloves, crushed
1 medium onion, finely chopped
1 cup dry white wine
juice of 1 lemon
1 teaspoon dried marjoram
2 tablespoons chopped fresh parsley
1 cup dried apricots
6 tablespoons olive or vegetable oil

Remove the breasts of each bird; save the carcass for a broth or soup. Using a small paring knife, make an incision into the meat and poke a slice of bacon into it; lard the breasts in this way throughout. Put the meat in a dish, preferably glass, and add all the other ingredients except for 3 tablespoons of the oil. Cover the dish and put in the fridge to marinate for 1 to 2 hours or overnight, if possible, basting once or twice.

When ready to cook the grouse, preheat the oven to 375°F.

Remove the grouse from the marinade. Heat remaining 3 tablespoons oil in a large frying pan on medium-high heat. When the oil is hot, put in the grouse and brown on both sides. Remove the meat to a baking dish, pour on the marinade, together with the apricots, and put in the oven. Roast, basting occasionally, for 1 hour.

Serve with rice and green beans or a salad.

SERVES 4.

9

Vegetables and Dumplings

The title of this chapter should probably be "Things Czechs Serve with Meat" and the contents should consist mostly of descriptions of various kinds of dumplings, with perhaps a footnote on vegetables. Indeed, there are so many different kinds of dumplings used in Czech cooking that it would be hard to provide an exhaustive account of them, and so I shall not even try to do so here. I grew up eating one basic dumpling, made primarily with flour and bread, and my penchant for it has lead me to ignore most other types. Still, variety is important, and so you will find a few different dumpling types at the end of this chapter, including the other main kind—the potato dumpling.

Czech dumplings are unique in that they come in largish loaves, about the size of a small bread, and are sliced before serving. Making dumplings is an art in itself, but slicing them also requires skill. A properly made dumpling should be light and fluffy and the slicing method should not cancel out this desired end. Using a knife is thus a no-no. A knife will most likely compress the dumpling and misshape it. Instead, use a long piece of thread, wrap it around the dumpling, and pull both ends tight. This method will yield perfect rounds without any loss in fluffiness. Learning how to use thread quickly and evenly takes some practice, but not too much.

In addition to savory, sliced dumplings, Czechs also use all sorts of small dumplings in soups and fill small, sweet dumplings with fruit for dessert (see the chapters on "Soups" and "Sweets"). This is not the end of it—pasta-like dough is also filled to make small, savory dumplings, similar to Polish pierogi or Italian ravioli. Various fillings may be used, such as seasoned ground meat or farmer cheese, and such dumplings make a wonderful meal all on their own.

As for vegetables, potatoes certainly top the list and there is almost as much profusion in potato recipes as there is in ones for dumplings. Some of these may be an acquired taste. Take, for example, *škubánky*, basically a mixture of mashed potatoes, flour, and some type of flavoring such as poppy seeds or cheese. This dish is quite heavy and, if you do not associate it with childhood comfort food, might seem rather odd.

Many other types of vegetables are used to accompany main dishes, especially root vegetables like carrots, parsnips, celeriac, and kohlrabi. These may simply be boiled or made into fancier dishes. Vegetables are often coated with egg and flour, sometimes bread crumbs, and fried; or they are stuffed and grilled or baked. Many of these dishes serve equally well as starters to a meal. What follows is not meant to be a complete inventory of what Czechs do with vegetables, since many of the simple preparations really do not require recipes and are common to many cuisines; instead, the point is to indicate a few of the methods by which vegetables are prepared so that you can adapt these to your own needs.

Poached Celery

We start with an incredibly simple, and some might think bland, preparation of the stalks of the celery plant, a part of the vegetable which receives much less attention in the Czech Republic than the root. Celery, to the cultured palate, is far from bland. The differences between an inferior, bitter plant and a tender and sweet, more white than green prize sample are enormous. Celery has, in fact, a pronounced flavor that may dominate a dish if too much of it is used. Poaching it keeps it mild and allows you to concentrate on the simplicity of the plant's flavor. If you can find choice white celery or come across a good batch of the green stuff, try this as is, or fancy it up by broiling the stalks with some grated cheese, such as Gruyère. The method used here would work equally well with kohlrabi, cauliflower, or leeks.

1 bunch fine celery stalks
2 tablespoons butter
1 cup dry white wine
salt and freshly ground black pepper
1 tablespoon chopped fresh parsley

Clean the celery well and trim off the tough bottoms and leafy parts from each stalk. Cut each stalk in half.

Bring a good deal of salted water to a boil. Put in the celery and parboil for about 5 minutes. Remove.

Melt the butter on medium heat in a large frying pan. Add the celery and fry gently for 1 to 2 minutes. Pour on the white wine and bring to a boil. Reduce the heat. Season with salt and pepper. Simmer, uncovered, for 5 minutes or until tender. Drain and serve sprinkled with parsley.

SERVES 6.

Stuffed Zucchini

Small zucchini are the best, being most tender, though larger ones do well in this recipe since they hold more stuffing and are baked. Zucchini may be prepared very simply, say, by cutting them into thin strips and frying them in butter or olive oil and lemon juice. Stuffing vegetables with a mixture of bread crumbs, onions, and some tastier ingredients like cheese, turns a common food into a fancy dish. This way of preparing zucchini may easily be used to cook celery (after parboiling), small eggplants, tomatoes, and so on.

4 medium zucchini
1 tablespoon butter or olive oil
1 medium onion, finely chopped
1 clove garlic, crushed
½ cup bread crumbs
½ cup grated cheese, such as Parmesan or Gruyère
2 tablespoons chopped fresh parsley
salt and freshly ground black pepper

Wash the zucchini, then cut them in half lengthwise. Do not trim the ends but leave them as you find them. Using a teaspoon, remove most of the insides of the vegetable, taking care not to break the skin. Finely chop the insides and reserve.

Preheat the oven to 400°F.

Heat the butter on medium in a frying pan. Add the onion and garlic and fry, stirring occasionally, until almost golden. Take off the heat. Mix in the zucchini insides, bread crumbs, ¼ cup of the cheese, and the parsley. Season with salt and pepper. Mix well.

Lay the zucchini halves on a baking tray. Fill each of them with some of the stuffing. Cover them with the remaining ¼ cup cheese. Put in the oven and bake for 15 to 20 minutes.

SERVES 4 TO 6.

Fried Tomatoes

All kinds of vegetables may be coated in batter, fried, and served as an appetizer or with a main dish. You may coat the vegetables in flour and then dip them in egg, or make a batter with flour. Large, thick slices of green or red tomatoes take to this treatment well. Try this recipe using cauliflower, zucchini, or onion.

1 whole egg
½ cup milk
⅔ cup flour
3 large, unripe tomatoes
3 tablespoons vegetable oil (or more if needed)
2 tablespoons chopped fresh parsley
1 lemon, cut into wedges

To make the batter, break the egg into a bowl and mix in the milk. Slowly add the flour, mixing well, until you have a fairly thick batter.

Preheat the oven to 200°F.

Cut the tomatoes into thick slices. Heat vegetable oil in a large frying pan on medium heat. When quite hot, dip a tomato slice in the batter, then place in the frying pan. Continue doing this until the pan is fairly full, but not crowded. Fry the tomatoes until lightly golden on both sides, about 7 to 8 minutes altogether. Remove and keep warm in the oven. Repeat this procedure, adding more oil if necessary, until all the tomatoes are fried. Serve sprinkled with parsley and with wedges of lemon.

SERVES 4.

Creamed Spinach

Perhaps the tastiest of greens, spinach is a versatile vegetable that may be used in soup and stuffings or on its own, either steamed or creamed. Spinach shrinks a whole lot when cooked, so make sure you buy a good deal so there is enough to go around.

- 1 pound fresh spinach
- 2 tablespoons butter or olive oil
- 1 small onion, finely chopped
- salt and freshly ground black pepper
- ½ teaspoon grated nutmeg
- ½ cup heavy cream
- 1 lemon, cut in wedges

Clean the spinach well and tear off the large stalks. Put in a large pot, cover, and place on low heat (the water left on the leaves will be sufficient for steaming the spinach). As soon as the leaves begin to wilt, give the spinach a good stir, cover again, and leave for another minute or so to cook.

Drain the spinach and squeeze out all the excess liquid. Chop it roughly.

In a frying pan, heat the butter on medium-low heat. Add the onion and fry until almost golden. Add the spinach, mix well, and cook for 1 to 2 minutes. Season with salt, pepper, and nutmeg. Pour on the cream, mix well, and cook for another 1 to 2 minutes. Serve with lemon wedges.

SERVES 4.

Cabbage Poached in Vinegar

Either red or green cabbage may be made this way. The secret to the dish is to cook the cabbage very slowly and not skimp on the butter or vinegar. Mixing fresh cabbage with some sauerkraut also works well.

4 tablespoons (½ stick) butter
1 medium onion, finely sliced
½ head red cabbage
⅔ cup red wine vinegar
1 tablespoon caraway seeds, crushed
salt and freshly ground black pepper

Melt 2 tablespoons butter in a large pot on medium-low heat. Add the sliced onion and fry, stirring occasionally, until almost golden.

Shred the cabbage as finely as possible, then add to the pot. Mix well, and cook for 2 minutes. Sprinkle on the crushed caraway seeds. Season with salt and pepper.

Cover the pot and reduce the heat to low. Cook, stirring occasionally, until tender but not mushy, about 30 minutes. Add the vinegar. About 10 minutes before serving, mix in the remaining 2 tablespoons butter.

SERVES 6.

Scrambled Vegetables

(Lečo)

A meal unto itself, any combination of vegetables may be prepared this way, though tomatoes and peppers should always be included. Slices of sausage may be also be added, but are not necessary.

- 2 tablespoons butter or vegetable oil
- 1 medium onion, finely sliced
- 2 medium leeks, sliced
- 2 medium green peppers, thickly sliced
- 4 medium tomatoes, thickly sliced
- 3 whole eggs
- 2 tablespoons chopped fresh parsley
- 1 teaspoon marjoram
- salt and freshly ground black pepper

Heat the butter or oil on medium-low in a large frying pan. Add the onion and fry, stirring occasionally, until almost golden. Add the leeks and fry for 2 more minutes.

Raise the heat to medium and add the green peppers. Fry, stirring occasionally, for 4 to 5 minutes. Add the tomatoes, mix well, and cook for another 4 to 5 minutes.

In a small bowl, beat the eggs with a fork. Mix the eggs into the vegetables and, stirring well, cook until done, 3 to 4 minutes. Mix in the parsley and marjoram. Season with salt and pepper. Serve with a good bread.

SERVES 4.

Beans with Tomatoes

Beans are a tasty and filling meal on their own and also go well with all types of meat dishes. This is especially true in the winter months when good quality fresh vegetables may be scarce. Beans are often prepared with smoked ham but do not need meat to be flavorful. Tomatoes are added here for taste and for color.

2 cups dried white beans
½ teaspoon baking soda (optional)
2 bay leaves
2 cloves
2 tablespoons lard or vegetable oil
1 medium onion, chopped fine
2 cloves garlic, crushed
2 large tomatoes, diced
2 tablespoons chopped fresh parsley
½ teaspoon thyme
salt and freshly ground black pepper

The day before serving, put the dried beans in a good deal of water to soak (add baking soda if you have it—it helps to tenderize the beans).

The next day, drain the beans and put them in a large pot. Cover them with plenty of water. Add the bay leaves and cloves. Bring to a boil, reduce the heat to medium-low, partially cover, and let simmer until done, about 1 hour.

Drain the beans, reserving 1 cup of the cooking liquid. Discard the bay leaves and cloves.

Heat the lard or oil in a frying pan on medium-low. Add the onions and the garlic and fry, stirring occasionally, until almost golden. Add the tomatoes, mix well, and cook for 3 to 4 minutes.

Combine the tomato-onion mixture with the beans. Add the cup of reserved cooking liquid, the parsley, and the thyme. Season well with salt and pepper. Heat through on medium for about 10 minutes.

SERVES 6.

Beans with Sauerkraut

The mild taste of beans goes well with sauerkraut for a filling side dish to accompany a roast or stewed meat. The smoked ham adds excellent flavor but may be omitted to accommodate vegetarians.

- 2 cups dried white beans
- ½ teaspoon baking soda (optional)
- ½ pound smoked ham
- 2 bay leaves
- 2 tablespoons lard or vegetable oil
- 1 medium onion, finely chopped
- 2 cups sauerkraut
- salt and freshly ground black pepper
- ½ cup sour cream
- 1 clove garlic, crushed

The day before serving, soak the beans in plenty of water with the baking soda, if you have it (it helps to tenderize the beans).

The next day, drain the beans and place in a large pot. Add a good deal of water to more than cover the beans. Add the smoked ham, in one piece, and the bay leaves. Bring to a boil, reduce the heat, partially cover, and simmer until done, about 1 hour.

When the beans are done, drain off their liquid and discard the bay leaves. Remove the ham, dice it, then return to the beans.

In a small frying pan, heat the lard or oil on medium-low. Add the onion and fry, stirring occasionally, until almost golden.

Mix the onion into the beans. Add the sauerkraut and season with salt and pepper. Put on medium heat and cook for about 10 minutes. Just before serving, stir in the sour cream and garlic.

SERVES 4 TO 6.

Sour Lentils

Lentils are easy to make, requiring no presoaking like beans, and taste very good. This simple recipe combines lentils with onion, thyme, and vinegar. Serve this dish with a roast or stewed meat.

2 cups lentils
2 bay leaves
salt
2 tablespoons butter or lard
1 medium onion, chopped
1 clove garlic, crushed
½ teaspoon thyme
½ cup red wine vinegar
freshly ground black pepper

Put the lentils in a pot and cover them with water. Add the bay leaves and a little salt. Bring to a boil on the stove, partially cover, reduce the heat and simmer until done, about 1 hour. Stir the lentils occasionally and add some water if necessary.

When the lentils are tender, heat the butter or lard in a small frying pan on medium-low. Add the onion and garlic and fry, stirring occasionally, until almost golden.

Add the onion, garlic, thyme, and vinegar to the lentils. Season with additional salt and pepper. Boil, uncovered, until fairly thick, about 10 minutes.

SERVES 6.

Potatoes with Bacon and Onions

It is hard to go for a day without potatoes in a Czech home, but this in no way implies monotony—there are so many different recipes for them that one would not have to eat the same dish for quite a while. The simplest way to prepare potatoes is to boil them with salt and caraway seeds and serve them with plenty of butter. Potatoes may be served as a meal in themselves, with some farmer cheese added for flavor, for example. Just about anything goes well with potatoes, though bacon and onions are ideal companions. Finally, a note of warning: Czechs are prodigious potato eaters, often consuming mass quantities of the tubers that would defeat the ordinary individual, so take this into account when preparing your meal.

8 large potatoes
salt
3 strips bacon, sliced
2 medium onions, sliced
2 tablespoons chopped fresh parsley
1 teaspoon paprika
freshly ground black pepper

Peel the potatoes and cut into quarters. Place them in a large pot with a good deal of water and add salt to taste. Bring to a boil, cover, reduce heat, and cook until tender, about 15 to 20 minutes.

Meanwhile, fry the bacon on medium heat until well-done but not crisp. Add the onions and fry until almost golden, stirring occasionally.

Drain the potatoes. Add the onions and bacon. Sprinkle on the parsley and paprika and season with additional salt and pepper.

SERVES 4 TO 6.

Sour Potatoes

Potatoes take almost all kinds of flavorings well, so try different herbs and spices with them. Parsley, caraway, and paprika are common favorites. Dill, especially when combined with sour cream, is also excellent.

8 large potatoes
salt
2 tablespoons butter or lard
2 tablespoons flour
1 cup milk
½ cup white wine vinegar
½ cup sour cream
2 tablespoons chopped fresh dill
freshly ground black pepper

Boil the whole, unpeeled potatoes in a good deal of salted water until tender, about 30 minutes.

Meanwhile, prepare your sauce. Melt the butter or lard in a frying pan on medium heat. Stir in the flour and cook for 2 minutes. Pour in the milk while stirring constantly. Reduce the heat and let boil for 1 to 2 minutes. Mix in the vinegar, sour cream, and dill. Season with additional salt and pepper.

Peel the potatoes and slice them thickly. Coat with the sauce and serve.

SERVES 4 TO 6.

Potatoes Baked with Cabbage

Potatoes and cabbage are two winter staples that happen to go together very well. Onions, bacon, and caraway seeds supply the additional zest, though the meat can be omitted if so desired. This dish is also very good with grated cheese.

- ½ head green cabbage
- 8 medium potatoes
- salt
- 4 strips bacon, sliced
- 1 medium onion, chopped
- 1 tablespoon caraway seeds, crushed
- ½ cup white wine vinegar
- freshly ground black pepper

Shred the cabbage as finely as you can. Put the potatoes, whole and with their peels on, in a large pot of salted water and bring to a boil; cook until tender, about 20 minutes.

Meanwhile, heat a large pot on medium heat, then throw in the bacon and fry until well done but not crisp. Add the onion and keep frying, stirring occasionally, until almost golden. Add the cabbage, mix well, and let cook for 2 to 3 minutes. Add the caraway seeds and additional salt and pepper. Cover and let cook about 20 minutes. Add the vinegar.

Preheat the oven to 400°F. When the potatoes are done, peel them and then cut them into thick slices.

Take an oven dish and place a layer of cabbage in the bottom, then some of the sliced potatoes, then some more cabbage, and so on until all the vegetables are used up. Place in the oven and bake for 30 minutes.

SERVES 4 TO 6.

Potato Mush

(Škubánky)

If you like potatoes a lot, you may like this dish, though it's probably a gamble for anyone not raised on it as a child. All sorts of toppings may be added to the basic recipe, though poppy seeds and cheese are the most common.

- 8 medium potatoes
- salt
- 1 cup flour
- 4 tablespoons lard or butter (½ stick)
- freshly ground black pepper
- ½ pound farmer cheese
- 2 tablespoons chopped fresh parsley

Peel and quarter the potatoes, then place in a large pot of salted water. Bring to a boil and let cook until tender, about 15 minutes.

When the potatoes are done, drain them, reserving ½ cup of the cooking liquid. Mash the potatoes well. Mix in the flour, pouring in some of the reserved cooking liquid as needed if the potatoes thicken too much. Mix in the lard or butter. Season with additional salt and pepper. Cook, uncovered, for 5 minutes on medium heat.

Serve with large dollops of farmer cheese, more butter, and parsley sprinkled on top.

SERVES 4.

Bread Dumplings
(Houskové Knedlíky)

These dumplings are a traditional part of Czech cooking and, if made well, are one of the most delicious ways to soak up sauce. Flour and cubed bread are combined to make large, loaf-like dumplings, which are then boiled and sliced with a thread. The lightness of the dumplings in part depends on the type of flour that is used. A rougher rather than a smoother flour is desired. If you can get it, "Wondra" brand is a good bet. Otherwise, mix together equal quantities of regular white flour and semolina.

3 cups white flour
3 cups semolina
1 teaspoon baking powder
1 whole egg
½ cup milk or so
1 teaspoon salt plus more for boiling
½ loaf French bread, cubed

Mix the flour, semolina, and baking powder together in a large bowl. Make a well in the center and break in the egg. Mix in some of the milk and 1 teaspoon salt, and then start mixing in the flour. Work the dough quite hard with a wooden spoon, adding a little more milk if necessary, until bubbles begin to form (about 10 minutes). Add some of the cubed bread and keep mixing. Keep adding bread until the dough is fairly saturated with it.

Plop the dough out onto a floured board or table. Divide the dough up into 4 pieces. Shape the pieces of dough into loaves by rolling them with your hands.

Bring a large pot of salted water to a rapid boil. Put in 2 of the dumplings and let cook for 12 minutes, then flip them over and cook for 13 minutes.

Remove the dumplings from the water and place on a cutting board. Take a long piece of sewing thread, slide it under one of the dumplings about ½ inch, then wrap it around the top of the dumpling and pull tight. You should have an even cut and a tender slice of dumpling. Continue cutting this way, placing the sliced dumplings in a covered serving bowl to keep warm.

SERVES 6.

Potato Dumplings

The closest approximation I can think of to these dumplings are Italian gnocchi, though in huge proportions. The principle is the same: mashed potatoes mixed with a little flour, bound, then boiled.

6 medium potatoes
salt
½ cup flour
2 eggs

Peel the potatoes, cut into quarters, and then boil until tender in a large pot of salted water, about 15 minutes. Drain off the liquid then mash the potatoes. Sprinkle on the flour and additional salt and mix well. Break in the eggs and mix well. Turn the mixture out onto a floured board or table and shape the dough into 2 or 3 large loaves.

Bring a large pot of salted water to a rapid boil, then put in the dumplings and cook, partially covered, until tender, about 20 minutes. Slice as described in the previous recipe (Bread Dumplings).

SERVES 6.

Stuffed Dumplings

(Varenĺky)

These are so good you'll make them over and over again, sometimes stuffing the dumplings with seasoned, ground meat, at other times with farmer cheese. Serve these hot, with melted butter and lemon wedges.

- 2 tablespoons vegetable oil
- 1 medium onion, finely chopped
- 1 pound ground beef
- 2 tablespoons chopped fresh parsley
- ½ teaspoon marjoram
- salt and freshly ground black pepper
- 1 cup flour
- 1 cup semolina
- ⅛ teaspoon baking powder
- 1 whole egg
- ½ cup milk or so
- 8 tablespoons (1 stick) butter, melted
- 2 lemons, cut into wedges

To make the stuffing, heat the oil in a frying pan on medium heat. Add the onion and fry, stirring occasionally, until almost golden. Add the ground beef and continue frying until it is browned. Take off the heat. Mix in the parsley and marjoram and season with salt and pepper.

To make the dough, mix together the flour, semolina, and baking powder in a large bowl. Add some salt to taste. Make a well in the center and break in the egg. Add some of the milk. Begin to mix in the flour gradually. Continue working in the flour, adding more milk if needed, until you have a thick dough.

Turn the dough out onto a floured board or table. Knead the dough for a couple of minutes, then roll it out with a pin fairly thin (about ⅛ inch). Cut the dough into 2-inch squares.

Put a heaped tablespoon of stuffing onto each square of dough, fold the dumplings in half across the diagonal, and seal the sides tight by pinching the dough together.

Bring a large pot of salted water to a rapid boil on high heat. Put in as many of the dumplings as will fit comfortably. Boil until tender, about 5 minutes or when all the dumplings have risen to the surface. Drain, put in a covered dish with a little butter, and serve with melted butter and lemon wedges.

SERVES 4 TO 6.

10

Mushrooms

For many people a mushroom is a mushroom: a small, smooth, white champignon. For others, mushrooms do not go with food at all, for these people seek hallucinogenic varieties. Between unimaginative homogeneity and abandon and encompassing both limits, lies a vast array of edible, inedible, poisonous, and even deadly wild fungi. The varieties and pleasures of spores may be little known to anyone who has not spent much time in the woods or does not happen to live in an epicurean city. Most grocers and supermarkets carried only champignon until quite recently, though now it is possible to find shiitake, portobello, and a few other kinds, without too much trouble. The woods still hold the greatest treasures, unless you are willing to pay an arm and a leg for chanterelles or porcinis. But beware, for the woods may also cost you your life if you do not know what you are picking and happen across the wrong cap.

My memories of mushrooms go back to the early years of my childhood, not to Czechoslovakia, where my family lived in the capital city of Praha and which we left when I was four, but to the woods of Kent, in southeast England, where I would walk with my mother, searching for *hřibky*, better known by the Italian name *porcini* or the Latin *Boletus edulis*. I do not remember eating them so much as looking for and stumbling across them, or picking huge baskets with my friends only to have them all thrown out by my mother when we got home because they were not the right kind, and for discovering huge caps, more than half a foot across, but not worth picking because they were riddled with rot or bugs. Walking through the woods with an eye out for something seems to bring great joy.

Like many Czechs, my mother would fry up slices of the mushrooms with scrambled eggs. Just as mushrooms are of one kind for some, so, for others, there is only one way of making wild mushrooms. The variety of colors, textures, flavors, and favorable accompaniments of wild mushrooms is truly vast, however, and an entire cuisine could be constructed around them.

As an adult I gave wild mushrooms little thought until I arrived in Newfoundland a few years ago. Living mostly in large cities I had lost the habit of walking the woods. I would use dried porcinis in soups and sauces but the fresh ones were usually beyond my price range, if they could be found at all. I would marvel occasionally at the mounds of wild mushrooms in the photographs of French and Italian cookbooks. Upon ordering a dish with wild mushrooms in a restaurant, I'd sort through the tiny chopped up ingredients searching for something I could recognize.

One day at Memorial University of Newfoundland, where I now work, I ventured to the Linguistics department to speak to Vit Bubenik, a Czech professor, who handed me a basket filled with *Boletus edulis*, chanterelles, and milk mushrooms. I ran back to the Philosophy department like a child with a prize. That day marked my ascent from combing beaches for rocks to scouring the woods for food, though I still fill my house with rocks and collect seaweed and driftwood washed up on the shores.

The rain, mild temperatures, and clean air of Newfoundland make for wondrous mushroom conditions and numerous wild varieties grow here, but mushrooms may be found in many kinds of woods all over the world. If you have never picked them, find someone reliable who has and consult a book, since the enterprise is dangerous. If picking is not for you, there are several varieties of wild mushrooms available dried and fresh, at good grocers and supermarkets, for the preparation of which the following advice and recipes should be useful. The following are but some tips for the complex and hazardous process of finding, identifying, cutting, carrying, cleaning, tearing, cooking, drying, and pickling these delicious spores.

Mushrooms are the surface-visible explosions of large swaths of underground spores. They come to the surface depending on type of spore and time of year, degree of temperature and moisture, and some magic. Their underground existence is a clue in their pursuit. Though there will always be variations in above-ground conditions that induce spores to surface, and though underground spores shift place through growth and atrophy, mushrooms are outgrowths of larger and deeper bodies and so are bound closely to their place. Shortly and sweetly, mushrooms come back.

Nor do mushrooms run away quickly. Once you have found a good place, it is likely mushrooms will return year after year. It is important to find a good place and perhaps keep it secret. Hunting for mushrooms is a craze in Europe. To succeed you ought to rise early, shake any followers, park or disembark your vehicle far away from where you intend to go, concentrate on generations of accumulated family wisdom, and pray for luck. In many places in North America, by contrast, mushrooms are shunned or kicked about for fun or simply ignored, making picking far easier. In Newfoundland, for example, a few locals and a handful of ex-Europeans search the hills and valleys, rarely coming across each other, and fearing little competition. Having found pounds upon pounds of your prize you may meet another kind of difficulty, however: few who are willing to eat them with you, out of ignorance or fear more often than dislike.

Finding mushrooms is a tricky and sometimes time-consuming endeavor, though also a highly pleasurable one. Some mushrooms grow all year-round, though not too many are found in winter and most congregate in the summer months. I am still a cautious picker, limiting myself to four or five varieties, due to a combination of inexperience, taste, and the limits of what grows in my extended backyard. I would search out truffles and morels if they grew here, but they do not seem to. I limit my discussion here to large brown-capped *Boletus edulis*, which may be cut into thick strips and fried or grilled like steaks; orange crinolined chanterelles; and the rather ugly looking orange and green red milk mushrooms aptly named *Lactarius deliciosus*.

Each kind of mushroom has a particular time of year, depending on weather conditions, in which it sprouts and particular types of places which are conducive to its growth. Chanterelles come out in late spring and last through mid-summer, *Boletus* are found all summer long, and

Lactarius deliciosus emerge in late summer and early fall. Mushrooms like wet and woody conditions, though some like clearings in woods, others the shores of streams or the fringes of woods. Trial and error and a good deal of practice, some luck, and a good guide are the best ways to get a sense of where and when to look. Sometimes mushrooms simply surprise you. I spent one long, peculiarly unfruitful day wandering through the woods with my daughter around my parents' house in the country, finding very little, only to come across a huge patch of red milk mushrooms under a spruce tree beside their house.

I find wandering for mushrooms a great way to enjoy the woods and run away from work, but it may also be precarious. I have yet to run across moose or bear but I have gotten lost, and with no sun, stars, moon, or highway noise to guide you, being in thick woods may quickly turn from fun to fright.

Identifying the right mushrooms to pick is more precarious still. The varieties which I seek are relatively easy to distinguish from foul-tasting similarities and have no exceedingly dangerous close resemblers. The color of the caps and stems, the structure of the underside of the cap, and the reaction of the flesh to a knife are all useful indications of what you might have found. A bitter taste on the tongue is a bad sign, but with some mushrooms you should not even go this far as they may be highly toxic in small quantities (cooking may reduce some toxicity in some mushrooms but leaves others just as vile or deadly as they are when raw); prior tastes from slugs and worms are often a good sign, but not invariably so (what is fine for a slug may not be so for you and some may not wish to go where a slug has been).

After finding your mushrooms, a few tips about collecting them and preparing them for cooking: First of all, you should always carry a small knife and basket with you when hunting. The knife is for cutting the mushroom at the base of its stem, to minimize the amount of dirt you pick up and to leave spores in the ground for the next growth. A basket holds mushrooms relatively stable, thus avoiding bruising and crushing, and also allows spores to drop on the ground as you walk, spreading their growth through the forest. In a pinch, I've found a sheet of newspaper works well if I've come unprepared or have found too much; avoid plastic bags or containers since they don't allow the mushrooms to breathe and build up moisture damaging to the meat.

Once you have your mushrooms at home, keep them in a cool, dark place. Clean them with a brush, scraping off any dirt on the stem with a paring knife. Clean assiduously, but do not wash mushrooms, since they soak up water and become mushy. But clean carefully, since nothing is more likely to spoil a meal than the crunch of grit. On holiday once in the south of France I bought mushrooms from a grocer, not realizing they were wild; without paying attention to their stalks, I folded them into a beautiful looking but unfortunately inedible omelette. Dried mushrooms should be checked for dirt and grit also since cleaning mushrooms is a painstaking and laborious process, which some may skip, but only if they are not to be doing the eating.

One more thing before we get to the cooking. A sharp knife is useful for cutting mushrooms from the ground and for turning them into even slices, but such should not be the destiny of all fungi. The cut of a knife produces an even slice precisely because the knife pays no attention to the structure of the flesh that is its object: mushroom, vegetable, or meat, a sharp knife cuts across any grain. Sometimes this is exactly what you want. Respecting the grain of the object may be better at other times and for some particular objects. If the grain of meaty flesh, vegetable, or mushroom has not been cut, juice is more likely to stay within the morsel. I have been tearing meat, vegetables, and mushrooms when possible to very good effect. Chanterelles benefit from such treatment for making fresh dishes but also, and especially, for drying.

Cooking mushrooms is the easy part. You can almost not go wrong if your mushrooms are good ones, and a little effort turns out spectacular results. What is it about mushrooms that fascinates people? Is it just the experience of finding one's own food, with a dash of peril and a sprinkle of exotica? No. The experience of foraging makes sense only when linked with the anticipation of a seared mushroom steak, redolent with garlic and lemon, or a plate of baby chanterelles dotted with parsley.

It is hard to pick out a basic mushroom taste to explain the appeal of fungi, though their texture and the way they soak up other flavors may be close to the mark. The abhorrence with which some people view mushrooms is some evidence to show that it is not just a slightly peculiar flavor that is at stake but the very feeling of the object on the tongue. And the same exact experience but with the opposite value may explain their great attraction. The texture of mushrooms together with their echo effect, their ability to take on and accentuate other flavors, is a major part of their culinary appeal.

Fresh wild mushrooms of all kinds may be made very simply or used in the most elaborate concoctions. If you like simple pleasures and especially if you have not tried a kind of mushroom before, slice it, heat a pan fairly hot with some butter or olive oil, sear the mushroom slices on both sides, add a little garlic and a sprinkle of lemon or vinegar, lightly salt and season with freshly ground black pepper, and eat. Some bread and a glass of red wine make fine accompaniment. Mushrooms are also excellent mixed with eggs, roasted alongside meat, chopped up into sauces and soups, formed into tarts, and so on. There are literally endless uses, though some types clearly benefit from one or another.

Meaty and juicy mushrooms that come in large sizes, like *Boletus*, are better on their own, flash fried, while red milk mushrooms require meat or vinegar to bring out their flavor. I provide a few simple recipes below that feature the taste of the mushroom with little adornment, but there are more complex recipes requiring wild mushrooms throughout the book, especially among soups, stews, and roasts. I would rarely if ever put mushrooms with fish or seafood, and I have yet to make mushrooms into dessert.

A few remarks about preserving mushrooms for future use, that is, drying, pickling, and freezing. If you are lucky, there will be times when you have too many mushrooms to eat. Last summer I picked a literal trunkload of chanterelles in the space of one afternoon. What to do now? Eat as many as you can and feed your friends, but that only goes so far. I find pickling some mushrooms very good and drying also works very well. Freezing is fine, but I find it changes the texture of the flesh.

Small, firm mushrooms are ideal for pickling. Simply flash fry the mushrooms then marinate them in a liquid high in citrus or vinegar, and they will keep for a few months and improve with age. Baby chanterelles and red milk mushrooms are both excellent pickled, but I find larger chanterelles do better dried. There is an opinion widely held that *Boletus* are excellent for drying, as indeed they are: evenly sliced caps and stems, alternating dark brown and cream colors like the black and tan of dried food. There is an opinion equally widely held that chanterelles do nowhere near as well desiccated and that they are prone to rot. I wish to dispel this rumor. Old, water-logged chanterelles will dry to look rotten because they are half rotten to begin with. Fresh chanterelles which are sliced thickly and dried insufficiently may also turn to rot more so than *Boletus* and other types. Fresh chanterelles that are torn into thin strips and dried until brittle, however, keep for over a year in glass, airtight containers. For the purpose of drying, buy a food dessicator or put the mushrooms on cloth on aluminum foil sheets and dry in a warm oven, door ajar, for a few hours, turning the mushrooms occasionally.

Fried *Boletus* Mushrooms
(*Hřibky*)

Boletus edulis *are the best of the family, though many other types are quite tasty too and only the* Satanus *(a reddish stem and underside) is to be avoided. These types of mushrooms may be as small as a large thumb but are usually bigger, sometimes up to half a foot or more in the diameter of the cap. The spongy, beige or greenish underside of the cap is cut off by some people but I would never do so; its texture is different from and less firm than the white stem and upper cap, but equally intoxicating. Prior to cooking, clean the mushrooms well with a dry cloth, scraping any dirt off the base of the stem.*

1 pound fresh *Boletus* mushrooms
3 to 4 tablespoons butter or olive oil
1 clove garlic, crushed
2 tablespoons chopped fresh parsley
2 tablespoons balsamic or red wine vinegar
salt and freshly ground black pepper

Slice the cap and stems of the mushrooms quite thickly (¼ inch).

Heat half the oil or butter in a large frying pan on medium-high. When hot, add half the mushrooms or so, making sure not to crowd the pan. Sear the mushrooms on one side for 2 minutes or so, then turn over and do the same. Remove the mushrooms to a plate, add the remainder of the mushrooms to the pan, and repeat.

Reduce the heat to medium low. Add the garlic, parsley, and vinegar to the pan, then mix in the fried mushrooms. Sprinkle on salt and pepper.

Serve as an appetizer with slices of good bread (baguette or rye loaf).

SERVES 4.

Fried Chanterelles
(Ližky)

Chanterelles, on the whole quite smaller than Boletus, *grow in packs or patches rather than alone. They are unmistakable (almost) due to their bright yellow-orange color and flower-like shape. The smaller, button-like mushrooms are preferable, though the older, large chanterelles, which can reach five inches or so in diameter, are not to be frowned upon, unless they are waterlogged and have begun to rot. Like all mushrooms, a high heat sears in their juice and flavor, rather than letting it flow out into a watery sauce.*

½ pound fresh chanterelles, cleaned
2 tablespoons butter or olive oil
1 clove garlic, crushed
1 tablespoon chopped fresh parsley
2 tablespoons lemon juice
salt and freshly ground black pepper
4 slices good toast, crust removed

Keep the small chanterelles whole and tear the larger ones in halves or quarters, with your fingers, starting at the top of the mushroom.

Heat the butter or oil on medium-high in a large frying pan. When hot, throw in the mushrooms (if all will not fit in comfortably, fry them in two batches). Sear them on one side for 2 minutes, then turn them over. Add the garlic, parsley, lemon juice, and salt and pepper to taste. Cook for another minute or so, then serve on top of toast slices with a glass of good red wine.

SERVES 4 AS AN APPETIZER.

Breaded *Boletus* Mushrooms

The simple frying of mushrooms may be varied in many ways, using lard instead of butter, or basil instead of parsley, etc. Frying breaded, large, thick slices of boletus *transforms the dish altogether. These may be served as a hefty appetizer or as a light lunch or supper.*

- 1 pound fresh *Boletus* mushrooms, cleaned
- ½ cup flour
- 2 eggs
- 2 tablespoons milk
- 1 cup dry bread crumbs
- oil
- 2 tablespoons chopped fresh parsley
- 1 lemon, quartered

Preheat the oven to 200°F.

Slice the mushroom caps and stems into ⅓-inch-thick slices.

Put the flour on a plate. In a bowl, whisk together the eggs and milk. On another plate, sprinkle the bread crumbs.

Take a mushroom slice, coat it with flour, dip it in egg, then cover it with bread crumbs. Repeat this procedure until all the mushroom slices are breaded.

Heat some oil in a large frying pan on medium. When quite hot, put in as many mushrooms as will fit without crowding the pan. Fry on one side until golden brown (2 to 3 minutes). Turn them over and fry until golden. Remove the mushrooms and keep them warm in the oven. Fry all the mushrooms as above.

Arrange the mushrooms on plates, sprinkle on parsley and add lemon quarters. Serve with good wine and bread.

SERVES 4 AS AN APPETIZER OR 2 FOR LUNCH OR DINNER.

Grilled Mushrooms

Any wild or domestic mushrooms will be good made this way, including Boletus, *chanterelles, portobello, shiitake, and champignon. Use the broiler in your oven or a grill. The cayenne in this recipe makes for a spicy dish, but leaving it out does no harm.*

1 pound mushrooms, cleaned
2 cloves garlic, crushed
2 tablespoons balsamic or red wine vinegar
4 tablespoons olive oil
1 tablespoon chopped fresh parsley
1 tablespoon chopped fresh basil
½ teaspoon cayenne pepper
salt and freshly ground black pepper

Preheat your broiler or grill.

Keep small mushrooms whole, halve the medium-size ones, and slice the big ones. Put the mushrooms in a bowl and add all the other ingredients. Mix well and let sit for 15 minutes.

Put the mushrooms on the grill on medium-high heat. Cook until golden on one side, then turn them over, wetting them with a little of the marinade. Once they are golden on both sides, serve with bread or as a side dish with a main course.

SERVES 4.

Wild Mushrooms Scrambled with Eggs

Just about any mushroom may be made this way. The combination of eggs and mushrooms is the classic, and in some cases, inescapable, combination in Czech kitchens. This dish should be made quickly rather than letting the ingredients stew and let out their juice. Serve eggs and mushrooms for a fancy breakfast or a simple lunch or supper dish.

- 2 tablespoons butter
- ⅓ pound fresh wild mushrooms, cleaned and sliced or torn
- 6 large eggs, whisked together
- 1 tablespoon chopped fresh parsley
- salt and freshly ground black pepper

Heat the butter in a large frying pan on medium-high. When the butter is sizzling, throw in the mushrooms and fry, stirring occasionally, for 2 to 3 minutes. Pour in the whisked eggs and mix together well with the mushrooms. Sprinkle on the parsley. Cook, stirring frequently, until the eggs are just set, 2 to 3 minutes. Serve with salt, pepper, and good toast or bread.

SERVES 4.

Roast Beef with Red Milk Mushrooms

The proposition that mushrooms, like sponges, soak up flavors very well is eminently true of the Lactarius deliciosus *or red milk mushroom. These usually rather small mushrooms have a motley, orange and green appearance but on the inside, depending on their freshness, they carry a deep red vein, similar to blood oranges. They are tasty on their own but develop true flavor when combined with vinegar and meat, especially a red meat like beef.*

1 (4-pound) sirloin tip of beef (or other suitable cut)
freshly ground black pepper
3 tablespoons oil
1 medium onion, finely chopped
2 cloves garlic, crushed
½ pound red milk mushrooms, or other wild or domestic kind, cleaned and sliced
2 tablespoons chopped fresh parsley
1 teaspoon marjoram
2 cups dry red wine
⅓ cup red wine vinegar
salt

Preheat the oven to 400°F.

Trim the beef of any excess fat, then cover it with pepper. Heat the oil in a large frying pan on high. When hot, sear the meat quickly on all sides, then remove it from the pan.

Put the meat in a large roasting pan. Add the onion, garlic, mushrooms, parsley, marjoram, 1 cup of wine, the vinegar, and salt to taste. Put the meat in the oven. After 15 minutes, baste the meat, add the remaining1 cup wine, and reduce the heat to 375°F. Roast the meat for a further hour or so, depending on how you like it done (1½ hours for well done), basting every 20 minutes and adding water as necessary.

Serve slices of beef adorned with plenty of mushrooms and juice, with roast potatoes and green beans or steamed cauliflower.

SERVES 6.

Beef Goulash with Fresh and Dried Mushrooms

Dried wild mushrooms, either Boletus *or chanterelles, are very good mixed with ordinary fresh champignons and add flavor to the latter. Make sure the dried mushrooms are clean (run water through them if you are not sure and feel the bottoms of the stems). Soak the dried mushrooms in hot water for about 15 minutes before chopping them and put the mushroom liquid, strained of any grit, in the stew.*

- 1 cup dry red wine
- ¼ cup red wine vinegar
- 2 bay leaves
- 1 to 2 ounces dried *Boletus* or chanterelles
- 2½ pounds stewing beef, cubed
- 4 tablespoons vegetable oil or lard
- 2 medium onions, chopped
- 2 cloves garlic, crushed
- ½ pound fresh mushrooms, sliced
- 1 teaspoon marjoram
- 2 tablespoons chopped fresh parsley
- 1 tablespoon paprika
- salt and freshly ground black pepper
- 2 medium potatoes, cubed
- 2 tablespoons butter
- 2 tablespoons flour

Put the wine, vinegar, 4 cups water, and the bay leaves to simmer in a large pot. Soak the dried mushrooms in a cup of hot water for 15 minutes. Remove any dirt from the mushrooms, then chop them roughly; strain and save the soaking liquid.

Trim any excess fat from the beef. Heat 2 tablespoons of oil or lard in a large frying pan on medium-high. When hot, add enough meat to cover the pan; brown on both sides, then transfer it to the wine mixture. Repeat with the remaining beef.

Reduce the heat to medium low, add a little more oil or lard, and add the onions and garlic; fry for a few minutes, then add this to the beef. Raise the heat to high, add the remaining oil or lard, then throw in the sliced fresh mushrooms. Fry for a couple of minutes and then add to the goulash. Add the marjoram, parsley, paprika, chopped mushrooms and salt and pepper to taste. Bring to a boil, partially cover, and let simmer for 1 hour. Add the potatoes and simmer, uncovered, until done (20 minutes).

Melt the butter in a small pan on low heat, then add the flour and, stirring constantly, cook for 5 minutes or so. Add a little of the hot goulash, then mix this roux into the goulash and let it boil for a couple of minutes. Check the seasonings for salt and pepper.

Serve with bread or rice and a salad.

SERVES 6.

Rice with Dried Mushrooms
(Kuba)

Kuba may be made with barley or rice, though I prefer the latter. This is a good dish for when there is nothing fresh in the house, when one is making do with dried goods or when you feel like something simple. Any dried mushrooms work, including Boletus *or chanterelles. The kuba may be finished on top of the stove or in the oven.*

⅔ cup dried wild mushrooms
2 tablespoons oil or lard
1 large onion, chopped fine
2 cloves garlic, crushed
1½ cups rice or barley
1 tablespoon caraway seeds, crushed
1 teaspoon marjoram
salt and freshly ground black pepper

Preheat the oven to 350°F.

Boil a little water and pour it on the mushrooms; let soak for 15 minutes. Drain the mushrooms, reserving the liquid, and then chop them fine.

Heat the oil or lard in a large, preferably ovenproof frying pan on medium. Add the chopped onion and the garlic and fry for 2 to 3 minutes, stirring occasionally. Add the rice or barley and cook for another couple of minutes, stirring constantly. Add the mushrooms, caraway seeds, marjoram, and salt and pepper to taste. Mix well. (If not using an ovenproof pan, transfer the rice mixture into an oven dish.) Pour on 3 cups water, and the mushroom liquid. Mix well. Cover the pan and set in the oven. Leave to cook 30 minutes or so.

A tomato or cucumber salad will accompany well.

SERVES 4.

Pickled Mushrooms

Any mushrooms, including the standard champignon, may be pickled to good effect, though the smaller, fresher kind are better. Lactarius deliciosus *or red milk mushrooms, are best made this way and the smaller chanterelles are excellent too. The herbs and spices in the recipe may be varied, of course; try cardamom, for example. Pickled mushrooms are better a few days after you have made them and will keep in an airtight jar in the fridge for a few months. I had the pleasure of serving pickled* Lactarius deliciosus *and champignon to Michel Serres, the great French philosopher and thinker of nature and communication. Spending two days with Serres in St. John's and preparing supper for him are, truth to tell, the reasons for the slight delay in the delivery of this manuscript to my publisher.*

3 tablespoons olive or vegetable oil
1 pound small, whole wild or domestic mushrooms, cleaned
1 small onion, finely chopped
2 cloves garlic
2 tablespoons chopped fresh parsley
1 teaspoon dried marjoram
1 tablespoon caraway seeds
salt and freshly ground black pepper
1 teaspoon hot pepper flakes (optional)
1½ cups white wine vinegar

Heat 1½ tablespoons of the oil on high in a large frying pan. When hot, add half the mushrooms and brown them quickly. Remove the mushrooms to a bowl and repeat with the remaining mushrooms.

Add the onion, whole garlic cloves, parsley, marjoram, caraway, and salt and pepper to taste. Add hot pepper flakes if using. Mix well.

Once the mushroom mixture has cooled, put it in a large glass jar with a lid. Pour on enough vinegar to cover the mushrooms, put on the lid, and let marinate in the refrigerator for a few days.

Serve with good bread as an appetizer.

SERVES 4 TO 6.

11

Sweets

A whole book could be written on the subject of Czech desserts, cookies, and cakes. As with many European countries, much attention is given to sweets in the Czech Republic and there are many fancy concoctions to be had. This chapter will barely do justice to all that could be said. I hope merely to outline some of the common, delicious ways of finishing a meal by presenting a few favorites.

Many Czech desserts are quite rich, featuring lots of cream, sugar, and eggs, but this is not invariably true. Fruit is used extensively, to fill cakes or dumplings, decorate tarts, make into fritters, or bake with a stuffing or sauce. Plums, strawberries, or apricots are wrapped in dough, boiled, and served with sugar, melted butter, and farmer cheese. Fruit dumplings are so good and are one of the very few desserts I know that may be turned into a meal in itself—try eating four or five and see if you're still hungry! All different types of strudels are made: a light, delicate pastry holding apples and raisins, or farmer cheese with some sugar, or a thick, poppy seed paste, for example. Fruit and fruit jam are used to sweeten *palačinky*, the Czech version of pancakes or crepes, and are baked into bubble cakes, plum cake being the most famous and delectable of these. Dried plums or prunes are turned into a paste and used to stuff *koblihy* (doughnuts) or other kinds of small cakes.

Layer cakes are common, as are Czech versions of coffeecake called *bábovka*. These also come in many varieties, though the marble effect is probably the best: a swirl of chocolate and vanilla dusted with confectioners' sugar. For Christmas, Czechs serve a special cake called *vánočka*, which is made by weaving together nine strands of dough into a large, multitiered cake. The dough is mixed with raisins and nuts and the whole cake is dusted with confectioners' sugar. Slices of *vánočka* are served with butter and honey at the end of the meal, though some prefer a slice before anything else, including the fish soup, is served.

Plum Dumplings

(Švestkové Knedlíky)

I start with my absolute favorite, sweet dumplings filled with halved, pitted plums. Any type of plum will do, really, but the dark-purple, oval prune plums are the best because they are not too sweet. If serving as a dessert, two or maybe three of these dumplings per person is ample, though four or five will do you for a light meal. You can also try making these dumplings with strawberries or apricots.

- 1 pound fresh plums
- 3 cups flour
- pinch of salt
- ½ packet (¼ ounce) dry yeast
- 1 teaspoon sugar plus additional for garnish
- ¾ cup warm milk or so
- 1 egg
- ½ cup (1 stick) butter, melted
- 1 cup farmer cheese

Wash and dry the plums, then cut them in half and remove their stones.

Mix together the flour and salt in a large bowl. Make a well in the center and put in the yeast and 1 teaspoon sugar. Mix in a little of the flour. Slowly add ½ cup of the milk, which has been warmed on the stove, and mix well. Do not mix in all of the flour. Put a warm, damp cloth over the bowl and leave for about 20 minutes or until the yeast mixture has risen a little.

Add the remaining ¼ cup of milk into the yeast mixture and begin to mix in the remaining flour. Break the egg into the flour and keep mixing it in until you have a thick paste.

Turn the dough out onto a floured board or table. Knead it very quickly and lightly just enough to have it form a ball, then, using a pin, roll it out quite thin (about ⅛ inch). Cut the dough into 2-inch squares.

Put half a plum in each square, wrap the dough around the plum, and seal the edges by pinching the sides together.

Bring a large pot of water to a rapid boil. Put about a dozen of the dumplings into the boiling water. Once the dumplings have risen to the surface of the water, boil them for another 5 minutes. Put a sieve next to the pot and transfer the cooked dumplings into it, piercing each of them with a fork to release their steam. Serve with sugar, melted butter, and farmer cheese.

SERVES 4 TO 6.

Apple Fritters

The basic concept of putting sliced fruit in batter works well for apples but may be modified for use with many other fruits. Apple fritters are easy to make and require only a few simple ingredients for a pretty and tasty dessert. Fritters may be served plain or with some whipped cream.

2 large apples
2 teaspoons sugar
4 tablespoons rum or brandy
2 eggs
pinch of salt
¾ cup flour
¼ cup milk
4 tablespoons (½ stick) butter
confectioners' sugar or whipped cream

Peel and core the apples, then cut them into ¼-inch rings. Put them in a bowl, sprinkle on 1 teaspoon of sugar and pour on 2 tablespoons of the rum or brandy. Mix well and set aside for about 30 minutes.

To make the batter, break the eggs into a bowl and mix together. Mix in the remaining 1 teaspoon sugar and the remaining 2 tablespoons rum or brandy, and a pinch of salt. Slowly add the flour, mixing well. Add as much milk as is required to form a fairly thick batter. Add the apple slices and mix well.

Heat 2 tablespoons of the butter on medium in a large frying pan. When the butter bubbles have subsided, placed the battered apple rings in the pan. Fry the apple fritters until golden brown, 3 to 4 minutes per side. Repeat until all the fritters are done. Serve with confectioners' sugar or whipped cream.

SERVES 4 TO 6.

Baked Apples

Apples, pears, and peaches, among other fruits, are delicious when baked briefly in the oven and stuffed with some raisins, nuts, honey, and so on. Baked fruit is excellent with whipped cream.

4 large apples
½ cup raisins
4 tablespoons honey
4 tablespoons (½ stick) butter
1 tablespoon cinnamon
whipped cream (optional)

Preheat the oven to 400°F.

Wash and dry the apples, then using a paring knife core them without piercing through one end of the apples. Mix together the raisins and honey. Spoon some of the raisin mixture into each of the apples. Place a tablespoon of butter on top of the stuffing in each apple. Sprinkle the cinnamon evenly on top of the apples.

Put the stuffed apples in a small, buttered baking dish. Place in the oven and bake until tender, about 30 minutes. Serve as is or with dollops of whipped cream.

SERVES 4.

Pancakes with Preserves

(Palačinky)

Czech pancakes are more like French crepes than American pancakes. They are thin and delicate and cook in 2 or 3 minutes. They may be filled by spreading some fruit preserves (try apricot or plum jam) over one side and rolling them up, then dusting them with confectioners' sugar or dolloping on whipped cream. You may also make fancier fillings of stewed fruit, farmer cheese, or poppy seeds (see pages 370–372).

1 cup flour
2 eggs
pinch of salt
¾ cup milk or so
6 tablespoons (¾ stick) butter
½ cup apricot jam
¼ cup confectioners' sugar
whipped cream (optional)

To make the batter, put the flour in a bowl, break in the eggs, add a pinch of salt, and pour in some of the milk. Start mixing the batter together, adding more milk as you go until you have a medium-thick consistency.

Heat a medium-size frying pan on medium. Add 1 tablespoon of butter. When the butter bubbles have subsided, ladle enough batter into the pan to make 1 large, thin pancake. Roll the pan around from side to side to spread the batter evenly. Once the pancake starts to set, shake the pan so that the batter does not stick. Fry until lightly golden, about 2 minutes, then flip over and brown the other side.

Continue melting butter and making pancakes until the batter is used up. Finished pancakes may be stacked between two plates and kept warm in the oven. Once all the pancakes are fried, spread 1 tablespoon of apricot jam on each, roll them up, sprinkle on confectioners' sugar, and serve with whipped cream if desired.

SERVES 4 TO 6.

Plum Cake I

This classic cake uses a yeast-raised dough. It is more substantial than the next version and less crisp, but the dough soaks up the juice from the plums excellently. Other types of fruit, such as apricots, strawberries, blackberries, and cherries, may also be used for good effect, but plums, and especially these slightly sour plums, are definitely the best.

½ cup milk
1 packet (½ ounce) dry yeast
2 cups flour
¼ teaspoon salt
4 large eggs
½ cup sugar
½ cup (1 stick) butter
1½ pounds prune plums, halved and pitted
confectioners' sugar
brandy or *slivovice* (optional)
whipped cream (optional)

To make the dough, first warm the milk a little, then stir in the yeast. Cover this mixture with a cloth and leave in a warm place for 15 to 20 minutes.

Pour the flour into a large bowl and sprinkle on the salt. Whisk the eggs well. Pour the milk mixture and the eggs into the flour, mixing well.

Mix the sugar and butter together well, until they form a rough cream. Mix the sugar and butter into the dough until all is well incorporated. Cover the dough with a cloth and let sit in a warm place for about 45 minutes.

Preheat the oven to 375°F.

Butter a large (9 × 13-inch) baking tin. On a floured board, roll out the dough to fit the pan then transfer it there. Stick plum halves, cut side up, all over the dough. Put the cake in the oven and bake for 35 minutes or until the cake is golden brown and free from the edges of the tin.

Serve slices of cake dusted with confectioners' sugar and glasses of brandy or *slivovice* if you have it. Whipped cream is also a nice accompaniment.

SERVES 6.

Plum Cake II

This thin cake is covered all over with plums, and their juices soak into the pastry to color it and infuse it with fruit flavor. Cherries, strawberries, raspberries, or apricots may be baked in the same way. Serve large squares of this cake with a mound of whipped cream.

- 1 cup granulated sugar
- 2 cups flour
- ¼ teaspoon baking powder
- ¾ cup (1½ sticks) unsalted butter
- 2 eggs
- 1½ pounds plums
- 1 tablespoon lemon juice
- 1 teaspoon cinnamon
- ¼ cup confectioners' sugar
- whipped cream

Preheat the oven to 350°F.

Put ⅔ cup granulated sugar, the flour, and baking powder into a mixing bowl and cut in the butter. Keep rubbing the mixture until it forms into a coarse meal. Beat the eggs together then work them into the flour and quickly form a dough.

Cut the plums in half and remove their stones. Put the plum halves in a bowl, pour on the remaining ⅓ cup granulated sugar, the lemon juice, and cinnamon, and mix well.

Butter a large, rectangular (9 × 13-inch) baking tray. Roll the dough out onto a board until it is ¼ inch thick. Transfer the dough to the tray. Space the plum halves, cut side up, all over the cake. Put in the oven and bake until done, about 30 minutes. Sprinkle with confectioners' sugar and serve with whipped cream.

SERVES 6.

Apple Strudel

Strudel dough takes time to make because you need a pastry that is very delicate such as puff pastry, but the availability of good phyllo pastry allows you to skip that step if you wish. Strudels may be filled with just about any type of fruit (though apples and cherries are favorites) or preserve, or some kind of cheese or poppy seed filling (see below).

2 pounds apples
½ cup plus 6 tablespoons (1¾ sticks) unsalted butter
½ cup granulated sugar
1 teaspoon ground cinnamon
½ cup raisins
zest of 1 lemon
1 package (1 pound) phyllo pastry or freshly made puff pastry (see below)
½ cup fine bread crumbs
confectioners' sugar
whipped cream

To prepare the filling, peel and core the apples, then slice them fine. Put them in a mixing bowl and add 4 tablespoons (½ stick) butter, the granulated sugar, cinnamon, raisins, and lemon zest. Mix well.

To prepare the phyllo, unroll it onto a flat surface. To prepare the fresh puff pastry, put it onto a floured board or table and using a pin roll it out very thin, about ⅛ inch, into a large rectangle.

Preheat the oven to 350°F.

Melt 2 tablespoons butter on medium heat in a small pan and throw in the bread crumbs. Brown them quickly.

Melt the remaining ½ cup butter. Slather the phyllo or pastry with a good deal, but not all, of the melted butter. If using phyllo, the sheets should be separated, buttered, and then layered. Sprinkle on the browned bread crumbs.

Spread the apple filling all over the pastry. Now roll up the strudel and tuck in the ends to make a long loaf. Place it on a buttered baking tin and brush with the remaining melted butter.

Put the strudel in the oven and bake for about 30 minutes or until golden brown. Let cool, then dust with confectioners' sugar. Serve thick slices with a dollop of whipped cream.

SERVES 8.

Bábovka

This is the Czech version of coffeecake and many different versions of the basic principle are possible: raisins or nuts are commonly used, the batter may be vanilla or chocolate flavored, or, as here, you can make a marble cake by combining a vanilla and chocolate layer. All that is absolutely required is the right kind of baking pan: a deep, circular one with a thin tube through the center. The finished cake is dusted with a little confectioners' sugar for a pretty and rich tasting dessert.

- 1 cup milk
- ½ cup plus 3 tablespoons granulated sugar
- 1 packet (½ ounce) yeast
- ½ cup (1 stick) butter
- 4 egg yolks
- 2½ cups flour
- 2 tablespoons cocoa
- ½ teaspoon vanilla extract
- ¼ cup confectioners' sugar

To prepare the yeast, warm ¼ cup milk on the stove and dissolve 1 tablespoon of granulated sugar in it. Take off the heat, make sure the milk is not hot, and add the yeast. Mix together and leave in a warm place for 30 minutes.

Put ½ cup granulated sugar in a mixing bowl and cut in the butter. Mix together well. Add the egg yolks and beat together well, until light and creamy (about 5 minutes). Mix in the prepared yeast. Gradually add the flour, mixing it in well, adding some more milk as required.

Divide the batter into two halves. Mix the cocoa with 2 tablespoons of granulated sugar and a little milk. Mix the cocoa preparation into one of the batches of batter. Mix the vanilla extract into the other batch. Cover both batches with a damp, warm cloth and leave to rise in a warm place for about 30 minutes.

Preheat the oven to 350°F.

Butter a 9-inch coffeecake pan, then lightly dust it with a little flour. Pour the vanilla batter into the pan, then carefully pour the chocolate batter on top. Put in the oven and bake until done (when a long baking needle or knife inserted into the cake comes out clean), 35 to 40 minutes. Let the cake cool, remove from the pan and turn right side up, then dust with confectioners' sugar and serve.

SERVES 8.

Chestnut Cake with Chocolate Sauce

You may use fresh chestnuts for this cake or take a harmless shortcut and use canned chestnut purée. This simple cake, combining nuts and flour, can easily be made using hazelnuts or almonds instead, and is tasty with or without the chocolate sauce.

- ¾ cup sugar
- ¾ cup (1½ sticks) unsalted butter
- 6 eggs, separated
- zest of 1 lemon
- ½ can chestnut purée
- 1 cup flour
- ¼ teaspoon baking powder
- ½ pound semisweet chocolate
- ¼ cup heavy cream

Put ½ cup sugar in a large mixing bowl and cut in ½ cup of butter, mixing the two together well. Add the egg yolks and beat the mixture well, until light and fluffy, about 5 minutes. Mix in the zest of the lemon. Fold in the chestnut purée.

Mix together the flour and baking powder. Gradually add the flour to the chestnut mixture, incorporating it well.

Preheat the oven to 350°F.

Beat the whites until stiff, then fold these into the batter. Butter a 9-inch round cake pan and then dust it lightly with flour. Pour in the batter, even it out, then place in the oven and bake until done, about 40 minutes (or until a knife inserted in the center comes out clean). Let the cake cool in its pan.

To make the sauce, melt the chocolate by putting it in a small pot and then setting this pot in a larger pot of hot water on medium heat. When the chocolate has melted, add remaining ¼ cup sugar and ¼ cup butter. Mix this together well, then incorporate the cream.

Take the cake out of its pan and arrange on a serving platter. Pour on the chocolate sauce and serve.

SERVES 6.

Christmas Cake
(Vánočka)

This cake is a fair amount of work but the occasion comes only once a year and the tender pastry is worth it. Vánočka *is even better a day or two after it has been cooked. Serve slices of the cake with butter and a good honey (it is also nice with a fruit preserve).*

¾ cup milk
½ cup sugar
1 packet (½ ounce) yeast
2 cups flour
2 cups semolina
1 cup (2 sticks) unsalted butter
4 egg yolks
½ teaspoon vanilla extract
zest of 1 lemon
pinch of salt
¾ cup raisins
¾ cup chopped almonds
1 egg white
confectioners' sugar

To prepare the yeast, warm ¼ cup milk on the stove, mix in 1 tablespoon granulated sugar, then stir in the yeast. Cover with a warm, damp cloth and leave in a warm place for 30 minutes.

To prepare the dough, mix the flour and semolina in a large mixing bowl. Cut in the unsalted butter using two knives until well incorporated. Add the egg yolks and the remaining granulated sugar and mix well. Add the vanilla, lemon zest, and a pinch of salt. Add the prepared yeast-milk mixture and just enough more milk to make a thick dough. Mix in the raisins and chopped almonds. Cover with a warm, damp cloth and leave in a warm place for 30 minutes.

Turn the dough out onto a floured board or table. Divide the dough into 4 larger and 5 smaller pieces. Using your hands, roll out each piece of dough into a long plait.

Preheat the oven to 500°F.

To arrange the cake, braid together the 4 longer strands to create the bottom layer. Then braid together 3 smaller pieces, and place on top of the bottom layer. Finally, twist together the remaining 2 strands and place on top of the middle layer. Secure the plaits with 6 or so toothpicks and let stand for about 30 minutes to rise more.

Brush the cake all over with the egg white then put it in the oven. Turn the oven down to 300°F. Bake for about 1 hour or until a knife placed in the center comes out clean. If the cake becomes golden before it is done, cover with aluminum foil. Let cool, remove toothpicks, then dust with confectioners' sugar.

SERVES 8.

Celestine Crusts
(Boží Milosti)

These simple but rich pastries are fried in butter and eaten while still hot. As the Czech name ("God's Graces") suggests, they are divine.

2 cups flour
⅔ cup unsalted butter
¼ cup granulated sugar
3 egg yolks
zest of 1 lemon
1 tablespoon rum
¼ cup heavy cream
confectioners' sugar

Pour the flour into a mixing bowl, then using two knives cut in ⅓ cup of the butter until it is well incorporated. Make a well in the center of the flour. Pour the granulated sugar into the well and add the egg yolks. Mix together the yolks and sugar, then add the lemon zest and the rum. Begin mixing in the flour until it is all incorporated. Add enough cream to make a thick dough.

Turn the dough out onto a floured board or table. Work it quickly with your hands to make it into a ball, then roll it out with a pin about ¼ inch thick. Cut the dough into diamonds or triangles 2 to 3 inches long.

Heat some of the remaining butter in a large frying pan. When hot, add as many of the crusts as will fit in the pan and fry until golden on both sides, about 5 minutes. Remove, drain on paper towels, and dust with confectioners' sugar.

SERVES 8.

Doughnuts
(Koblihy)

Czechs make all kinds of small, stuffed cakes to eat as snacks or after a meal. These are fried in oil but versions of the same recipe may also be baked. Freshly made doughnuts are nothing like what you buy in the store and are worth the trouble. They may be filled with fresh fruit, jam (especially prune preserves), farmer cheese, or poppy seeds. Quick recipes for the latter three fillings follow. Instead of stuffing these cakes you may add raisins and nuts to the dough and fry small balls of this to make šišky.

½ cup milk
¼ cup granulated sugar
1 packet (½ ounce) yeast
½ cup (1 stick) unsalted butter
2 large eggs
1 tablespoon rum
zest of 1 lemon
½ teaspoon vanilla extract
pinch of salt
1 cup flour
1 cup semolina
2 cups vegetable oil
confectioners' sugar

To prepare the yeast, warm the milk a little on the stove, dissolve 1 tablespoon of the granulated sugar in it, then stir in the yeast. Cover the mixture with a warm, damp cloth and leave for 20 minutes.

To prepare the dough, pour the remaining 3 tablespoons sugar into a mixing bowl and cut in the butter. Add the eggs and beat the mixture until light and fluffy, about 5 minutes. Add the rum, lemon zest, vanilla extract, and salt. Mix in the yeast and milk. Mix together the flour and semolina. Gradually fold the flour mixture into the sugar and eggs, adding a little more milk if necessary to make a thick dough. Cover the dough with a warm, damp cloth and leave in a warm place to rise for 30 minutes.

Turn the dough out onto a floured board or table. Work it with your hands briefly to make a cohesive ball, then roll it out about ¼ inch thick with a pin. Cut the dough into circles with a large glass jar. Put a tablespoon of jam, fresh fruit (apricots, strawberries, raspberries, etc.), or one of the fillings below onto each piece of dough. Form the dough around the stuffing and pinch the sides together to seal. Leave the doughnuts to rise for another 20 minutes or so.

Heat the oil on medium-high in a large frying pan or deep-fat fryer. When quite hot, put in as many doughnuts as will fit comfortably. Fry until done, turning over once, about 5 minutes. Remove the doughnuts and let drain on paper towels. Dust with confectioners' sugar and serve.

SERVES 6.

Prune Filling

You may find a good prune preserve at a specialty store, but the homemade version is easy and probably much better.

- 1 pound prunes, pitted
- ¼ cup (½ stick) unsalted butter
- 1 tablespoon rum
- ¼ teaspoon ground cloves
- zest of 1 lemon

Put the prunes in a pot and just cover with water. Bring to a boil, reduce the heat, and simmer, uncovered, for about 30 minutes. If there is quite a bit of liquid left with the prunes when cooked, drain some off. Either mash the prunes or purée them in a food processor.

Melt the butter and mix it into the puréed prunes. Add the rum, cloves, and grated lemon zest. Taste and add a little sugar if needed.

Cheese Filling

Farmer cheese is best for this type of filling and ricotta is pretty close, but if neither of these is available use a fine cottage cheese.

- ½ pound farmer cheese
- 3 egg yolks
- ⅓ cup sugar
- ½ teaspoon vanilla extract

Mix all the ingredients well and taste; add more sugar if necessary.

Poppy Seed Filling

Use this filling for doughnuts, cakes, tarts, pancakes, or strudel.

- ¼ cup (½ stick) unsalted butter
- ⅓ cup sugar
- 2 cups poppy seeds
- ½ cup heavy cream
- zest of 1 lemon
- ¼ teaspoon ground cloves

Melt the butter in a pot on medium-low heat, then pour in the sugar and mix well. Add the poppy seeds, mixing well, then pour in the cream. Add the lemon zest and the ground cloves. Cook for about 10 minutes, stirring occasionally.

Fruit Bubble Cake
(Bublaňina)

This cake starts with a basic sponge cake into which sweet whole cherries are sunk throughout. Leaving the pits in is fine and maximizes one's juice quotient, as long as you warn guests. If pitting the cherries, do so over the dough so juice is conserved. Other types of fruit, especially berries, are also very good in this cake.

- 4 eggs
- ¼ teaspoon salt
- ¾ cup granulated sugar
- ¾ cup flour
- 1 teaspoon vanilla extract
- ⅔ pound cherries, stems removed
- confectioners' sugar
- whipped cream (optional)

Preheat the oven to 350°F.

Beat the eggs with the salt and granulated sugar until the mixture is quite light and stiff. Fold in the flour and mix in the vanilla extract.

Butter a medium-size (9 × 13-inch) rectangular or 9-inch round cake pan, then pour in the cake batter. Either plop unpitted cherries into the batter or cut cherries in halves over the batter, letting the juice drip in, and letting fall cherry halves but no pits.

Bake in the oven for 20 minutes or until the sides separate from the pan and a needle inserted in the cake comes out clean.

Let the cake cool, then dust it with confectioners' sugar. Serve with or without whipped cream.

SERVES 6.

Crumble Berry Cake

A very simple and delicious cake which cannot go wrong, because if it does you cannot tell the difference: everything is supposed to be crumbly in the first place. The dough is made by smearing together flour, butter, sugar, and lemon zest. This crumble is then spread on the bottom of a cake pan and topped with blueberries or sliced strawberries and a little sugar. Mix several berries together if you like.

- 1½ cups flour
- ¾ cup sugar
- ½ cup (1 stick) butter
- 1 teaspoon grated lemon zest
- 2 cups fresh blueberries, cleaned
- whipped cream

Preheat the oven to 375°F.

Put the flour and ½ cup sugar in a medium-size bowl. Cut in the butter and mix in the lemon zest. Using your fingers, work the dough until it comes together in clusters.

Butter a medium-size (9 × 13-inch) rectangular baking sheet or a 9-inch round cake pan. Crumble in the dough, making sure the pan is well covered everywhere.

Mix the blueberries with the remaining ¼ cup sugar, then spread them across the crumbled dough. Bake in the oven for 15 to 20 minutes.

Serve warm or cooled with whipped cream.

SERVES 6.

Czech Wedding Cake
(*Svatebný koláč*)

There are a variety of such cakes, based primarily on the combination of fillings of the yeast-raised dough. Common mixtures include jam, poppy seeds, and farmer cheese. These round cakes look lovely and are highly portable.

½ cup milk
1 packet (½ ounce) dry yeast
2 cups flour
¼ teaspoon salt
4 large eggs
1 cup granulated sugar
1 cup (2 sticks) butter
1 cup poppy seeds
2 egg yolks
confectioners' sugar

Warm the milk a little, take it off the heat, and stir in the dry yeast. Cover the milk, put in a warm place, and leave to sit for 15 to 20 minutes.

Pour the flour into a large bowl and sprinkle on the salt. Whisk the eggs together well. Pour the eggs and the milk-yeast mixture onto the flour, and mix well.

Whisk or blend together the granulated sugar and butter, until you have a light and creamy mixture. Fold this into the dough. Cover the dough with a cloth and let sit in a warm place for about 45 minutes.

In a small bowl, mix together the poppy seeds, and egg yolks.

Preheat the oven to 375°F.

On a floured board, roll out the dough a little, until it is ¼ inch thick or so. Use a small saucer and a knife to cut out round pieces of dough.

Butter a couple of large baking sheets. Take a round of dough and, using your fingers, depress the center of the dough a little to make room for some filling, but leave the edges raised. Put the round of dough onto the baking sheet. Spoon some of the poppy seed mixture onto the center of the dough and spread it around evenly but leave the edges clean. Continue to fill the dough rounds in just this way.

When both baking sheets are filled, put them in the oven and bake for 20 minutes, or golden brown. Let cool and serve sprinkled with confectioners' sugar.

SERVES 8.

Czech Cheese Cake
(*Linecký tvarohový koláč*)

Using cheese for baking sweets is common in the Czech Republic, as it is almost everywhere. Fortunately, however, Czech sweets are more varied than the rather monotonous line of cheesecakes that often suffocates an American dessert menu. Still, cheesecakes are popular and are usually made with a rough kind of fresh cheese, resembling farmer cheese or ricotta. Cottage cheese, while somewhat similar in texture, should really be avoided for these purposes. Raisins are very good mixed with farmer cheese, as are other types of dried fruit, nuts, and a little liqueur.

1½ cups sugar
1 cup (2 sticks) butter
4 egg yolks
2 cups flour
¼ cup milk
1 pound farmer cheese or ricotta
½ cup raisins

Whisk or blend together 1 cup of the sugar and the butter very well, until you have a light and creamy mixture. Add two egg yolks and mix together well. Fold in the flour and a little milk, if necessary, to make a dough.

Butter a medium-size 9-inch round cake pan. Spread the dough on the cake pan.

Preheat the oven to 375°F.

Press the farmer cheese through a sieve. Mix in the raisins, the remaining ½ cup sugar, and 2 egg yolks. Spread the cheese mixture over the dough. Put the cake in the oven and bake for 30 minutes or until lightly golden on top.

SERVES 6.

Baked Doughnuts

(Buchty)

These doughnut-type cakes are rich with butter and dense fillings, jammed together on a tray in the oven, then ripped apart for individual consumption. A good jam, typically made from prunes or apricots, will do well as a filling. Also try farmer's cheese mixed with a bit of sugar, or sweetened poppy seeds bound with an egg yolk or two.

- ½ cup milk
- 1 packet (½ ounce) dry yeast
- 2 cups flour
- ¼ teaspoon salt
- 4 large eggs
- ½ cup granulated sugar
- ¾ cup (1½ sticks) butter
- 1 cup prune jam
- confectioners' sugar

Warm the milk a little, take it off the heat, stir in the yeast. Cover the milk and let it sit in a warm place for 15 to 20 minutes.

Pour the flour into a large bowl and sprinkle on the salt. Whisk the eggs together well. Pour the milk-yeast mixture and the eggs into the flour and mix well.

Whisk or blend together the granulated sugar and ½ cup (1 stick) butter until you have a light and creamy mixture. Fold this into the dough. Cover the dough with a cloth and let sit in a warm place for 45 minutes.

Preheat the oven to 375°F.

Tear off a tennis ball–size chunk of dough and work it with your hands into a round shape. Poke two fingers into the dough to make a small well, fill it with a tablespoon of jam, then cover up the depression. Fill all the doughnuts in this way then let them sit for another 15 minutes or so.

Butter a large (9 × 13-inch) baking sheet. Melt the remaining ¼ cup butter. Place the filled cakes close together on the sheet and drizzle the melted butter on top. Put the cakes in the oven and bake for 30 minutes or until golden brown. Tear the cakes from each other and serve warm or cooled, sprinkled with confectioners' sugar.

SERVES 8.

Fried Pastries with Assorted Fillings
(*Vdolečky*)

These small, oval-shaped pastries are made from a yeast dough, filled with a jam, such as apricot, prune, strawberry, or partridgeberry (similar to cranberry), and a soft farmer cheese or a little yogurt or sour cream. They are very rich and very delicious.

- ½ cup milk
- 1 packet (½ ounce) dry yeast
- 2 cups flour
- ¼ teaspoon salt
- 4 large eggs
- ½ cup granulated sugar
- ½ cup (1 stick) butter
- 1 cup farmer cheese
- 1 cup good jam
- ½ cup vegetable oil
- confectioners' sugar

Warm the milk a little, take it off the heat, then stir in the dry yeast. Cover the milk with a cloth and let sit in a warm place for 15 to 20 minutes.

Pour the flour into a large bowl and sprinkle on the salt. Whisk the eggs together well. Pour the milk-yeast mixture and the eggs into the flour and mix well.

Whisk or blend together the granulated sugar and butter until you have a light and creamy mixture. Fold this into the dough. Cover the dough with a cloth and let sit in a warm place for 45 minutes.

Find or make a small oval shape, the size of a tea saucer (e.g., cut one out of cardboard).

On floured board, roll out the dough until it is about ¼ inch thick. Using your oval shape and a knife, cut out as many oval pieces of dough as you can.

Take a piece of dough, and, using your fingers, depress the middle a little to make room for some filling. Spread a tablespoon or so of farmer cheese in the middle of the dough, then cover this with a spoonful of jam. Fill all the cakes this way.

Heat vegetable oil in a large frying pan on medium. Put in as many of the cakes as will fit comfortably. Fry them gently until golden brown, about 5 minutes. Serve warm or cooled sprinkled with confectioners' sugar.

SERVES 8.

12

Beers, Wines, and Spirits

Certain debates make sense. Which is better, French or Italian cuisine? There is no debate, however, about the weakness of Czech wines compared to the better European varieties. This does not mean that Czech wines are not fit to drink, for they are, and some are quite good, but the best Czech wines do not compete with the best French, Italian, or Spanish wines.

There is also no debate, in many Czech minds, concerning the absolute premier status of Czech beers, especially and notably Pilsner Urquell, the first and best lager in the world. In Germany, England, Scotland, or Belgium you'll find arguments on this issue, but not in the Czech Republic. Beer drinking is popular and intensive among Czechs, who are the greatest consumers of beer per capita in the world, a considerable accomplishment considering some of the fierce competitors.

Czech beers are well made and the best, like Pilsner Urquell, rival good wines in their purity of constitution, demanding conditions of production, and complexity and satisfaction of taste. Beers are consumed in mass quantities, as elsewhere, for the primary purpose of intoxication but beer is also the common accompaniment with food, more so than wine, and beer is appreciated for its contributions to meals.

The world historical claims of the Czechs are strong when it comes to beer, but there is at least one other contender for universal or world-object status among drinks, the herbal spirit Becherovka. There are numerous good tasting brandies and liqueurs made by Czechs, but many of these have competent rivals or clear superiors elsewhere. *Slivovice*, a plum brandy, stands out among these. The distilled herbal drink Becherovka, however, is rather unique and especially prized, and a taste for it is developed and refined. Becherovka's medicinal properties are purported to be numerous and profound, so much so that it is rumored to be an elixir of life. Perhaps a world historical moment lays here in wait.

BEERS

The story begins over 150 years ago in a town called Pilsen, sixty kilometers or so west of Prague. As is true of many novel creations, the time is ripe for something new: a few things have come into existence that had not been and something wears out that has been and has done for a long time. Refrigeration by mechanical means is newly possible, bacteriology has emerged as a science from the experiments of Louis Pasteur, and clear glass has begun to appear in many forms, including drinking vessels.

The old way of brewing beer, without refrigeration, and, therefore, by fermenting the yeast on top of the mash, is prone to accident by spoiling. A series of such accidents befalls the town of Pilsen in the 1830s. Imagine the despair of having to abandon thousands of gallons of finely made but foul tasting beer. Such despair or something like it leads to a revolutionary change in the art of brewmaking in Pilsen and the formation of a common brewery in 1842.

The Pilsen revolution is the first ever application of cool or bottom fermentation techniques to brewing. Cool fermentation reduces the likelihood of the beer spoiling and it also produces a lighter colored, clear lager. Such a golden and pure liquid, in contrast to dark stouts and murky ales and porters, calls out for display in clear glass, rather than the then standard earthenware.

New creations often depend on the circumstances being right, in this case on new technological means and crafts, but they also require artisanship. The great popularity and even hegemony of lager today bears witness to the tasteless potential results of cool fermentation and the mass production that is possible on its basis, but such beers have little in common with Pilsner Urquell or other good lagers.

The brewmasters of Pilsen had a history of fine artisanship with which to seize the new opportunities of the 1840s. The beer contained natural ingredients alone and still does. The water is excellent, soft and fresh tasting. The "Urquell" in Pilsen means source and refers to the spring from which the water for the beer is taken. Pilsen and other areas surrounding the north and west of Prague are famed for their springs, notably Karlovy Vary (Carlsbad), which were and are places of sojourn and health-seeking due to their high quality water.

Fine two-row barley, as opposed to the coarser six seed varieties, are used exclusively for the malt. The barley cones are dried for five months, ground, and boiled thrice in soft water. The strained barley mash is then mixed with Saaz hops and cooked for ten hours in copper kettles. One of the many good things about all natural ingredients is that if large quantities of Pilsner are drunk chances of a severe hangover are significantly reduced as compared with drinking a beer replete with additives and preservatives.

The aging process used today for Pilsner Urquell is much the same as it was in the 1840s, though switching to giant steel containers to hold the beer may be on the horizon. Currently, once cooked, the beer is put in large oak barrels and stored in cellars. The climate of the cellars, in terms of its stable temperature and moisture, is important for the final result. The beer finishes its aging in even larger wooden barrels in limestone caverns.

If pasteurized, the beer could be bottled and exported, and the Czechs lost little time in spreading their invention across Europe. The unpasteurized and preferable draught beer, better on the very premises it is made, is also exportable in aluminum and clay barrels.

Pilsner Urquell is served traditionally in ½ liter glasses with handles. It should have a substantial (1inch or so) creamy head. The liquid is clear and light golden in color, with a high percentage of dissolved carbon dioxide. And the beer has taste. Unlike copycat mass produced varieties which bring lager a bad name, Pilsner Urquell, when served chilled but not freezing cold, has a sophisticated and multiple range of flavors, suggestive of burnt caramel, molasses, and apples, among others.

Pilsner Urquell and other Czech beers have many imitators. Budvar or Budweiser, for example, has just finished a long and successful legal battle with the American copycat beer. The Czech original and the American copy have almost nothing in common, however.

There are numerous other quality beers in the Czech Republic. Pilsner itself comes in three strengths (12, 14, and 18 degrees) and the brewery produces a dark beer as well. Other notable lagers include Cambrinus, Senator, Prusovice, and Radegast. U Fleku is a good stout.

WINES

Bohemia is the Czech province of beer making, and little good wine is made there. One exception is a white wine called Ludmilla coming out of Zamek Mělník, a castle headed at one time by the Count or *Kniže* Lobkovic and responsible also for Lobkovicé beer.

Moravia is the province for wine. Like other eastern European countries, such as Hungary and Bulgaria, the standard wines, both white and red, are drinkable, especially if lightly chilled on a hot day, but rarely rise beyond such simple pleasures. Southern Moravia is the wine center of the province. A couple of good reds and whites may be found there. Czech wine is drunk quite extensively within the country, though little is exported. Good Moravian reds include Svatovavřinecké and Mešní. Drinkable whites are Rulanské and Miller-Turgan. Some wines, especially white, may be quite sour, though a decent table wine is not hard to find. There is also a champagne-like sparkling wine, Bohemia Sekt, which is drinkable and cheap.

SPIRITS

Almost any aperitif, digestif, liqueur, or other spirit may be found in the Czech Republic, though few are unique to or find their roots in the country. A fair amount of rum and vodka is drunk, but these are made elsewhere for the most part. The quality and range of fruit brandies, emanating mostly from southern Moravia, is notable, however. Clear and crisp in taste, similar to French *eau de vie* and Italian *grappa*, the fruit brandies are often drunk with dessert or as a digestif by themselves. They may be quite strong but are not usually sweet.

Fruit brandies are made privately as well as commercially, and their range of quality is thus wide, from extremely rough and sharp drinks to smooth and refined ones. The best and most famous of these brandies is *slivovice*, which is made from prune plums (the same plums used in making plum dumplings and plum cakes). The bouquet and taste of a fine *slivovice*, such as Jelinková, is easily comparable to some of the better *eau de vie*. A dinner party may get out of hand if there are too many bottles of *slivovice*. Another favorite fruit brandy is made from apricots (*merunkovice*).

The truly unique spirit of the Czech Republic is Becherovka, though even Becherovka's lineage is not pure, originating in England and crossing over to Germany at one point. Becherovka is a clear, strong drink usually served after food as a digestif. It is always served cold, from the freezer straight up or with some ice; it may also be mixed with tonic water. Many restaurants in the Czech Republic still offer shots from the distinctive flat, green bottle on the house at the end of supper.

The taste of Becherovka is uncommon, at first more medicinal than pleasurable, but one is told one develops a liking for it upon repeated exposure. It has a bittersweet, complex flavor. Perhaps the initial displeasure is worth it, since Becherovka's blend of herbs is designed to ease digestion and extend life.

The secret recipe for Becherovka came to the Czech Republic from an English physician, Dr. Fobrega, who lived for a time among the springs of Karlovy Vary. Dr. Fobrega befriended a Czech, Mr. Josef Becher, and in 1807 he entrusted his friend with his elixir of life. Mr. Becher began commercial production of the spirit in 1841 and the spirit has been made exclusively in the Czech Republic ever since, except for a brief period after World War II, when a relative of Becher started up production across the border in Germany.

Like Pilsner Urquell, Becherovka was made possible by some fortune together with new craft, but neither would become a world-object without a good deal of skill in production. Part of the secret of Becherovka is its ingredients, the twenty or so herbs that flavor the spirit. But the secret has other, less tangible moments. The springs of Karlovy Vary, the reason for Dr. Fobrega's presence in Bohemia, are also part of the success of Becherovka. The water from the springs is of exceedingly high quality, soft in texture and fresh and clean in taste. The way in which the herbs are prepared, the climate, and the cellars in which the spirit is cooled and stored all contribute in some way to the quality of the drink. For these and other reasons, Becherovka and drinks like it are unique, irreplaceable, and incapable of precise, qualitative duplication.

The water in Karlovy Vary, along with the beauty of the landscape, has been a draw for many to Bohemia in the past. The legacy of the place extends to beer, wine, and spirits. The water is also bottled and sold simply as water. One of the better sparkling mineral waters from Karlovy Vary is Mattoni. Have a couple of glasses of Mattoni with your wine or beer at dinner, and a shot or two of *slivovice* or Becherovka to finish up: the heavy feeling of a sated stomach should make way for a more blissful sense.

springs [illegible]

[illegible] so [illegible] had [illegible] and the [illegible]

[illegible] and that [illegible]

[illegible] started [illegible] to [illegible] them.

Like [illegible]

[illegible] but the second [illegible] less than [illegible]

also part of the [illegible] what [illegible]

[illegible] in texture [illegible]

The [illegible] they [illegible]

[illegible] the quality of [illegible] and [illegible]

[illegible]

[illegible] has been [illegible]

[illegible] place [illegible]

[illegible] Kol'd simply [illegible]

[illegible]

[illegible]

[illegible] in a band [illegible]

Recipe Index

www.ingramcontent.com/pod-product-compliance
Lightning Source LLC
Jackson TN
JSHW011352130125
77033JS00023B/652
* 9 7 8 0 7 8 1 8 1 2 1 0 8 *